Winged Stallions & Wicked Mares

Winged Stallions & Wicked Mares

Horses in Indian Myth and History

WENDY DONIGER

Illustrations curated by
ANNA LISE SEASTRAND

University of Virginia Press | *Charlottesville and London*

Publication of this book was assisted by a grant from the Page-Barbour
and Richard Lecture Fund

University of Virginia Press
© 2021 by Wendy Doniger
Printed in the United States of America on acid-free paper

First published 2021

9 8 7 6 5 4 3 2 1

Library of Congress Cataloging-in-Publication Data

Names: Doniger, Wendy, author. | Seastrand, Anna Lise, other.
Title: Winged stallions and wicked mares : horses in Indian myth and history /
    Wendy Doniger ; illustrations curated by Anna Lise Seastrand.
Description: Charlottesville : University of Virginia Press, 2021. | Series: Richard
    lectures | Includes bibliographical references and index.
Identifiers: LCCN 2020037878 (print) | LCCN 2020037879 (ebook) |
    ISBN 9780813945750 (hardcover) | ISBN 9780813945767 (ebook)
Subjects: LCSH: Winged horses. | Horses—Mythology. | Hindu mythology. | Mares—
    Mythology.
Classification: LCC GR830.W57 D55 2021 (print) | LCC GR830.W57 (ebook) | DDC
    398.24/5296655—dc23
LC record available at https://lccn.loc.gov/2020037878
LC ebook record available at https://lccn.loc.gov/2020037879

For Penelope Chetwode Betjeman
(February 14, 1910–April 11, 1986)

and also for Sidi, Nandi, Rebel, Damien,
Smif, and Babur

Contents

viii | Contents

Illustrations

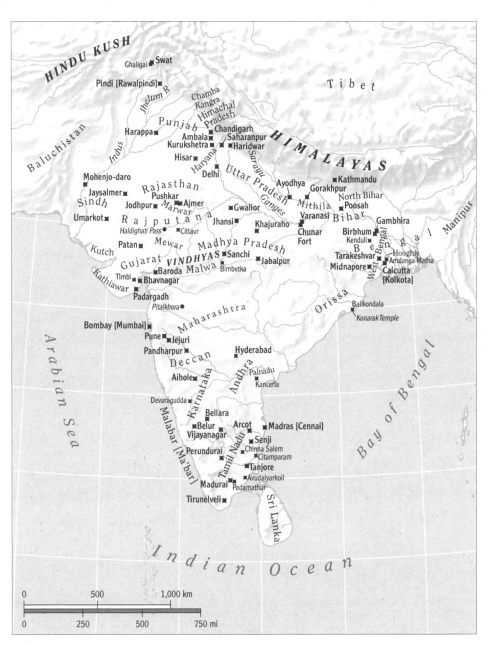

MAP OF INDIA

Preface

I discovered India and horses at the same time. I was twenty-two, in 1963, and it was my first visit to India. Flying from Calcutta to Kathmandu, I happened to be seated next to a woman who turned out to be Penelope Betjeman, née Penelope Valentine Hester Chetwode. She was the daughter of Field Marshal Sir Philip Walhouse Chetwode, 1st Baron Chetwode, who had been commander of the British Forces in India from 1928 to 1935. Penelope told me that, though she had lived in Delhi from her eighteenth to her twenty-fifth birthday, she was only now trying to learn Hindi, because, back in the day, "we only learned the imperatives of all the verbs." (She said this deadpan; she never joked.) In 1938, in England, Penelope had been photographed with her white Arab gelding Moti in the drawing room of Lord Berners (Gerald Hugh Tyrwhitt-Wilson, 14th Baron Berners, 1883–1950), while he painted a portrait of the two of them.[1]

Now, in Kathmandu, in 1963, Penelope (who was staying with the Maharaja in his palace) rode in a small race on the miniscule track on the palace grounds; disdaining to use the whip as the other jockeys did, she allowed them all to lap her twice, on two full circuits, and as she finally came into the home stretch she patted her pony's neck, "to demonstrate kindness to animals," she later explained to me.

When I moved to Oxford in 1965, Penelope taught me to ride, on her own Arab gelding Sidi, and then kept my horses in her stable at the Mead, in Wantage, Berks.: first the cob Nandi, who taught me how not to fall off; then the Connemara pony Rebel, who taught me how to jump fences; and finally the Anglo-Arab Damien, whom I bought from Penelope's friend Myles Dillon in Ireland, Dillon whose works on the shared literature of ancient Ireland and India I had read for years. And so India came into my horse world again. Penelope and I rode Sidi and Damien up on the Berkshire Downs, and rode them to hounds with the Old Berks, and jogged and ambled them home on a loose rein in the long English

FIGURE 1. Penelope Chetwode Betjeman and her Arabian horse Moti having their portrait painted by Lord Berners in the drawing room of his Berkshire home, July 4, 1938. (Photo by Fox Photos/Hulton Archive via Getty Images)

FIGURE 2. Wendy Doniger on her Anglo-Arabian horse Damien, at the Mead, Wantage, Berkshire, 1968. (Photo taken by Penelope Betjeman)

evenings, their hooves echoing through the narrow, silent streets of the sleepy villages as we talked about India.

Back in the United States, I stayed closely in touch with Penelope by mail as I rode my Arab Smif (named after my son's imaginary friend) up in the Berkeley Hills from 1975–78, and finally my wonderful Arab Babur (named after the great equestrian emperor of India), who came to me as an unbitted three-year-old in 1980 and died out at grass at the age of thirty-two.

Penelope returned often to India, usually taking groups trekking on horseback up into the Kulu hills, where she visited the wooden temples that she had written about for years.[2] On April 11, 1986, riding at the head of a group in those hills, she halted her horse and dismounted properly, then continued to slip to the ground, dead. On that spot there is a plaque with an inscription that ends, "She died in these hills she had loved so long."

Now, more than three decades later, I have written this book, in grateful memory of Penelope and our horses.

Acknowledgments

I began writing this book for the Radhakrishnan Lectures at All Souls College, Oxford University, in May of Trinity Term, 1986. (Romila Thapar was there, and Richard Gombrich, Bimal Matilal, and Andrew Sherratt, and I benefited greatly from their feedback.) Penelope Betjeman was to be there too, but she died just weeks before my lectures began. I lost heart in the book then, and dropped the reins until January 1996, when I visited several North Indian studs to find out more about breeding horses in India; the breeders were most generous with their time, and I learned much that was of great interest to me. I am particularly grateful to Mrs. Naju Bhabha for giving me introductions to some of the best studs in India. I am also deeply indebted, for their wisdom and hospitality, to Dr. Handa, of the Poonawalla Stud, Sholapur Road, in Pune; Mr. Chenoy, of Venkateshbagh, Ghorpuri, Pune; Dr. Faroukh Wadia and Statira Wadia, of the Wadi Stud, Pune; Mr. Martin Mahendra, of Broad Acres; and the Kunigal Stud near Bangalore.

In February 1997, I developed the Radhakrishnan Lectures into the Richard Lectures at the University of Virginia. But then I put the book out to pasture again until 2017, when Eric Arthur Brandt, editor in chief of the University of Virginia Press, persuaded me to resurrect the Richard Lectures and magically translated my antediluvian computer files into Word files that enabled me to pick up the conversation almost in midsentence. I am deeply indebted to him for putting the book back into harness, as well as for standing by the book through the whole course, bringing it home on a tight rein. And I must also thank the University of Virginia for inviting me to give the generously endowed Richard Lectures in the first place.

It only remained, I thought, for me to put the horseflesh (back) on those seminal essays by drawing upon all I knew about horses in India. But I see things quite differently now from the way I saw them back in 1986, and I had to rethink the entire book, which turned out to be an unexpectedly exciting voyage of (re-)discovery. Over the years, I had thought aloud about horses with a number of colleagues and publishers, occasions that supplied many of the ideas in this book. I am grateful to *Incognita* for commissioning my article "The Tail of the Indo-European Horse Sacrifice," in 1990; to the *London Review of Books* for inviting me to write the essay "Crazy about Horses," in 1993; to the Association of Asian Studies, for my 1998 Presidential Address, "'I Have Scinde': Flogging a Dead (White Male Orientalist) Horse," later published in the *Journal of Asian Studies;* and to Kimberley Patton, for inviting me to write the essay, "A Symbol in Search of an Object: The Mythology of Horses in India," for *A Communion of Subjects* in 2006. Threads and shreds of all of these have been reworked and woven back into the larger fabric of this book.

I am also grateful to all the people, starting back in the 1980s, colleagues and students, who gave me ideas and information that appear in my notes only as "personal communication from. . . ." Some of them are no longer here for me to come back to in search of more information, others very much alive as of this writing and helpful to me again after all these years: Karen Anderson, Elayaperumal Annamalai, Elena Bashir, Madeleine Biardeau, Stuart Blackburn, Devangana Desai, Simon Digby, Peggy Egnor, Joan Erdman, Kathleen Erndl, Carl Ernst, Henry David Ginzburg, Ann Grodzins Gold, Richard Gombrich, Leonard Gordon, Alex Gunasekara, Eric Gurevitch, James Harle, Susan L. Huntington, Stephen Inglis, Francesca Kelly, Peter Kepfoerle, Bimal Motilal, Sandra King Mulholland, Kirin Narayan, Father Selva Raj, Suzanne Rudolph, Andrew Sherratt, David Shulman, Gunther Sontheimer, John L. Stanley, Ulrike Stark, Romila Thapar, Robert Thurman, Gary Tubb, Herman Tull, Dominik Wujastyk, and Glenn Yocum. I am grateful to David Robertshaw for so many mind-boggling conversations in the spring of 1989, when he was professor and chair of the Department of Physiology at Cornell University's veterinary college and I was the A. D. White Professor-at-Large. I am indebted to James Nye and Laura Ring for their patience in guiding me through the mysteries and marvels of Regenstein Library. I owe a great debt to John Nemec for a generous and sharp-eyed reading of a penultimate version of the text, and to Katherine Ulrich for a number of brilliant suggestions, too many to acknowledge individually, in her reading of the final version, and for making the index.

Anna Lise Seastrand immediately understood my dream of what this book should look like and tirelessly tracked down all sorts of marvelous images that she alone knew where to find.

As always, Raine Daston cheered me on and gave me precious advice and arcane bits of information and articles and books, from the starting gate right through the home stretch.

A Note on Translation

Throughout this book, all the translations from the Sanskrit are mine unless otherwise specified. Translations from other languages are based on texts supplied by the scholars of those languages, though I have taken the liberty of rephrasing them for consistency. And here is a final prefatory word of caution: So much time has elapsed since I first wrote about "contemporary" attitudes to horses in India that much of what was true in the 1980s may no longer be true now, two decades into the twenty-first century. Things in Indian villages hang on for an awfully long time, but even in India, things do change. Words like "now," "nowadays," and "even today," particularly but not only in the later chapters, should therefore be taken with a grain of *haldi*.

Winged Stallions & Wicked Mares

1 | ✧ | Horses in Indian Nature and Culture

Life's like Sanskrit read to a pony.
—LOU REED, "What's Good: The Thesis"

I n this book, I want to explore three strands—the nature of horses, the history of India, and the Sanskrit and vernacular storytelling traditions—to see how they twined together to form the mythology of horses in India, paradoxically rich despite the rarity of real horses.

HORSES AS INVADERS

Most of the peoples who entered India over the centuries rode in on horseback. First came the Vedic people formerly known as Indo-Europeans (more properly, Indo-European speakers), who brought their horses with them from we know not where (probably the Caucasus), and then Greeks and Scythians, riding over the Northwest passes. Carvings at Sanchi, some dating from the second century BCE, depict a number of northwestern foreigners—in this case mostly Greeks—on horseback.[1] Turks and Mongols (the latter to become known in India as the Mughals) brought Arabian horses from Central Asia and Persia, overland and by sea. Then came the British, who brought Cape horses from South Africa and Walers from New South Wales in Australia. Most of these people came peacefully, as traders or migrants, but some came to conquer. It was largely because they had horses, or better horses, or more horses, or bigger horses, or all of the above, that the invaders were able to overpower the Indian people who did not have such horses.[2]

To understand some of the reasons for the continual movement of horses into India, we need first to understand two different but intersecting aspects of horses: the physiology and mentality of horses, and horses as humans have used them.

Horses move around in search of new grazing land, which they need constantly because, unlike cows (who tend to bite off the blades of grass), horses (whose teeth are rather dull) pull up the roots of the grass or nibble it right down to the ground so that it doesn't grow back, thus quickly destroying grazing land, which may require some years to recover. Horse breeders leave such fields fallow from time to time to allow the grass to regenerate, but horses in the wild, left to their own devices, range constantly to find new territory, moving on to literally greener pastures, the broad open spaces, eminent domain. (As Virginia Woolf remarks, in *Orlando,* chapter 3, "The gipsies followed the grass; when it was grazed down, on they moved again.")

The ancient Indo-European horse owners mimicked this behavior as they responded to the need to provide grazing for their horses once they had domesticated them and kept them from their natural free-grazing habits. They rode roughshod over other peoples' land and took it over for their own herds. This spirit was expressed in their very vocabulary; the Sanskrit word *amhas* (constraint)—from which comes our "anxiety" and the German *Angst*—expressed the terror of being fenced in or trapped. (The archvillain of the *Rig Veda* is the serpent Vritra, "The Restrainer," who coils up around the mountains and holds back the waters.) And the opposite word, *prithu* (broad and wide), is the name of the first king, the man whose job it was—like that of all the Indian kings who followed him—to widen the boundaries of his territory, to create *Lebensraum* for his people and his horses.[3] *Prithivi* (a feminine form of *prithu*) is a Sanskrit word for the earth, with its wide-open spaces that such kings must always conquer. It was not merely, as is often argued, that the horse (and more particularly the horse-drawn chariot with its spoked wheels) made possible conquest in war; the horse came to symbolize conquest in war through its own natural imperialism.

INDIAN CLIMATE AND PASTURAGE

But the land of India did not welcome horses.

It is not easy for horses to find good grazing land in South Asia, for they are not well adapted to conditions in most of the area, most of the time. (Of course, the climate has changed in various ways over the centuries, but the basic patterns have prevailed throughout the historical period that concerns us, from 3000 BCE to the present.) Horses hate the humid heat of the Indian plains, and during the monsoon rains their hooves soften in the wet soil and pieces break off, causing painful, recurring sores.[4] The violent contrast between the monsoon and the hot season makes the soil ricochet between swampy in one season and hard, parched, and cracked in another. One ancient Indian textbook of horses insists that you should not ride horses in the three months of the hot season but should ride in the three months of the winter season,[5] and another text says, "Winter, the cool month, and spring are for riding horses; in summer, autumn, and the rains, the riding or harnessing of horses is forbidden."[6] Though the Indian soil apparently has enough lime and calcium to support cattle, it is not good soil for horses; contemporary breeders now add calcium, manganese, iron, and salt to the horses' diet. There are very few tropical areas in which horses do well (Southeast Asia is one), and even there it takes a great deal of work, and money, to keep them healthy.[7]

Horses breed with difficulty or feebly in the extreme south of the Indian peninsula, and the suitability of the land for horses declines sharply toward the south and the east of the subcontinent.[8] The Deccan Plateau and Central India provide suitable grazing land, but this becomes parched between May and September.[9] Even during the grazing season, which lasts only from September to May, the grasses are sparse and not good for fodder. And since the best soil is mostly reserved for the cultivation of greens and vegetables to feed a large population many of whom cannot afford to eat meat, there is relatively little room for horses even in those places where more nutritious fodder grasses are found (such as the eastern extensions of the arid zone in the north and northwest and particularly in Rajasthan, where horses have been bred successfully for centuries). Stall feeding, essential during the dry months, is out of the question for subsistence farmers, and in any case stall feeding is never as good for horses as active grazing.[10] Since there is no extensive pasturage, most horses are stabled as soon as they are weaned, unable to exercise or develop full strength or fitness.

The best places in the world to breed horses are Kentucky and Ireland, with their blue grass and their Emerald Isle, both of them rich in limestone calcium. But the horses that dominate the equine history of India were bred in, and imported from, Central Asia and the Persian (or Arabian) Gulf states. These horses are the Arabians (who are also the ancestors of all Thoroughbreds). Parts of that world are often as hot as India, but much of it is significantly cooler, and, more to the point, these areas do *not* have the Indian monsoon, which is much more of a problem for horse breeders than is the dry heat. Moreover, the soil there has more of the minerals essential for the thriving of horses, particularly calcium, than the Indian soil has. Finally, horses are bred in Central Asia and the Gulf only in *some* places, not in the middle of the hottest deserts but in adjacent oases, just as it is possible to breed pretty good horses in *some* parts of India, such as Rajasthan, which have deserts and oases.

From breeders whom I consulted in North India in 1996, I gathered that the main centers of horse breeding in India then were in the Punjab, Maharashtra, and Karnataka; Pune, Mumbai, and Kolkota were the best breeding centers for Thoroughbred horses, mostly for racing. Again and again I heard that Kathiawar horses are good for long distances in the desert, but too slightly built, and not big or fast or strong enough, for cavalry use. Indian stud owners did find some places suitable for breeding horses, but they worried that you need better pasturage than you can get in India.[11] And if no new stock is imported, the height of horses in India diminishes dramatically in just a few years. As one breeder told me, wistfully, "If we had pasturage all year round, the horses would be an inch taller."[12] And every rider knows that a good big horse will beat a good little horse. Or, as the author of the Persian *Mirror of Princes* put it, "Buy large horses, because even though a man may be fat and of goodly figure he has an insignificant appearance on a contemptibly small mount."[13]

As early as the fifth century BCE, the Greek historian Herodotus wrote, "In India, all the four-footed beasts and the birds are very much bigger than those found elsewhere—except only the horses."[14] Yet the early Indians did, at least, *imagine* very big horses. An unusual, perhaps larger than life beige sandstone sculpture of a horse survives from the Gupta period (fourth century CE).[15] It measures approximately eighty inches at the poll, which would make it about sixty-four inches at the withers, or sixteen hands high,[16] and solid in every limb, a big, heavyset cart horse with a Roman nose, a stubborn eye, and a truculent jaw, with ears apparently broken off but leaving the impression that they are flattened back in anger—not a mount for a trepid rider. Yet, when we consider that South Indian sculptors many centuries later produced terra-cotta horses twenty-five feet high, we might consign this horse to wishful thinking.

In medieval India, even in regions "comparatively highly developed and prosperous . . . the horse [did] not breed well."[17] Sufi paintings often depicted emaciated horses,[18] perhaps because the Sufis regarded horses as metaphors for the body's insatiable desires. But these images of wretched horses may also have been responding compassionately to the difficult conditions under which most horses (and many people) suffered in India. In the nineteenth century, John Lockwood Kipling remarked of Indian horses that "the animals that take their chance with the poor are always light in form and often of spectral slenderness."[19]

Europeans have been quick to condemn the Indian subcontinent as a place to raise horses. Marco Polo (1254–1324), who visited India in around 1291, noted the sorry state of horses in Malabar: "[I]t is my opinion that the climate of the

FIGURE 3. Freestanding sandstone horse, found at Khairigarh in Uttar Pradesh, fourth century CE. In the State Museum, Lucknow. (Courtesy of the John C. and Susan L. Huntington Photographic Archive of Buddhist and Asian Art; photo by John C. Huntington)

province is unfavourable to the race of horses, and that from hence arises the difficulty in breeding or preserving them. . . . A mare, although of a large size, and covered by a handsome horse, produces only a small ill-made colt, with distorted legs, and unfit to be trained for riding."[20] Centuries later, in 1814, the British veterinarian and adventurer William Moorcroft observed: "There are few breeds of Horses raised in the North-West, which can work with vigor, during the hot months, in India. Sooltan Muhmood Ghuznuwee was obliged to withdraw his foreign cavalry from service during the hot season."[21]

INDIAN FODDER

Problems of climate were compounded by problems of nutrition.[22] Marco Polo insisted that horses in India died not just from the climate but from unsuitable feeding; when they bred, they produced "nothing but wretched wry-legged weeds.[23] . . . For food they give them flesh dressed with rice and other prepared meats, the country not producing any grain besides rice."[24] The Mughal emperor Akbar's historian Abu'l Fazl (1551–1602) testified that in addition to grass when available, and hay when there was no grass, horses were fed boiled peas or beans,

FIGURE 4. Emaciated horse and rider, Bijapur, Karnataka, c. 1625. (Metropolitan Museum of Art, 44.154)

flour, sugar, salt, molasses, and ghee (clarified butter, used both for cooking and in Hindu rituals).[25] Other sources agree that, lacking the right sort of fodder grasses and hay, people in India fed horses mainly wheat, barley, and horse gram (*kollu,* Sanskrit *chanaka,* a kind of pulse related to the chickpea) and mixed these grains with all sorts of stuff: cow's milk, coarse brown sugar, and sometimes even boiled mutton mixed with ghee.[26]

No oats were grown in India until the nineteenth century, and even today, you can't grow hay in South India.[27] M. Horace Hayes, in his 1878 study *A Guide to Training and Horse Management in India,* provides an itemized list of the sorts of fodder that were available for horses in India, accompanied by a tragic chorus of complaints about their inferior quality. Here is what he says about oats:

> Oats. This grain, when grown in India, possesses a far larger proportion of husk to flour than that produced in England, hence its lower value as an article of food. . . . Although our Indian oats are far below the standard, still they are much superior, as a food for horses, to any other grain which we can procure. . . . In order to make up for the inferior quality of the oats, we may, with great advantage, supplement them by an addition of gram.[28]

He goes on to talk about gram ("It is objectionable on account of its tendency to cause diarrhea"), rice, and grass ("In some districts it is necessary to convert a quantity of it into hay for consumption during the rains").[29]

In particular, Europeans criticized Indians for feeding their horses ghee, a disastrous diet for herbivores. (The fool in Shakespeare's *King Lear* is said to have "in pure kindness to his horse, buttered his hay" [2.4.128].) Lockwood Kipling complained:

> The climate is not favourable to the pig-like roundness of form shown in all modern Indian pictures [of horses]. . . . But by rigorous confinement and careful stuffing with rich food even this condition is approached. Many horses belonging to persons of rank are fattened like fowls in France, by the grooms thrusting balls of food mixed with ghi [ghee], boiled goats' brains, and other rich messes down their throats. And, as may be expected, very many die of diseases of the digestion and liver under the process.[30]

Mr. T. Wallace, Lockwood Kipling's contemporary and professor of agriculture and rural economy at the University of Edinburgh, agreed:

> In addition to ordinary food, [the horses in India] got mixed with it 2 lbs. of sugar and from 1 to 2 lbs. of ghi daily. The first result of this feeding would be a rapidly thriving condition, accompanied with a sleek and glossy coat and an increase of fat; but the ultimate and most natural consequence proved to be the gradual breaking down of the system in each case at its weakest point through over-pressure.[31]

This regimen was said to result in many diseases, and in particular deaths from "fatty degeneration of the liver."

These problems were exacerbated when imported horses had to adapt to Indian foods.[32] Jean-Baptiste Tavernier, a seventeenth-century French merchant and traveler, wrote:

> The horses imported to India, whether from Persia or Arabia or the country of the Usbeks, undergo a complete change of food, for in India they are given neither hay nor oats. Each horse receives for its portion in the morning two or three balls made of wheaten flour and butter, of the size of our penny rolls. There is much difficulty in accustoming them to this kind of food, and often

four or five months pass before it can be accomplished. The groom is obliged to hold the horse's tongue in one hand and with the other he has to force the ball down its throat. In the sugar-cane or millet season they are given some at midday; and in the evening, an hour or two before sunset. They receive a measure of chick-peas which the groom has crushed between two stones and steeped in water. These take the place of hay and oats. . . . As neither barley nor oats are to be had in this country, . . . the horses are given some of these peas every evening, and in the morning they receive about two pounds of coarse black sugar, . . . kneaded with an equal weight of flour and a pound of butter. . . . During the daytime the horses are given some grass which is torn up in the fields, roots and all, and is most carefully washed so that no earth remains.[33]

Both Wassaf, a fourteenth-century Persian historian, and Marco Polo commented upon "the effect of the mishandling and unsuitable diet given to the imported horses in South India."[34]

Feeding ghee to horses is a really bad idea. But a Vedic text mentions a horse who was set free so that he could eat ghee,[35] and the *Arthashastra* recommends the feeding of ghee to mares and foals (and a mash including meat and liquor for working horses).[36] Apparently this practice continued into the modern period. Ranjit Singh's 14.1 hands prize stallion Pigeon, who lived to the age of thirty-five, in 1858, was said to be "as fat as possible," since his daily diet was "two-and-a-half pounds of sugar, two-and-a-half pounds of fine flour, and one-and-a-half pounds of clarified butter (*ghi*)."[37] And the 1880 *Gazetteer of the Bombay Presidency* wrote of the typical horse from Kutch: "His ordinary food is a mixture of pulse (*math*, Phaseolus aconitifolius) and millet (*bajri*, Penicillaria spicate), with in addition, in the cold season and after hard work, a mess of flour, molasses, and clarified butter. Before any extremely hard expedition the old outlaw custom of giving the horse a feed of boiled goat's or sheep's flesh is said sometimes to be still kept up."[38] The ghee indictment may be one of those canards that got repeated over and over, but people do tend to feed their most precious animals the things that they themselves like best, which often proves disastrous.

THE CARE OF HORSES IN INDIA

Some have argued that culture, rather than nature, is what kept horses from thriving in India. It has often been said (by people who may or may not have known what they were talking about, and who may or may not have wanted to slander the Indians) that, compounding problems caused by the inhospitable climate and lack of access to appropriate fodder, Indian kings and their servants simply did not know how to care for horses properly, that, in addition to feeding them enormous quantities of ghee and mutton, they made other mistakes in their care that kept their horses from thriving.

Marco Polo made several complaints:

> In consequence, as it is supposed, of their not having persons properly qualified to take care of them or to administer the requisite medicines, perhaps not three hundred of these [original five thousand in this particular herd] remain alive, and thus the necessity is occasioned for replacing them annually. . . . They all die because, they say, they have no grooms to come to them in sickness and know how to give a remedy; nor do they know how to care for them, but they die from bad care and keeping.[39]

Lockwood Kipling made similar complaints about the quality of Indian horse husbandry:

> The horse of the Indian noble . . . is imperfectly nourished in its early youth. . . . In India it seems impossible to persuade people that money spent on a growing beast is money invested. All they see is present loss. Then it is tied up during the greater part of its life, not merely secured by the head but tethered by heel-ropes . . . for Orientals have a passion for tying things up. A group of young horses in a pasture, free to exult in their strength, is a sight not seen in India, with a few exceptions to be presently noted.[40]

And he quotes Mr. T. Wallace, to the same effect:

> I spent some hours in one stable where over one hundred of the finest horses—Arabs, Barbs, Marwars, and Kathiawars—that India could produce were tied up and actually fed as fat as pigs. Horses that had cost Rs. 18,000 and Rs. 20,000 were kept in close boxes with most imperfect ventilation and were taken out only for show at rare intervals, and not at all for regular exercise.[41]

Marco Polo suggested that it was no accident that there were no "properly qualified" people to look after horses in India: "The merchants who bring these horses to sell do not allow to go there, nor do they bring there, grooms, because they wish the horses of these kings to die in numbers soon, on purpose that they may be able to sell their horses as they will; from which they make very great wealth each year."[42] Polo similarly accused the merchants of the Gulf of refusing "to let any horse-doctor travel to Ma'bar to teach the inhabitants better 'because they are too glad to let them die at the King's charge.'"[43]

Stephen Inglis, who did extensive field work among the potters of South India in the twentieth century, noted their similar indictment of the foreign horse trade: "One of my favorite stories is how the wily Arabic traders kept the secret of shoeing horses from the South Indians for centuries and so the poor beasts were simply ridden until their hooves wore down and they died. This added to the popular notion of the horse as an ephemeral, semi-divine creature (and made for steady business at the Arab end)."[44] And this practice—or, more likely, the mythology about this practice (for, in fact, North Indian farriery enjoyed a considerable reputation among Muslims)[45]—had important repercussions upon the mythology of the horse in India. Much of this criticism, from Marco Polo and the Delhi sultans to the British, reeks of foreign prejudice and imperial self-justification. Surely, at the very least, the foreign horsemen could have used their own good horse sense when it came to feeding and exercise, and also brought along some of their own grooms and vets.

THE EXPENSE AND LUXURY OF HORSES IN INDIA

As a result of the failure of Indian rulers to develop a successful program for breeding the sorts of horses they wanted in India, for whatever reasons, the importing of horses was "India's main extravagance."[46] There was an extensive and well-documented trade in the importing of horses throughout Indian history, particularly from Western and Central Asia, through the Northwest territories.[47] It is likely that Persian horses were imported into India from about 600 CE, and that the increased demand for Persian and Arabian horses first arose from the perceived threat posed by Arab cavalry, sometime after the conquest of Sindh by the Arabs in 712 CE.[48] Centuries later, when these foreign dynasties had been established, a steady stream of Central Asian imports was still "seemingly vital to the virility of Muslim rule."[49] The Deccan sultans and their opposite numbers, the martial Hindu kings of Maharashtra, Rajasthan, and Vijayanagar, imported Arabian horses on a large scale, "in order to improve the breed of cavalry horses in their own districts."[50] The best horses were imported from Central Asia ("Turki" horses), Iran, or Arabia ("Tazi" horses, from the Sanskrit *tajika*).[51] Wassaf remarked, "There is therefore a constant necessity of getting new horses annually and consequently the merchants of Islamic countries bring them to Ma'abar."[52]

It was not just a fad, a kind of inverted proto-Orientalism, in which what was foreign was good, what was native was bad. That sort of mythology did indeed develop, but it had a realistic base, too. New bloodlines have always had to be constantly reimported. It is true of horse breeding everywhere, but particularly where conditions are not good for horses, that breeders need a periodic infusion of new stock to maintain and improve the breed,[53] and in India it has been the custom to important new blood every five years or so.[54] Even the plucky little Tonga ponies who used to ferry tourists around the streets of Indian cities and villages needed the periodic infusion of foreign blood to maintain the breed.[55] For breeding purposes, it is better to import mares than stallions, and indeed the Indians seem to have imported mares more often than stallions.[56]

After each initial conquest, the rulers replenished their herds of horses with new stallions and mares imported from outside India. Ancient Sanskrit and Tamil sources (such as the *Arthashastra* and *Sangam* texts) observe that horses had to be imported, probably from Parthia, to which the Arabian trade was later added. Ninth- and tenth-century CE Sanskrit inscriptions tell us the northern route: through Kabul, Peshawar, Pindi, Kangra, Ambala, Delhi, and Gwalior,[57] the route through which the Vedic Indians and, later, the Turks entered India (and the territory that is also described in Rudyard Kipling's *Kim*).

But from the earliest recorded period in Indian history there was, in addition to the overland route from Central Asia, also a southern route, by sea from Arabia to ports in South India. A sixth-century CE Christian monk, Cosmas Indicopleustes, mentions the shipping of horses from Persia to the ruler of what is now Sri Lanka, who bought them for military purposes.[58] Ancient Tamil poems speak of "horses brought from distant lands beyond the sea."[59] A Tamil anthology of poems composed from the second to the fifth century CE mentions, among wares arriving at the seaport of Kaviripoom, "the tall galloping horses that came from the waters."[60]

Large numbers of horses were imported into the Pandyan kingdom, which, being in the remote south of India (the land least favorable to the breeding of horses), probably had the greatest need of them. South Indians, particularly in the vicinity of Madurai, even into the late twentieth century still told stories about the Pandyan kings' energetic importation of horses from Arabs, Greeks, and others.[61] And there is still more information about the lust for horses in the later dynasties of the Nayaks and Vijayanagara kings.[62] One of the sixteenth-century South Indian kings of Vijayanagara is reputed to have imported 13,000 horses annually for his own personal use and for his officers.[63] The horses landed at the

Portuguese colony of Goa and at other ports south along the Malabar coast. Portuguese traders like Payez, Nunez, and Diaz wrote extensively about the horse trade, in which 10,000 Arabian and Persian horses were imported into Malabar every year, despite their high cost.[64] A sixteenth-century mural recently discovered in the *gopuram* (entrance tower) of a temple in the district of Tirunelveli portrays the arrival from the Gulf of a ship laden with horses.[65]

This constant importing of new bloodlines made Indian horses extremely expensive. Some of the money came from Hindu temple revenues and the tax on courtesans attached to the temples.[66] Both foreign and Indian sources testify that South Indians imported as many as 14,000 horses a year, valued at 2,200,000 dinars of "red gold."[67] In Marco Polo's time, a horse cost five hundred *saggi* of gold, or one hundred marks of silver.[68] Polo remarked of the Pandyan ruler of Madurai, "No horses being bred in this country, the king and his three royal brothers expend large sums of money annually in the purchase of them from merchants of Ormus, Diufar, Pecher and Adem etc."[69] According to William Moorcroft, "The Khumbaet Rajahs formed a breed, the Katheewar [Kathiawar], at an expense almost exceeding belief." Indian fictional texts also reflect this extravagance: the Rajasthani hero Pabuji found no suitable horse until he remembered that Deval Charan had "crossed the seven seas and brought back *costly* horses."

Heavy losses at sea are one reason for the high cost of imported horses.[70] Indian kings had to pay for all horses lost on the voyage;[71] or, to put it differently, "it was said that the Vijayanagar rulers would pay even for dead ones."[72] This was a major consideration; since horses cannot throw up, seasickness can often become fatal; horses with upset stomachs develop severe colic and can die of a twisted gut. The folk etymology for the so-called horse latitudes (high pressure belts at latitudes 30°–35° N and 30°–35° S) tells us that when the Spanish shipped large numbers of horses to their colonies, and the ships became becalmed in the "horse latitudes," they sometimes threw the horses overboard to conserve water.[73] Shipping such "fragile and valuable cargo in a pitching East Indiaman on a six-month journey halfway round the world" was a costly and risky venture.[74] As Moorcroft notes: "As to Horses brought by sea, the freight of each from the Persian Gulph will be two hundred Rupees, and if stowed close during bad weather, some will probably be farcied and glandered [two very dangerous diseases of horses], as occasionally happens to Arab Horses imported at Calcutta."[75] When M. Horace Hayes discusses the management of horses on board ship, he laments: "Fully half of the horses which come from England to India, suffer more or less from inflammation of the feet (*laminitis*) from long standing."[76] British horses also became more scarce, and even more expensive, when so many of them were used, and killed, in the Napoleonic Wars (1803–15).[77] Importing horses at sea was therefore particularly perilous, but horses brought in overland also underwent hardships and losses.

In addition to being prohibitively expensive, horses in most parts of India have never been very useful. They do not pull the plow or give milk as cows and goats and buffalo do; horses in India seldom carry a pack; and except in Rajasthan, Sindh, and the Punjab, they are seldom ridden. They don't do farmwork as well as bullocks or water buffalo or donkeys (which are, unlike horses, desert adapted) or mules. Camels and elephants also do most of these jobs better. But at economic subsistence levels, villagers can't afford horses or camels. If a farmer had enough money to buy a horse, he would use it instead to buy a water buffalo, or two bullocks. Moreover, human beings in India often do the work of beasts of burden; human labor there is cheap.[78]

There is therefore no native, village tradition of using horses in India as there is among the natives of places like Ireland or Egypt, where the *people* kept horses.[79] The only common use for horses in India was, formerly, for military purposes. Nowadays, most people in India have never even seen any equine but the half-starved Tonga ponies and the small, rather cowed horses that a Hindu bridegroom traditionally rides to his wedding. For most Indians, horses are mythical beasts, like unicorns. Yet that equine mythology has always been vital to the history as well as to the art, religion, and literature of India. And that paradox is the driving force of this book.

THE DOMESTICATION AND WILDNESS OF HORSES

The history of horses in human religious conceptualization begins with the first evidence of their domestication, with the archaeology not merely of images and texts but of bones and bits.

The earliest relationship between horses and humans was that of hunting; before horses were domesticated, they were one of the many animals that galloped across cave paintings as they were hunted for food. But once domestication took place, the primary relationship between horses and humans became that of taming, which becomes a metaphor that dominates the mythology of horses in the historical period. Hunting and taming are intrinsic to the mythology of horses, whereas nobility, for instance, is not, though nobility appears in many horse myths as a common result of the economic conditions under which horses were kept.

When horses were first domesticated rather than hunted, they were still regarded as food, though their ritual importance and their intimacy with humans eventually kept them from being eaten by most horsey cultures,[80] even by some of those cultures that did kill them in sacrifices. After that, they were used first as riding animals and, later, put to harness.[81]

No one nowadays ever sees truly wild horses, because "wild" horses now are merely feral, domesticated animals that have reverted to the wild. But the heroes of stories told by non-horsey people often try to erase or destroy the imagined wildness of horses, usually by overpowering them through human violence. In such myths, the fact that horses remained foreign, other, to the culture of the storytellers, and feared by them, sometimes produces a sadistic version of taming, in which the humans are more violent than the horses. But where horses are known and loved, the metaphor of taming often takes on a more mutual aspect.

Many myths testify to the other side of the transaction of taming, to the role of horses in drawing humans from the tame into the wild. In the mythologies of India and Greece, as well as in medieval Europe and Britain, we read of princes who are lured by white stags[82] or white hinds or white swans or white unicorns—or white horses—from the safe territory of the royal parks to the thick of the forest, to the Other World, where they may meet their princess or encounter their dragon, or both (or both in one female dragon), but where, in any case, they learn what they need to know. Horses are liminal creatures, who lead humans from the world of the tame into the world of the wild, the magic, supernatural world of the gods and anti-gods—up to heaven, or down to the watery hell of the cobra people.

A twelfth century CE Sanskrit philosophical text, the *Yogavasishtha,* tells us that King Lavana was sitting on his throne when a magician waved his peacock-feather wand and introduced a man from Sindh, leading a horse. As the king gazed at the horse, he remained motionless on his throne, as if in meditation. After a few minutes he awoke and told his story: He thought he had mounted the horse and gone out hunting alone; the horse bolted and carried him far away, until he arrived at a jungle where he met a low-caste woman ... And the king now narrated a long adventure, all of which turned out to be both a momentary illusion and a real experience that had lasted for many years.[83] But it was the beautiful horse that had bewitched him and literally carried him away.

Many horsemen, and even more horsewomen, speak not of the "breaking" of horses but of their "gentling," the harnessing (or yoking, derived from the Sanskrit word *yoga,* "joining") of their wildness for our good, but not necessarily for their ill. Humans can never entirely succeed in taming horses; this is the charm and the challenge of an intimate association with an animal that always retains some measure of his primeval freedom. Horsepower is what we still use as a touchstone, a basis for other sorts of mechanical power. But horses are not machines; people who work with horses know that you are never in total control, that you never entirely tame a horse, who remains at some level always wild. There is a cowboy saying about this: "Never was a horse that couldn't be rode; never was a rider who couldn't be throwed." In the taming of a horse, force is used, but so is persuasion. At a certain moment, force becomes useless; there are some things that no one can make a horse do unless the horse wants to do it, unless he understands what is wanted of him and is willing to give up his physical superiority in exchange for something that he derives from his contact with humans.

And so horses, both in actuality and in Indian myths and rituals, are not tamed but, on the contrary, they *un*tame the humans. The stallion in the Vedic horse sacrifice was said to wander freely for a year, attended by the king's men, to claim for the king whatever grazing land the horse cared to wander through. This was a symbolic expression of freedom — political, of course, but also sexual, spiritual, what you will. And when the stallion was killed, he transferred those freedoms to the king. So, too, ordinary horses transfer to their riders some of their own wildness and freedom. One might, perhaps, think of this, too, in sacrificial terms, as a sacrificial exchange, not a sacrifice *of* a horse, but a sacrifice *by* a horse. And it is this exchange that is mythologized in the narratives of people who have horses, narratives about horses that speak, that weep, that love their riders and willingly give their lives for them.

THE MATING OF HORSES

City kids usually catch their first glimpse of the mating game when they see dogs doing it, but farm kids see horses mating, and no one who has seen horses mating ever forgets it. Cows and bulls go about it in a relatively calm and businesslike manner, but mares and stallions are ferocious in their foreplay, and the violence of their coupling burns into the retina of the unconscious of any witness. Ernest Jones and the Freudians see horses, despite their domestication, as symbolic of raw, natural sexuality. This is certainly true of horses in Indian mythology.

But the basic, brute sexual symbolism is complicated by conflicting concepts of the gender of the horse. Real horses come in both male and female forms, of course, but symbolic horses are usually one thing or the other. We Anglophones[84] use the word for the male animal, "horse," to designate the breed in general, stallions and mares and geldings, when we refer to "the horses in that field" (just as, contrariwise, we use the word for the female animal, "cow," for cows, bulls, or steers — "the cows in that field"). The horse is "he," unless we specify a mare or stallion. The stallion, a large, powerful, impulsive, and aggressive animal who bites and tramples, symbolizes macho sexuality. But mares bite and trample too, and are notoriously, sometimes dangerously, skittish about mating, thereby running head-on into many sexist cultural stereotypes of gender that make the mare a problematic female symbol: if the horse genus (*equus*) is essentially male, the mare is somehow unnatural, a kind of category error. Moreover, if *equus* is male and therefore appropriately fierce and violent, and females (human and animal) as a gender should be gentle and acquiescent, the stallion is the "right" animal, the good animal, while the mare, who can also be fierce and violent, is wrong, and evil.[85] By contrast, the cow, in India and beyond, symbolizes all that is generous, gentle, and maternal. For cows did better than mares in the transition from life on the steppes to intensive breeding and reproductive management, and this observed contrast further enhanced the mythology of evil mares (whores) and good cows (mothers).[86]

Male dominance led Indians (and others) to prefer the missionary position in intercourse, male/rider on woman/mare, and in India the image of the woman riding astride the man in the sexual act was called the "perverse" or "upside-down" position.[87] In Europe, women riders (think: Joan of Arc) supplied the unconscious imagery for the medieval witch, who may appear as a horse, transform a man into a horse and ride him, become a man-eating mare, or ride on her phallic broomstick to her bestial orgies with Satan.[88] The "nightmare," though etymologically unrelated to the word for the female horse (for it comes from the Old English *mare,* meaning "hag"), takes on explicit equine overtones from an early period in European mythology, through the attraction of assonance (Indo-European **mer, *mor,* "death"; French *mère,* "mother"; and English *mare,* "female horse"). The nightmare is a female monster closely related to the female demon known as the *succubus;* she presses down on a sleeping man's chest, producing a feeling of suffocation or forcing him to have sex with her. In India, sexually voracious female monsters had the heads of horses and the bodies of human or demonic females.

The ways in which horses interact with humans greatly influence our views and myths of horses and of our relationships with them. Horses have been dramatically altered by the history of their contact with humans. The physical changes are obvious (greater size, longer legs that are skinny and fragile), but so are the psychological changes, such as their nervousness, particularly in mares subjected to intensive breeding. Mares in the wild breed with far greater success than mares in captivity, who tend to have a relatively low level of fertility, thus requiring multiple matings that waste a lot of stallion power. Of course, it is humans who breed mares for beauty and speed, rather than for ease of conception or parturition; they corrupt them, then stigmatize them for the difficult, dangerous foaling that the humans themselves have purchased in the service of beauty and speed.

A mare will welcome the stallion only when she is in heat, and she may kick him in the head if she isn't. In the wild, where mares and stallions are always together, the gentleman can sense when the lady is or is not in the mood and will generally avoid dangerous and demoralizing rejections. But when you have fenced a mare in, you have to make a special assignation with her, and you can't always tell when she's in season; and when she isn't, watch out. Worse still, mares tend to be testy and capricious even (or, indeed, sometimes especially) when in heat, and their unfortunate tendency to kick the stallions who try to mount them often inflicts permanent damage or impotence. The equicidal tendency of such mares would dampen the enthusiasm of the most passionate stud, making such an unfortunate stallion what breeders call a "dud stud." The mare thus comes to represent desirable beauty and speed, purchased at the price of danger (to the male) and infertility. This then is the naturalistic basis for the myth of the deadly mare, demonized in the eyes of humans (and, presumably, stallions).

Despite the availability of artificial insemination (which is used by almost all breeders of prize bulls), most breeders of prize Thoroughbreds insist on going to the considerable expense and trouble of having the stallion cover the mare in their presence, to make sure that the semen actually belongs to the stallion under contract. Deceit and trickery have always been, and are now more than ever, factors in horse breeding. Think of all the "doubles" and "ringers" that horse copers use, and the ingenious sleights of hand in Dick Francis novels. In fact, blood typing on semen now ensures what stallion it comes from, but still people usually insist on having the stallion there in the flesh, just to be certain (or for the fun of watching?).

THE WINGS OF HORSES

The need to control mares and stallions for breeding is the most dramatic instance of the more general need to tame horses altogether. An Indian story that tells how horses lost their wings functions as a metaphor for the domestication and taming of horses. The *Ashvashastra* version of the myth features Indra, king of the gods, and Shalihotra, a mythical figure to whom are attributed several important Sanskrit works on medicine, including veterinary medicine. The story also involves Gandharvas, magical demigods closely associated with horses. (Their name is cognate with the Greek "centaurs," though the Greek and Indian mythologies are quite different.) Gandharvas have wings, as horses no longer do:

Formerly horses were born with wings, and moved in the sky like the Gandharvas, wherever they wanted, everywhere. Seeing them so full of power, proud of their power, but capable of becoming vehicles [*vahanas*], Indra said to Shalihotra, the great sage who was standing beside him, "There is nowhere in the triple world where they cannot go; therefore, take away their wings." Sending for a weapon made of reeds, Shalihotra cut off the wings of the horses, as Indra had commanded.

When all the horses had lost their wings, they were miserable, overcome with suffering, bleeding heavily, and they said to the sage, "Why have you cut off our wings, when we had not committed any offense? Good people do not act like this. You must therefore be a refuge for all the horses here, so that they will always be happy." The sage was filled with pity, as they were so unhappy, and he replied to them: "I did this because Indra commanded it, even though it was hurtful to you. Therefore, I will do something to make you happy, to make you thrive and earn respect throughout the universe. Become the vehicles of the gods—the Sun, Indra, and others—and this will make you respected among the kings of the earth. Whatever king nourishes you with pasture grass and water and so forth will certainly become very difficult to conquer. Lakshmi, goddess of fortune, will never abandon such a king, even if he is devoid of all good qualities and surrounded by powerful enemies. And I will establish the supreme art of healing, to nourish men and cure their diseases. Therefore, some of you go to the earth, or go to the underworld if that will make you happy, and others go to heaven, by my command, wherever you will find peace." And in this way, the sage Shalihotra calmed down the horses. And from that time on, horses wander in this world, and the art of curing them, that Shalihotra invented, is here too.[89]

This is the founding myth of harnessing the power of wild horses.

The myth of the winged horses permeates Indian literature. The *Rig Veda* refers to special horses on several occasions as "winged," as does the *Ramayana,* and there is a widespread Indian folk tradition of mythical demonic winged horses that dominated the mountains.[90] Among the tribal myths of Middle India, it is said that a demonic winged horse, or two horses, endangered the god's creation of the first human beings; as a punishment, the god cut off the wings of the horses and reduced them to the condition of riding and pack animals.[91] According to other Indian folk traditions, horses originally had wings, and the hard places called "chestnuts" on their legs are the scars in the place where the wings originally grew.[92] (We speak of the fluffy hair on the lower legs of ponies and rough-bred horses as "feathers," perhaps a distant echo of that same myth.) An illustrated text, in Hindi, depicts the taming of the celestial horses, the cutting off of their wings, in a series of lurid and bloody paintings.[93]

The Tamil poet C. Subrahmaniya Bharathi (1882–1921) incorporated into a whimsical satire on the *Ramayana* an even more whimsical satire on the myth of the horses' wings. His version of this story, which involves Rama, the hero of the *Ramayana,* and Ravan, the villainous ruler of the island of Lanka, went like this:

> When Ravan heard the news that Ram had come to invade Lanka, he began to roar with laughter: "Hahaha!" The sound of his laughter was so loud that the sun couldn't bear the noise and fell down, and the horns of the sun's seven horses broke. The sun came and fell at the feet of Ravan, beseeching him tearfully: "My horses have the boon of immortality. They are swifter than other horses, but their horns have broken. From now on, everyone in the world will laugh at me. What shall I do?" Out of compassion for the sun, Ravan said to Brahmadeva [the creator]: "From now on, you must create horses without horns. That way, there will be no reason for anyone to laugh at the sun's horses." Since that day, Brahma has created horses without horns.[94]

Despite their winglessness (not to mention their hornlessness), horses continue to fly throughout Indian folklore.

HORSES IN THIS BOOK

The ancient Indians saddled horses with a wide range of interrelated symbolic phenomena: power, royalty, divinity, sexuality, and, more particularly, flying, taming, and freedom. Horses were essential to the religious imagination of India. This book is an attempt to sketch out the development of that imagination, first in the Vedas, then in the two great Sanskrit epics, the medieval Puranas, the scientific textbooks, the vernacular epics, and contemporary art and folklore. Horses make a significant appearance in Buddhism, in Mughal art and literature, and under the British Raj. They were important to villagers who had never touched a horse. Even in the modern period, after Independence, Marwari horses inspire controversy over the question of who, among Indians or non-Indians, has the right to define the right sort of Indian horse. In each period, we need to understand as much as we can of the actual history of the people telling the stories before we can understand their stories.

The Indian ambivalence toward horses is both intrinsic and culturally constructed. Horses are often, if not always, regarded with mixed feelings: they are both tame and wild, both male and female, both divine and demonic, both solar and chthonic, both sexy and infertile, and both native and foreign. But in India this intrinsic ambiguity is enhanced by a different sort of ambivalence fostered by the place of horses in Indian history, by their association first with the people of the Vedas and the *Mahabharata* and then with Arab, Turk, Mongol, and British equestrians. In successive phases of mythology, horses are associated first with positive male values, in the Vedas; then with negative, gynophobic values, in the Vedas, Epics, and Puranas; and then with positive female values, in the glorified mares of Arab-influenced Rajput narratives. Certain basic themes crop up again and again even in different Indian subcultures, but at the same time each subculture has its own ideas about horses. Buddhist horses, Mughal horses, Tamil horses, tribal horses both are and are not like Vedic horses.

I will try to trace, in the following chapters, the history behind the stories that Indians told about their horses, and the history of those stories. As horses turn out to be an intrinsic part of Indian myth, art, folklore, and literature, anything like an encyclopedic coverage of their full cultural range would be unreadable. Since I never met a variant I didn't like, I have included a number of different versions of stories that were told over and over again, never quite the same, across the centuries. (Readers who find such variations tedious are advised to skip the indented paragraphs and their framing analyses.) In the end, I offer here, embedded in the context of the history of horses in India, my favorite Indian stories about horses.

2 | ✿ | Horses in the Indo-European World but Not in the Indus Valley

3000 to 1500 BCE

The story of horses in India begins outside of India, in the broader Indo-European world, and involves archaeology as well as texts. These sources demonstrate both how central horses have been to Indian civilization from the very start and how they have been, from the start, foreign to the subcontinent.

INDO-EUROPEAN SPEAKERS

Nineteenth-century German and British linguists, building on some eighteenth-century hunches, uncovered connections between members of a language family (a rather dysfunctional family, but a family) that included ancient Greek, Latin, Hittite (in ancient Anatolia), Vedic Sanskrit (in ancient India), the Celtic and Norse-Germanic languages, and, ultimately, French, German, Italian, Spanish, English, and their friends and relations. All of these languages are alleged to have broken away from a single parent language sometime in the fourth millennium BCE, a language that linguists call Indo-European (or Indo-Germanic or Indo-Aryan) or, more cautiously, *Proto-Indo-European, as easy as *PIE.

The reconstructed, hypothetical (nowadays we would say virtual) forms of Indo-European are usually designated, like *PIE, with an apologetic or apotropaic asterisk. The Indo-European map is linguistic, linking languages together in a group that is distinct from other groups containing other languages such as, for instance, Chinese, or Hebrew, or Tamil. The evidence that the Indo-European languages are related lies primarily in their grammar and vocabulary. Thus "foot" is *pada* in Sanskrit, *pes, pedis* in Latin, *pied* in French, *fuss* in German, *foot* in English, and so forth. The earliest example of an Indo-European language that we have is a fourteenth-century BCE Anatolian treaty in Hittite that calls on the Hittite version of several Vedic gods.[1] Horses and horsemanship have long been central to investigations of Indo-European history, especially to the much-vexed question of the homeland of the *PIE speakers, and the arguments concerning horses have depended primarily upon archaeological and textual evidence.[2]

There is much debate about the hypothesis that the Indo-European speakers followed a diffusionist, centrifugal cultural movement from a political center, like an airline hub. If so, where was the hub? Probably somewhere in the area of the Caspian and the Mediterranean, perhaps in southern Russia, the Caucasus or the northern Black Sea or the Sea of Azov. (Arguments that the original *PIE home was India, though not indefensible, are driven more by nationalism than by scholarship. It is likely that the Indo-European speakers reached India no earlier than 1500 BCE.) But the mythical land of the family home might just as well be thought of as *Indo-Europe, the land East of the Asterisk.

The early Orientalists designated the Indo-European speakers with the San-skrit word "Aryan," the word that the Vedic people had used to refer to them-selves, meaning "Us" or "The Good Guys," long before anyone had a concept of race. Properly speaking, "Aryan" designates a linguistic family, not a racial group; there are no Aryan noses, only Aryan verbs, no Aryan people, only Aryan-speaking people. The Indo-European speakers were a people only in the sense of a linguistic continuum; the blood of many different peoples flowed in their veins. But the story became a thoroughly racist myth when the Nazis got ahold of it. (The Nazis, incidentally, also grotesquely distorted the ancient Indian good-luck symbol of the swastika, a Sanskrit word that simply meant "a good thing.") And so "Aryan" became a word that, like "gay" or "holocaust," no longer means what it once meant, and we can't forget what we now know about it; we can't regain our earlier naïveté. Since the Aryans were presumed to come from the Caucasus, they were also called Caucasians, which also became a racial designation. People always think about race when you say "Aryan," even though you tell them not to. It is therefore best (however cumbersome) to avoid using the "A" word, and to call the people who spoke or speak Indo-European languages "Indo-European speakers."

INDO-EUROPEAN HORSES AND HORSE SACRIFICES

The Indo-European speakers were mad about horses; wherever they went, they left horse bones and horse trappings, and often paintings or sculptures of horses. They shared the word for "horse": *H_1ekwo-, or *ekwos to its pals, the *PIE word for "horse," yields the Latin equus, Gallic epos, Greek hippos, Sanskrit ashva, old English eoh, English equine, and so forth, with further variants in languages that include Luwian, Tocharian, Tacharian, Venetic, Anglo-Saxon, Gaulish, Old Irish, and Old Church Slavonic (which also has a word for "horse groomer").[3] A Mittannian named Kukkulis, whom the Hittite king Sepululiumas employed as Master of the Horse, composed the earliest book we know of that deals with nothing but horses (a book that has a word for "horse trainer"), in about 1360 BCE.

The first archaeological evidence of the domestication of horses consists of bits, supporting other evidence that by 3000 BCE people in northern and central Europe kept small numbers of horses for riding, and by 2000 BCE signs of horses appear regularly on Bronze Age domestic sites in central Europe.[4] The technique of riding horses spread in the Near East, first from Anatolia and northwest Iran, by the end of the second millennium BCE,[5] and by the ninth or eighth century BCE horses were widely used as personal mounts.[6]

The Persians tell of a battle between an evil black horse and a good white horse, whose victory released the fertilizing rains; and the Iranians regarded white horses as symbolic of the sun.[7] Rituals involving horses, more particularly rituals that involve the killing of a white stallion, are attested throughout the Indo-European world.[8] Horses were sacrificed among the Armenians, Massagetes,[9] and Scythians, of whose spectacular royal burials and sacrifices Herodotus gives us a hair-raising description.[10]

But it was with the Vedic Indians and the Romans that horses truly came into their own as a religious symbol. The Greek mythological sources are supportive of but not truly analogous with the Vedic and the Roman in any detail; in particular, though horses were sacred to Poseidon, there is no evidence that the Greeks ever actually sacrificed horses. But it is an Irish text that supplies the best counterpart for the Vedic and Roman horse sacrifices, forming a triangle on which the Indo-European evidence rests, however shakily.

The facts of congruence are impressive, though grotesquely dissimilar in the weight and substance of the three sources. The Vedic ceremony is by far the best documented, both in terms of the contemporaneity of the ritual with the text describing it (both from 900 BCE, but referring back to Rig Vedic hymns to the horse, perhaps half a millennium earlier) and in the volume of data: hundreds and hundreds of lines of Sanskrit texts. The Roman ritual is a poor second, cursorily described by Polybius, Plutarch, and Festus,[11] with worrisome discrepancies and lacunae. The Irish ritual is even more problematic, having been described only in the twelfth century CE, by a Christian clergyman who could scarcely believe his eyes, so appalled was he by the obscenity of the rite.[12]

Yet the parallels are truly striking. In India, a ritually consecrated white stallion was killed after a chariot race; the chief queen then pantomimed copulation with the stallion.[13] In the Roman Pales festival (Parilia) in April, a horse was mutilated (perhaps castrated),[14] and in the Roman October festival, the right-hand horse of a winning chariot was sacrificed to Mars on the Field of Mars; its tail—more precisely, the organ designated by the Latin term *cauda*—was carried to the Regia, where its blood was sprinkled on the altar (Plutarch) or the hearthstone (Festus). In Ireland, the king pantomimed (or performed) copulation with a live mare who was afterward dismembered and cooked; the king bathed in her broth and drank it, and the broth was then distributed to the people. The common thread in all three is the killing of an equine. In two of the rituals (India and Rome), the horse is a stallion; in two of the rituals (India and Ireland), there is a sexual union as well as a death. These motifs, together with others (such as the communal meal, the presence of mares and queens, and the chariot race), form the basic vocabulary or building blocks, a kind of Erector set, if you will, out of which the three different religions built three different configurations of the ritual of a horse sacrifice. A bit of ancillary support is offered by evidence that, among the ancient Norse, a white horse symbolizing the sun and accompanied by women was killed in a ritual that involved obscene references to the phallus of the horse, ritual castration, and an intoxicating drink.[15] Tantalizing, suggestive details of the Vedic ritual can be heard echoing through the corridors of Indian literature for many centuries.[16]

DRAVIDIAN SPEAKERS AND THE INDUS VALLEY CULTURE

Humans must have ridden astride before they yoked a horse to a chariot; once a horse has been gentled or tamed, it is natural enough to swing one's leg over him. Certainly this is more likely to have happened before anyone got around to constructing anything as elaborate as a horse-drawn chariot. A simple noseband, or even a rope around the neck, could have sufficed for a young boy or girl bareback on a quiet animal. Horses are very useful in herding cattle, which is always easier to do from horseback in places where the grazing grounds are extensive.[17] The systematic riding of a horse, however, and in particular the harnessing of a horse, necessitated a more efficient method of control, that is, a bit. There is evidence of bits from early sites in the Indo-European world, before there is any evidence of chariots.[18]

For a long time, however, scholars argued that humans drove horses in harness before they rode astride, and this is because our first historical (in contrast with prehistorical) records are monuments of royal cults, in which chariots were the dominant form of equitation. The earliest historical evidence is of chariots; the visual evidence of the Babylonian friezes and the literary evidence of Homer and the *Rig Veda* (the earliest Indian text) depict chariots, not horses ridden astride. But before that, and continuing among common people, horses were generally ridden rather than driven. As Michael Witzel has put it, "Indo-Aryan nobility fought from chariots, and the commoners on horseback and on foot."[19] This contrast takes another form in mythology, where the equine metaphor of driving horses harnessed to a chariot was intellectual, political, and aristocratic, in contrast with the metaphor suggested by mounting, more physical, sexual, and plebeian. The two techniques give rise to very different sorts of mythologies and histories.

Horses yoked to spoked chariots are the key to an ongoing argument about the origins of Indian civilization.[20] The smug theory, held by nineteenth-century British and European scholars, that a cavalcade of blond-haired, blue-eyed "Aryans" drove their spoked chariots through Eurostan and into India, c. 1500 BCE, bringing civilization with them, has been challenged on both academic and political grounds.[21] As our certainty about the Indo-European conquests has melted away, new answers have thrown their hats into the ring, many of them just as politically driven as the "Aryan-invasion" theory and, like most politically driven theorizing, ranging from plausible (if unsupported) to totally bonkers. The general consensus (among scholars, both Indian and European) is that the Indo-European speakers simply settled gradually and quietly in India, or (among Hindu nationalists) that they started out in India and then conquered the rest of the world.

In 1856 came the discovery of the great cities of the Indus Valley, though their importance was fully appreciated by scholars only after 1917, and widely discussed only in recent decades. The extraordinarily rich material remains of this culture, which we call the Indus Valley Civilization (IVC) or the Harappan Civilization (named after Harappa, one of the two great cities on the Indus River, the other being Mohenjo-Daro), an area now in Pakistan, date from about 3000 BCE. Arguments about the identity of the people of the IVC have often turned on the language of the script that appears on numerous small seals: are they in an Indo-European language or in another language, perhaps an ancient form of Dravidian, the non-Indo-European language family of India and Pakistan? Since no one has yet succeeded in deciphering the script,[22] the debaters seek their evidence among the archaeological remains. Arguments based on a tantalizing treasure trove of often enigmatic images hover just beyond our reach, taunting us with what might well be the keys to the roots of later Indian civilization. The evidence that the IVC met a violent end is now generally debunked,[23] though some scholars continue to argue that the authors of the *Rig Veda* destroyed the IVC cities.

Which brings us to the horses. The English have a saying, "No foot, no horse."[24] I would say, "No horse, no *PIE." The archaeological evidence supports the hypothesis that, wherever Indo-European speakers arrived, they rode and/or drove, rather than walked; their horses trotted in at the same time as their languages. There are (despite spurious arguments to the contrary) no horses in the IVC remains, neither bones nor bits nor images on the seals. No Indus horse whinnied in the night. As Romila Thapar put it, "The horse, the animal central to the Rig Veda, is absent from the Harappan seals" and is "unimportant, ritually and symbolically, to the Indus civilization."[25] Even were we to accept any of the rather farfetched arguments for a stray bit of equine bone here or there in the IVC, or the image of a horse among the many other animals, from monkeys to rhinos, that figure abundantly on Harappan seals, we would have to grant that horses rarely if ever appear. Horses became important figures only in the Vedic age. The IVC was therefore neither invented nor destroyed by Indo-European speakers such as, to take a case at random, the authors of the *Rig Veda*. Most scholars now agree that "there is a gap of some centuries between the two cultures, as the descriptions of ruins and simple mud wall/palisade forts (*pur*) in the Rigveda indicate. . . . The local people (*dasyu*) of the small, post-Harappan settlements . . . are said not even to understand 'the use of cows.'"[26] Whatever contributions the two cultures made to later Indian culture they made separately, the Vedas leaving an unbroken verbal trail, ridden by many a sacrificial horse, the IVC offering archaeological materials that may or may not be the source of many later Hindu visual images[27]—but little, if any, evidence of horses.

So there were probably no horses, and therefore no Indo-European speakers, in the IVC, since wherever there are Indo-European speakers, there are horses. But it does not necessarily follow that where there are/were horses, there are/were Indo-European speakers. The simple, and long-held, assumption that every horse is an Indo-European speaker's horse is incorrect.[28] We must beware the trap of the excluded middle: though all crows are black, not all black birds are crows. Other people also domesticated horses at an early period, both far beyond India and inside India,[29] and it didn't happen all at once even in Central Asia. The ancestor of the horse, the so-called Dawn Horse, or *Eohippus,* much smaller than the modern horse, lived throughout Europe as well as North America in the Eocene age, some sixty to forty million years ago.

Good, albeit slim, evidence that horses were domesticated in India at a very early period, long before the IVC and even longer before the presence of the Indo-European speakers (however they got there), has been found in various Indian sites. Megalithic remains may represent the source of a pre-Indo-European equine tradition in some Indian tribes or villages. There is evidence of domesticated horses from the nineteenth century BCE in the excavations in Ghaligai in the Swat valley.[30] The remains of horses have been found in the megalithic burial mounds of the Deccan,[31] perhaps dating from as early as sometime between the seventh and twelfth century BCE.[32] In 1922, in Baluchistan (now in Pakistan), Walter Granger discovered the Baluchitherium, the largest land mammal ever found, a perissodactyl twenty-two feet at the withers, the ancestor of the tapir/ rhino/horse.[33]

These sites contain horse bones and human bones, as well as horse bits and sidepieces of bridles. The first-century CE Greek historian Arrian was wrong when he recorded that Indians did not use bits, as early terra-cotta representations of horses bridled with bits clearly show.[34] Horse paraphernalia (such as bits) in Maharashtra and south of the Narmada River during the time of the IVC (though not in the IVC) suggest an extensive network of horse trade from northwest India.[35] We know that there was a great deal of trade between India and the ancient Near East; there is therefore no reason why horses could not have reached India from various Near Eastern sources before the arrival of large numbers of Indo-European-speaking equestrians. Horses may have come from Arabia, through Sindh; or by sea, from Syria and Nubia, and the west coast of Iran. But these horses would have been scattered, not part of a concentrated horsey culture like that of the Vedic Indians. Whatever bits of horse lore there might have been in India in the second millennium BCE may well have survived and reemerged in the local folklores of India, but it was overridden by the elaborate equestrian traditions that the Indo-European speakers brought with them.

3 | ✿ | Horses in the Vedas

1500 to 500 BCE

tallions are heroes, and mares villains, in the oldest Indian text, the *Rig Veda* (composed in Sanskrit in northwest India, c. 1500 BCE), and in the supplements to the *Rig Veda,* the Brahmanas (c. 900 BCE) and the Upanishads (c. 600 BCE). These Vedic texts present a consistent vision of the horse as a stallion, martially and sexually potent, the ultimate macho sacrificial animal. In the *Rig Veda,* the horse represents the "Aryas," as they called themselves, against the indigenous inhabitants of India, the "slaves" (*dasyus*), whom they associated with the serpent Vritra. But the Vedic texts also contrast the good stallion with the dangerous mare, a scenario that is rooted in the conditions of breeding horses in India and that continues to dominate Indian mythology until the medieval period. In this earliest period of recorded Indian literature, the stallion represented martial and political aggression and aggrandizement, particularly the invasion of hostile territory, as he would continue to do in later Indian history. And Upanishadic horses already begin to symbolize the unbridled passions that pose a danger for Indian ascetic traditions.

Three Rig Vedic hymns tell us that the Ashvins, twin equine gods, gave a man named Pedu a horse that had the power to destroy snakes.[1] This is part of a widespread mythology in which the horse that conquers the snake represents us against them (as in the icon of St. George, on horseback, killing the dragon). In a tenth-century temple in Tamil Nadu, a freestanding statue of a winged horse rears up, with his front feet resting on the hoods of a five-headed serpent. David Shulman connects this icon with Pedu: "It is," Shulman says, "almost as if the Tamil village shrine were offering us a graphic representation of this almost forgotten Vedic symbol."[2]

THE SACRIFICIAL STALLION IN THE *RIG VEDA*

The sacrificial horse must be male, like all Vedic sacrificial animals. The *Rig Veda* contains several hymns to the sacrificial horse. One identifies him with the sun and fire, and with several gods, including Indra, King of the Gods and God of the Storm (like his Indo-European cousins Zeus, Jupiter, Wotan, and Odin), the god to whom most horse sacrifices were offered. The poet closes by imagining the arrival of the winged horse in heaven and reminds him not to forget his human friends:

> When you whinnied for the first time, as you were born from the ocean, with the wings of an eagle and the forelegs of an antelope—that was your great birth, Swift Runner. . . . These are the places where they rubbed you down when you were victorious; here are the marks where you put down your hooves. . . . From afar, in my heart I recognized your soul, the bird flying below the sky. I saw your winged head snorting on the dustless paths that are easy to travel. . . . The chariot follows you, Swift Runner; the young man follows, the cow follows, the love of young girls follows. The troops follow your friendship. The gods entrusted virile power to you. His mane is golden; his feet are bronze. He is swift as thought, faster than Indra. . . .
>
> The celestial coursers, reveling in their strength, fly in a line like wild geese, the ends held back while the middle surges forward, when the horses reach the racecourse of the sky. Your body flies, Swift Runner; your spirit rushes like wind. Your mane, spread in many directions, flickers and jumps about in the forests. The racehorse has come to the slaughter, pondering with his heart turned to the gods. The goat, his kin, is led in front; behind come the poets, the singers. The Swift Runner has come to the highest dwelling-place, to his father and mother. May he go to the gods today and be most welcome, and then ask for the things that the worshipper wishes for.[3]

The sacrificial horse (like many a racehorse today) has a goat as his companion, but in India the goat was also the usual animal killed in ordinary sacrificial rituals, less elaborate than the great horse sacrifice, the *ashvamedha*.

Another hymn describes, and blesses, in strikingly concrete images, all the grim paraphernalia of the slaughter, as well as the dismemberment, the cooking, and the eating of the horse. The poet then apologizes to the horse for all of this gruesome ritual and even for possible mistreatment of the horse during his life:

This goat for all the gods is led forward with the racehorse. . . . The hewers of the sacrificial stake and those who carry it, and those who carve the knob for the horse's sacrificial stake, and those who gather together the things to cook the charger—let their approval encourage us all. . . . The charger's rope and halter, the reins and bridle on his head, and even the grass that has been brought up to his mouth—let all of that stay with you even among the gods.

Whatever of the horse's flesh the fly has eaten, or whatever stays stuck to the stake or the axe, or to the hands or nails of the slaughterer—let all of that stay with you even among the gods. Whatever food remains in the stomach, sending forth gas, or whatever smell there is from his raw flesh—let the slaughterers make that well done; let them cook the sacrificial animal until he is perfectly cooked.[4] Whatever runs off your body when it has been placed on the spit and roasted by the fire, let it not lie there in the earth or on the grass, but let it be given to the gods who long for it. Those who see that the racehorse is cooked, who say, 'It smells good! Take it away!', and who wait for the doling out of the charger's flesh—let their approval encourage us. . . .

If someone riding you has struck you too hard with heel or whip when you shied, I make all these things well again for you with this prayer. . . . Let not the dear soul burn you as you go away. Let not the axe do lasting harm to your body. Let no greedy, clumsy slaughterer hack in the wrong place and damage your limbs with his knife. You do not really die through this, nor are you harmed. You go to the gods on paths pleasant to go on. The two bay stallions, the two roan mares are now your chariot mates. . . .

Let this racehorse bring us good cattle and good horses, male children and all-nourishing wealth. Let the goddess Infinity make us free from evil. Let the horse with our offerings achieve sovereign power for us.[5]

The poet is quite shameless in acknowledging, in gory detail, the harm that has been done to the horse—though he glorifies his death—in order for his patron to have the things he wants from life. An image in a manuscript of the *Ramayana* depicts the Brahmins at their grim tasks in the horse sacrifice.

THE VEDIC MARE: SARANYU

The Vedic ritual of the sacrifice of a stallion is balanced by the Vedic myth of a goddess who takes the form of a mare named Saranyu ("Fleet"). The Veda wraps the story in a riddle,[6] but here is a brief summary of the plot:

FIGURE 5. Brahmins preparing the horse for sacrifice. Rishyashringa and the Brahmin priests are severing the limbs of the horse and cleansing them in the sacred waters of the river Sarayu. From a manuscript of the *Ramayana* originally produced in Udaipur, 1712. (© The British Library Board, Add. 15295, f. 34)

The blacksmith of the gods[7] gave his daughter, Saranyu, in marriage to the Sun,[8] and she gave birth to twins, Yama and Yami. Then the gods concealed the immortal woman from mortals; they put in her place a female of-the-same-kind (*savarna*), and gave that look-alike to the Sun. Saranyu took the form of a mare; the Sun took the form of a stallion, followed her, and coupled with her. From that were born the twin equine gods called the Ashvins. She abandoned them, too.

As the later Indian tradition attempts to unlock the riddle of Saranyu, it draws upon many deep-seated, often conflicting, ideas about human and divine sexuality and deception. In place of the statement that the gods concealed Saranyu from her husband, later texts blame Saranyu for the separation and speculate on various reasons for her flight from her husband: as the sun, he was too hot for her; as a mortal, he was not fit to mate with an immortal; and so forth.

In the *Rig Veda,* the female in this story is explicitly an immortal, while her husband, the Sun, is a mortal (one of those mortals from whom the gods hide her); he was born to die,[9] for he dies each night/autumn and is reborn each dawn/spring. That Saranyu's husband and child are closely connected with death is as clear as anything in this riddle. Yama is often said to be the first one who died,[10] and he becomes the god of the dead. Saranyu's double is said to be of-the-same-

FIGURE 6. The birth of the Ashvins. Folio from a *Harivamsha*, Lahore, Pakistan, Mughal empire, c. 1585–90. Opaque watercolor, gold, and ink on paper. 16⅛ × 11¾ in. (Los Angeles County Museum of Art, from the Nasli and Alice Heeramaneck Collection, Museum Associates Purchase [M.83.1.7]; digital image © Museum Associates / LACMA, Licensed by Art Resource, NY)

kind (*savarna*) as Saranyu, of the same sort, or type, or appearance, or of the same color or class (*varna*), but, unlike Saranyu and like the Sun, the double is mortal.

The double produces no children, but Saranyu in her own persona produces a child whose name (Yama) means "twin" and who is then usually regarded as twins. As the mare, she produces the twin Ashvins, who are liminally immortal: they are often depicted as centaurs, half horse and half anthropomorphic gods (or half divine horse and half mortal humans), like the Greek Dioscuroi or the Roman Gemini, Castor and Pollux. The Sun is acquainted with mares: the seven bay mares that pull his chariot are sometimes said to be his seven daughters.[11]

Saranyu's ambivalence toward her husband splits the story into two contrasting sexual episodes: as a goddess, she leaves him; as a mare, she receives him. Though someone other than Saranyu herself makes the female look-alike, she herself abandons both "the twin" (Yama) and the equine twins; there are no other children. Saranyu is the Vedic evil mother.

But as this story is retold in later mythology, an essential change is made: Saranyu herself, rather than the gods, makes the look-alike, who is now usually called the Shadow (or mirror image, Chaya). And the Sun, not at first realizing that a substitution has taken place, begets a mortal child upon the Shadow. Only after realizing his mistake does he pursue the mare Saranyu and beget the equine twins on her.[12] The story is narrated in detail in a commentary on the *Rig Veda* in which the children continue to proliferate: now not only does the Shadow have a son, but Saranyu has yet another son (her third birthing, and her fifth child, if you count Yama-the-Twin and the Ashvins as two sets of two):

> Saranyu's father willingly gave her in marriage to the Sun, and Saranyu bore him the twins Yama and Yami. Out of her husband's sight, Saranyu created a female who looked like her. Tossing the two children to this female, she became a mare and went away. But in ignorance of this, the Sun begat Manu upon that female. . . . Then the Sun became aware that Saranyu had departed in the form of a mare, and he took the form of a horse and went quickly after her. Saranyu, knowing that it was the Sun in the form of a horse, approached him for coupling, and he mounted her. But in their haste the semen fell on the ground, and the mare smelled that semen because she desired to become pregnant. From that semen that was inhaled twins were born, the famous Ashvins.[13]

By conceiving through her nose, the mare is placing smell, the reliable equine criterion for the appropriate sexual partner, above vision, the flawed human (and, apparently, divine) criterion. Whereas vision made the Sun mistake the wrong female (created "out of his sight") for his wife, and made the mare at first mistake him for someone else, ultimately smell allows Saranyu the mare both to recognize her true mate and to conceive by him. The procreative powers of equine sniffing are cited in a Brahmana: "The creatures that the Creator made did not procreate. He changed himself into a horse and sniffed at them and they procreated."[14] The statement that the Ashvins were conceived from the nose (*nasat*) may also have been inspired by a desire to account for their Vedic epithet of Nasatyas, "Nose-beings,"[15] though the name is elsewhere said to mean "not false" *(na-a-satya,* literally, "not-not-true" or "not-not-real")—an interesting assertion in light of the fact that they are the "true" sons of Saranyu, in contrast with their not-equine, and not-immortal, brothers. Some later texts regard Revanta, another offspring of the Sun and the Shadow, as the ancestor of all horses.[16]

But in many texts the child born of the Shadow is Manu, the ancestor of humankind. Both of his parents are mortal, flawed, and doomed. The mortality of the Sun is a pivotal point of the myth in all its variants, and in most of them Manu is the son not of the first wife, the true wife, the immortal wife, but of the replica, a mortal. As anthropogonies, these stories are saying that the primeval human children, our ancestors, were abandoned by their mother. And on the metaphysical level, the myth of Saranyu (or Samjna, "the Name," as she is called in many later variants) seems to be saying that we, the descendants of Manu, are the children of the image, the Shadow—the children of illusion, not the children of the real thing. These myths embody the later Indian philosophical view that we are born into illusion, live in illusion, and can only know illusion. Clearly, this is a deeply religious story, not merely (or not even primarily) a story about parents and children (human and equine). For, in addition to psychological questions regarding stepmothers, rejected children, and unwanted husbands, the Saranyu story raises theological questions about the origin of the human race and human death, about appearance and reality, about the relationship between male and female divine powers, and between humans and the divine and the equine.[17]

DOUBLY FERTILE MARES AND BARREN MULES IN THE BRAHMANAS

Saranyu's connection with twins is part of a broader mythology about another sort of "doubleness" that all mares have: the ability to be impregnated by the males of two different species, a stallion or a male donkey (called a jack or a jackass; the female donkey is a jenny). A mare is, in this sense, two-faced. (Donkeys are the victims of another sort of duplicity, vaguely reminiscent of the myth of Saranyu: when breeders put a jack donkey to a mare to breed a mule, some jack donkeys won't do it unless they tease him first with a jenny, a female of his own species, a "shadow" mare, if you will.)

The Brahmanas tell us that a mare has "double" seed, since she can accommodate both the stallion and the jack donkey:

Prajapati ("Lord of Creatures," the Creator) created the creatures and then laid hold of them in the twelfth month; therefore the females bear their young for ten months and bring them forth in the eleventh. The female mule went away from these female creatures as Prajapati was laying hold of them. Prajapati followed the female mule and took away her seed, which he then wiped off on the mare. Therefore the mare has double seed, and therefore the female mule is barren, for her seed had been taken away.[18]

Prajapati starts the process of reproduction going and then brings it to its fruition by touching the females, ending their pregnancy and bringing about their parturition. Like Saranyu, the female mule (confusingly called a mare-mule) decamps, apparently in order to avoid giving birth; Prajapati then punishes her, appropriately, by making it impossible for her ever to give birth at all. He "wipes off" the female mule's seed on the mare, which means that he transfers the seed to the mare; the barrenness of the mule results from (and corresponds to) the double fertility of the mare. The nature of this double fertility is not made explicit in this text, but another Brahmana tells us, "A mare with a foal is the sacrificial fee, for she gives birth to both a horse and a mule."[19]

The barrenness of the mule is proverbial in India. The mule in Sanskrit is called *ashva-tara* (female, *ashva-tari*), "a sort of a horse" or "more than a horse." The grammarian Patanjali, in the second century BCE, says that the "*tara*" suffix denotes superior quality: "What is called a horse [*ashva*] can walk four leagues. What is called a better horse [*ashva-tara*] can walk eight leagues."[20] But the grammarian Panini, in the fourth century BCE, had said that, on the contrary, the "*tara*" suffix denotes thinness, which is to say deficiency, and a seventh-century CE commentator explains: "A horse [*ashva*] comes from a mare as mother and a stallion as father; the deficiency of a mule [*ashvatara*] is that it has something else [i.e., a donkey] as its father."[21]

One Brahmana explains the mare's doubleness by linking her with her male counterpart, the jack donkey, and describes the transfer of seed not from a female mule to a mare but from a male mule to a jack donkey: "When Prajapati was laying hold of all these creatures, the male mule ran away from them. Prajapati followed the mule and took his seed, which he then wiped off on the donkey and on the mare and on cattle and on plants. Therefore the donkey has double seed, and therefore the mare has double seed."[22] This passage explains why the male mule is barren, while the donkey can impregnate either a female donkey or a mare, and a mare can be impregnated by either a stallion or a jack donkey.

Mares, donkeys, and oversexed women are linked together in land-grant stones called Gardabha stones (donkey stones), from about the tenth century CE, throughout a belt that extends along Gujarat, Andhra, Maharashtra, and Orissa. These stones bear the following inscription: "If anyone takes this land, a donkey or another animal will do this to your mother."[23] Some of the boundary stones in Gujarat are engraved with horses or donkeys copulating with women, and on them is inscribed, "Whoever comes beyond this boundary, let his mother copulate with a horse." This is also a common Gujarati curse: "If you do such and such, let your mother copulate with a horse."

The double-sexed (which comes to mean oversexed) Vedic mare, whom we first encountered in Saranyu, will haunt later Indian mythology. Throughout Sanskrit literature, a mare is equivalent to what Europeans would call a bitch, more precisely a bitch in heat. In the *Kamasutra,* the "mare's trap," a position that can only be done with practice, is one in which the woman, "like a mare," grasps the man with the lips of her vagina, so tightly that he cannot move.[24] And in the Epics and Puranas a mare is a metaphor for the insatiable appetites of a woman out of control.[25] A character in a Sanskrit play from the fourth century CE remarks that fate, which comes in pursuit of a man by day or night, in good luck or bad, is like a filly that has broken loose from the reins and is "unbridled," or, as we might say, has "kicked over the traces."[26]

In the *Rig Veda,* there is a verb that means "to desire horses,"[27] that is, to wish to own lots of horses, said of certain men. In later Sanskrit, however, another verb appears, said only of mares, consisting of the noun for "horse" (*ashva*) plus the verbal suffix meaning "to desire"; the resulting verb is *ashvasya, ashvasyati,* "to desire [that is, to lust for] a horse [i.e., a stallion]."[28] We say, in English, that a cow is "bulling" when she shows signs of being in heat (such as trying to mount other cows), but we do not say that a mare in this condition is "stallioning"; Sanskrit, however, has a verb that lets you say that. The twelfth-century poet Harsha, for instance, applies this verb to mares who passionately desire the horses (here regarded as stallions) that draw the chariot of the Sun.[29]

THE HORSE SACRIFICE IN THE BRAHMANAS

The stallion ritually consecrated for the Vedic horse sacrifice "wandered" for a year, returned, engaged in a chariot race (in which he was generally the right-hand horse of the winning team),[30] and then was killed by suffocation. The political agenda of this sacrifice is blatant. During the year of his "wandering," the king's men "set free" the consecrated white stallion and an army "followed" him and claimed for the king any land on which he grazed. But in fact, though a stallion in the wild will indeed wander in search of new grazing land, a horse that has been stabled will not stray far from that stable when he's loose; he'll come back home to be fed. The idea that he will wander away as he used to do in his salad days up in the hills of Central Asia was by this time an anachronism, a conscious archaism. Now he had to be actively driven in order to make him "wander" away from home. ("Doubtless some manipulated the wandering of the horse to save face," Romila Thapar remarks dryly.)[31] So the "following" army would sit down each night and decide whether or not they dared to cross over the border to the next territory; and then they would herd the horse to go where they thought he ought to go. If they were met by opposition, they would fight the owners of the land thus transgressed and so establish the "right" of their stallion to graze there. The charade of the horse's chance wandering masked the human control of the horse's itinerary, just as the ceremonial chariot race at the end of the year must have been rigged to ensure that the sacrificial stallion was the winner (as he always was), and the Vedic sacrifice in general hoped to control the chance catastrophe of death.[32] The ritual that presented itself as a casual equine stroll over the king's lands was in fact an orchestrated annexation of the lands on the king's border. No wonder the Sanskrit texts insist that a king had to be very powerful indeed before he could undertake a horse sacrifice.[33]

A correlation between the horse and the king is frequently made in the course of asserting the horse's physical and quasi-political superiority over the other animals. And indeed in the Vedas, as in ancient Greece, there was "a common predisposition toward the anthropomorphizing of horses and the concomitant hippomorphizing of humans."[34] The horse is said to rule over his "subjects" in the animal kingdom like a king and to be physically dominant like a warrior.[35]

The horse sacrifice was designed to restore the king who had been sullied by the bloodshed necessitated by his office. But new things could go wrong during the period when the horse was said to wander freely. So restorations were prescribed if the horse mounted a mare, or became lame, or got sick but not lame, or if the horse's eye was injured or diseased, or if the horse died in water. And finally: "If the horse should get lost, [the sacrificer] should make a sacrificial offering of three oblations. . . . And if enemies should get the horse, or if the horse should die, . . . they should bring another horse and consecrate it by sprinkling it with water; this is the restoration for that."[36] And so there were stand-ins for the horse who was a stand-in for the king.

THE OBSCENITY OF THE HORSE SACRIFICE

The horse is, according to the Vedic texts, the most virile animal,[37] and the fertility and potency of the sacrificed stallion were enhanced by special ritual laws keeping him away from mares during the year preceding the ceremony.[38] The powers of the horse were transferred to the king in the course of the sacrifice, through the king's identity with Indra, the king of the gods:

> The horse is Indra.[39] . . . Indra ran the race with a horse-drawn chariot; therefore the horse, loudly neighing and snorting, is connected to Indra.[40] . . . The horse is virility; therefore the priest makes the horse turn around again so that this virility does not turn away from the sacrificer. He places fire in the horse's footprint. The horse is virility; he places the fire in virility.[41] . . . The gods put virility and physical strength into Indra with offerings of horses[42]. . . . The priest then fumigates the sacrificial vessels, saying, "I fumigate you with the dung of the stallion, the impregnator." For the stallion is an impregnator.[43]

And so forth, and so on.

The queen represented the fertile earth that the king both ruled and impregnated; the ceremony was intended to produce a good crop for the people and offspring for the king.[44] The human queen who is essential to the horse sacrifice in the Vedas and Brahmanas may have absorbed some of the role of the mare in the ancient Indo-European horse sacrifice. The queen in the ritual acts as an intermediary who transfers to the king the seed of the stallion, and with it the royal and magical powers of the stallion.[45] Even in the *Rig Veda* there are hints that the ritual may have included the mimed copulation of the queen with the stallion; one Vedic poem may be a satire on the horse sacrifice, with a sexually challenged male monkey playing the role of a mock stallion.[46]

But the Brahmanas are the first texts to describe the horse sacrifice in any detail. In the course of the sacrifice, four of the king's wives (the chief queen, the favorite wife, the rejected wife, and a fourth wife)[47] mimed copulation with the stallion (after he had been killed), and other women (one maiden and four hundred female attendants) played subsidiary roles. The presence of several queens also introduced into the Indian ritual a political factor, the jockeying (*sic*) for favor among the queens that became a metaphor for political intrigue, "co-wife" (*sa-patni*) being a synonym, in Sanskrit, for "enemy." A Gupta coin depicts

FIGURE 7. Gupta coin of a horse sacrifice, with a queen on the obverse side, probably from Samudra Gupta, 330–36 CE. *Obverse:* Caparisoned horse facing left before a decorated sacrificial post, which rests on a pedestal. *Reverse:* Female figure facing left, wearing a gown and earrings, holding a fly whisk (chowrie) over her right shoulder and a cloth in her left hand, with a halo around her head. At her feet, a lotus, and in left field, a spear with ribbons. *Obverse inscription:* The King of Kings, performer of the Ashvamedha, conqueror of heaven. *Reverse inscription:* One who has the power to perform the Ashvamedha sacrifice. (© The Trustees of the British Museum, 1847, 1201.361)

a horse facing a sacrificial post and, on the obverse, a queen. The politics of sex are matched by the eroticism of political power.

Here the judgment of obscenity rears its head. The texts of the horse sacrifice include a lot of obscene banter about the size and character of the horse's phallus[48] and specify that the stallion should have an erection.[49] The chief queen pantomimes copulation with the stallion, but she complains that the stallion—who is, after all, dead at this point—is not, in fact, performing well: "No one is 'marrying' me; the little horse is sleeping."[50] This action is accompanied by verses (spoken by priests) that even the liturgical texts themselves regarded as obscene and for which they therefore prescribe a "perfumed" verse to be recited at the end, to wash out the mouths of the participants.[51]

The Vedic Indians were embarrassed by the obscenity of the horse sacrifice, and this embarrassment contributed to its eventual desuetude.[52] In the *Ramayana,* King Dasharatha performs a horse sacrifice in order to beget a son. His chief queen, Kausalya, "spends one night with the horse, her mind steadfastly fixed on her desire for dharma,"[53] while two other wives of the king also "unite with the horse," and as a result of this ceremony, the three queens give birth to Rama and his brothers.[54] This text hints at the sexual nature of the horse sacrifice by immediately prefacing it with another long, famous (and in some

FIGURE 8. Queen Kausalya performs the horse sacrifice (*left*). She then spends the night next to the body of the horse (*right*). From a *Ramayana* text originally produced in Udaipur, 1712. (© The British Library Board, Add. 15295, f. 33)

Buddhist retellings very funny and very dirty) story about the notoriously chaste sage Rishyashringa, who had never seen a woman.[55] (His mother was an antelope; it's a long story). An ancestor of Dasharatha had had Rishyashringa seduced by courtesans and brought to the capital to perform the king's horse sacrifice. (In the Buddhist version, the chaste sage mistakes the courtesans for men with two peculiar but delightful growths on their chests, and something missing from between their legs . . .). Dasharatha now sends again for Rishyashringa (this time without the courtesans) and engages him to perform the sacrifice, and the queens lie down with the horse. An illustration of the *Ramayana* depicts Dasharatha's chief queen, Kausalya, lying down beside the horse.

The *Harivamsha* (c. 300–500 CE) tells a satirical story about a horse sacrifice begun by King Janamejaya but interrupted by the god Indra, the deity to whom horse sacrifices were offered. It seems that Indra, overcome by desire for the wife of King Janamejaya, one day took advantage of the occasion of a horse sacrifice to combine the roles of sacrificer, recipient, and victim:

> Janamejaya was consecrated for the sacrifice, and his queen approached the consecrated stallion and lay down beside him, according to the rules of the ritual. But when Indra saw the woman, with her flawless limbs, he desired her. He himself entered the stallion and mingled with the queen. And when

this transformation had taken place, Indra said to the priest in charge of the sacrifice, "This is not the horse you consecrated. Get out of here."

The priest, who understood the matter, told the king what Indra had done. The king cursed Indra, saying, "From today, kings will no longer offer horse sacrifices to this king of the gods, who is fickle and cannot control his senses." And he fired the priests and banished the queen.

But then the king of the Gandharvas calmed the king down by explaining that Indra had wanted to obstruct the sacrifice because he was afraid that the king would surpass him with the merits obtained from it. To this end, Indra had seized upon an opportunity when he saw the consecrated horse, and he had entered the horse. And the woman with whom he had coupled in that way was actually an Apsaras [a celestial nymph, traditionally the wife of a Gandharva]; Indra had used his special magic to make the king think that it was the queen, his wife. The king of the Gandharvas persuaded the king that this was what had happened.[56]

The *Arthashastra* remarks (perhaps alluding to this story) that Janamejaya used violence against Brahmins and perished, and a commentary on that passage in the *Arthashastra* adds that Janamejaya whipped the Brahmins (the *Harivamsha* just says that he fired them) because he suspected them of having violated his queen, though in reality it was Indra who had done it.[57] The ending of the story in the *Harivamsha,* which forbids not all horse sacrifices but only horse sacrifices consecrated to the god Indra, reflects the historical fact that Indra, a Vedic god, was no longer worshipped by the time the *Harivamsha* was composed.

Indra steals sacrificial horses on many occasions throughout Indian mythology, since he is jealous of his title as the one who performed a hundred horse sacrifices (even though he himself is usually the recipient), and he therefore tries to prevent other kings from doing this. He also changes his shape from time to time in order to seduce married women (most notoriously Ahalya, the wife of the sage Gautama, an occasion on which Indra invents adultery).[58] Perhaps the Vedic stories of Indra's horse thefts gradually morph into Epic and Puranic stories of Indra's adulteries, as religious practices shift from horse sacrifices to asceticism[59] and from a fairly casual Indo-European sexual code to later Indian strict marital chastity (for women). A man who stole a king's horse transferred the king's royal and martial power to himself; a man who cuckolded an ascetic (or had him seduced by a woman) usurped his victim's magic powers.

In the epilogue, a Gandharva persuades the king that it was all an illusion. But was it? Was the god really there? Or has the Gandharva revealed the deeper illusion, the illusion that in every horse sacrifice the sacrificial horse is Indra and not just a horse? The horse sacrifice is similarly demystified and satirized in a twelfth-century text in which Kali, the spirit of the degenerate Kali Age, watches the coupling of the sacrificer's wife with the sacrificial horse and announces that the person who made the Vedas was a buffoon—though the text hastens to assure us that Kali is no pandit.[60] And in a fourteenth-century Sanskrit doxography, Brihaspati, author of the Charvaka heresy,[61] is said to have mocked the Vedic ritual in which "the sacrificed wife takes the phallus of the horse."[62]

In the eleventh century, the Arab scholar Alberuni, who lived in India for much of his life, described the horse sacrifice as he knew it to be practiced: the horse is a mare, who "wanders" before the sacrifice (just as the stallion did, in the Vedic texts), and the attendants who follow her proclaim, "She is the king of the world. He who does not agree, let him come forward." Alberuni does not mention any sexual act at all.[63] He seems to have missed the point. And wherever did he get the idea that the sacrificial horse was a mare?

When Ralph T. H. Griffith translated the texts of the horse sacrifice into English in 1899, he left out the episode of the queen and the stallion, and he remarked: "This and the following nine stanzas are not reproducible even in the semi-obscurity of a learned European language."[64] That learned language was, of course, Latin, into which other lewd bits of Sanskrit were traditionally translated. (When scholars encountered such passages in Latin texts, such as Catullus, they simply left them in Latin, in the midst of the English translation. If the translators of Catullus had known Sanskrit, they might have translated those bits of Catullus into Sanskrit in return, but this does not seem to have happened.)

Recently (September 23, 2019), someone in India posted an email which purported to clarify the meaning, and deny the obscenity, of the horse sacrifice (Ashvamedha). Here are a few excerpts:

ASHWAMEDHAM MEANS "INTELLIGENCE GATHERING BY HORSE" (IN MODERN PARLANCE IT IS "VOTE OF CONFIDENCE")..
ASHWAMEDHAM IS A RITUAL, NOT A BLOOD SACRIFICE..
HINDUS DID NOT DO ANIMAL SACRIFICE TILL THE WHITE INVADER CAME TO INDIA..LEAVE ALONE RAMAS MOTHER QUEEN KAUSHALYA USING THE DEAD HORSES PHALLUS AS A DILDO IN FRONT OF ALL.

MEDHA IS A FEMALE BABY NAME . . WHICH HINDU WILL NAME HER
CHILD "SACRIFICE?"
WENDY DONIGER PUT ASHWAMEDHA ON THE COVER OF HER
BOOK.[65]

So the horse sacrifice, including the *Ramayana* version of that embarrassing episode of the queen and the dead stallion, is still, apparently, a bone of contention
in certain circles in India.

THE SEVERED HORSE HEAD

The Vedic sacrificial horse was killed not by beheading but by strangulation or
suffocation, and was then dismembered, at which point the head would be sepa-
rated from the body. But the idea of a severed horse head (sometimes connected
with an anthropomorphic body) is a persistent image in Indian mythology and
visual art.[66] The *Rig Veda* refers rather cryptically to a myth about the head of a
Vedic sage named Dadhyanch who learns the secret of "the mead," the elixir of
immortality, which revives the sacrificed horse.[67] The Brahmanas tell us more:

> Dadhyanch knew the secret of the mead and the secret of the sacrifice: how
> the head of the sacrifice is put on again and becomes complete. Indra threat-
> ened to cut Dadhyanch's head off if he told this secret to anyone. The Ashvins
> asked him to tell them the secret and made this provision: they first cut off his
> head and laid it aside, then placed the head of a horse on his neck, and then
> he told them the secret through the horse head. Indra cut off that head, the
> Ashvins brought back his own head and restored it, and all was well.[68]

"The head of the sacrifice" is the head of the sacrificial horse. The Ashvins, being
only partly divine, as well as part mortal and part horse, are at first not allowed
access to the secret hiding place of the elixir of immortality, but they gain it in
the course of the story by giving the sage Dadhyanch a horse head (temporarily),
mimicking the form that this text (and others) assume that the Ashvins themselves have. This text also adds the secret of the sacrifice—that is, the secret by
which the mutilated victim is made whole again, in this case the secret of ex-
changing a human head for a horse head and then back again.

We will encounter Dadhyanch again in later periods of Indian mythology,
sometimes under the name of Dadhichi. We will also encounter other horses who

speak, as well as people pretending to be horses who speak and people talking to horses in the expectation that they understand human speech. In the *Ramayana*, for instance, when Rama is leaving the city, the people beg him not to go; a group of aged, learned Brahmins address their pleas not only to Rama but to his horses, saying, "You understand what we are asking, for creatures have ears, especially horses."[69] Sometimes, as in the tale of Dadhyanch, even (or only) when it is severed from the horse's body, the horse head speaks.

HORSES IN THE UPANISHADS

The very first words of the oldest of the Upanishads, the *Brihadaranyaka,* are a meditation on the sacrificial horse:

> The head of the sacrificial horse is the dawn. His eye is the sun, his breath the wind, and his open mouth is the fire that all men share. The body of the sacrificial horse is the year. His back is the sky, his stomach the middle region, his underbelly the earth, his flanks the quarters, his ribs the middle quarters, his limbs the seasons, his joints the months and fortnights. The contents of his stomach are the sand, his intestines the rivers, his liver and lungs the hills. The hairs on his body are the plants and trees, his forequarters the rising sun and his hindquarters the setting sun. When he yawns, lightning flashes; when he shakes himself, it thunders; and when he urinates, it rains. His neighing is speech itself. . . . He became a steed and carried the gods; he became a racehorse and carried the Gandharvas; he became a charger and carried the anti-gods; he became a horse and carried the humans. The sea is his counterpart; the sea is his womb.[70]

The same attention to minute anatomical detail that characterized the Vedic and Brahmana sacrificial texts is here joined to a cosmic vision of the horse as the world.

This Upanishad also goes on to speculate about the relationship between horses, the sacrifice, death, and the Sanskrit word for "horse." In a passage just a few verses after the one quoted above, the body of Death himself dies and begins to swell up (*ashvat*), as dead bodies do; but Death still has a mind, and he wills his swelling body to become a horse (*ashva*). Then: "Death believed that the horse should not be fenced in in any way. At the end of a year, he sacrificed it as a sacrifice to himself, while he assigned the other animals to the gods."[71] Elsewhere it is said that Agni, the god of fire, is like a hungry horse who had been yoked but now must be set free.[72] Again we encounter the idea of the horse running free, in the face of all the evidence of his confinement.

THE INCEST MYTH, THE WILD AND THE TAME

Another passage from this Upanishad takes the core of the Saranyu myth—the idea of a wife taking the form of a mare to flee from her husband (to whom, the text begins by saying, her father had given her)—and combines it with a myth about an incestuous father:

> The first being split his body into two, creating a husband and wife. He mated with her, and from that mating human beings were born. She thought to herself, "He created me from himself; how could he mate with me? I will hide myself." She became a cow; but he became a bull and mated with her again, and from that mating cattle were born. Then she became a mare, and he a stallion; she became a female donkey, and he a male donkey. And again he mated with her, and from their mating were born all the animals that have a single hoof. Then she became a nannygoat, and he a billygoat; she a ewe, he a ram. And again he mated with her, and from their mating goats and sheep were born. In this way he created every male and female pair that exists, right down to the ants.[73]

Now we are given a new motive for the flight of the female: she is fleeing, unsuccessfully, from her father, and from rape. And now the mare takes her place, after the cow, among all the other animals in creation.

There is a fine symmetry to this list, which encompasses all the defining species of the ancient Indian animal world. At the two ends of the spectrum are humans and ants. Right after humans come the pairs of other mammals, including the female counterparts of the macho sacrificial trio: the cow (the mate for the bull or buffalo), the mare and the female donkey (which we have seen to be the two consorts of the stallion), and the nanny goat and ewe. (The goat and sheep are often joined in a single Sanskrit noun, *ajavi*, goat-sheep, and in fact the two animals, though not of the same species, are very closely related.)

The central macho trio, and their female counterparts, constitute the main members of the class of animals known in Sanskrit as *pashu* (cognate with the Latin *pecus*, the English "impecunious" [out of cash, i.e., cattle]). I have translated *pashu* as "cattle," but it more properly designates the domestic animals that one raises for food and for sacrifice, in contrast with the wild animals or *mrigas* that are hunted for food (from the verb *mrig,* "to hunt"). Ancient India thus classifies all the animals according to the way they are killed and eaten. (That's all I'll say, in this book, about contemporary Hindu claims to primeval vegetarianism.)[74]

The incest myth in the *Rig Veda* tells of the father's attempt to mate with his daughter, an act that the gods oppose.[75] The Brahmanas expand upon this theme, speaking of wild animals (rather than the domestic animals that we have seen in the later Upanishadic version of the myth): when the Creator tried to commit incest with his daughter, she became a female wild animal (*mrigi*) and he became a male wild animal (*mriga*). When the gods intervened to prevent the act of incest, they created an avenging god who beheaded the Creator in his wild animal form.[76] But the domestic animals come in here too, for the gods rewarded the avenger by making him lord of cattle (*pashus*), and so he is called Pashupati (a name of the god Rudra, later Shiva).[77]

From our standpoint, humans and ants are equally remote from the central group of domesticated animals, but in the Indian view the humans are a part of it.[78] *Pashus* are animals fit to be sacrificed to the gods; they are the livestock of the gods, the food of the gods. Human beings are simply the best of these animals; what horses are to humans, humans are to the gods.

HARNESSING THE HORSES OF THE PASSIONS

One of the later Upanishads, the *Katha Upanishad,* uses the metaphor of harnessed horses to describe the control of human emotions:

> Think of the self as a rider in a chariot, and the body as the chariot. The intellect is the charioteer, and the mind is the reins. The senses are the horses, and the objects of the senses are the paths all around them. When a man lacks understanding and fails to control his mind, his senses disobey him, as bad horses disdain the charioteer. But when a man has understanding and controls his mind, his senses obey him, as good horses respond to the charioteer.[79]

Where the Vedas valued the martial power of horses, the Upanishads feared their sensual power. One Sanskrit word for an aphrodisiac is "something that turns a man into a racehorse" (*vaji-karana*).

The lawmaker Manu, in the first century CE, cautioned: "The wise man should strive to restrain his sense organs, which run wild among alluring sensual objects, as a charioteer restrains his horses."[80] Even the *Kamasutra* (c. second century CE), which is in general a powerful advocate for sensual pleasure, compared the passions to dangerous horses that must be controlled:

> Just as a horse in full gallop,
> blinded by the energy of his own speed,
> pays no attention to any post
> or hole or ditch on the path,
> so two lovers blinded by passion
> in the friction of sexual battle
> are caught up in their fierce energy
> and pay no attention to danger.[81]

A sixteenth-century text agrees about the problem and suggests a solution: "When horses run unrestrained over rough terrain, the wise check them with the reins and tie them with a rope. And when the senses run rampant across the terrain of sense objects, the wise check them by showing them the defects of this view and bind them to the truth with the rope of the heart."[82]

Horses as symbols of unbridled, or bridled, passions form a motif that we will be able to trace throughout Indian literature. In the *Mahabharata,* to which we now turn, appetites that are difficult to tame are symbolized by the underwater mare with the doomsday fire in her mouth, held in check not by the reins of the mind but by the waters of the great ocean.

4 | ✿ | Horses and Snakes in the Underworld in the *Mahabharata* and *Ramayana*

300 BCE to 300 CE

CHARIOTEERS AND BARDS

Horses run through the *Mahabharata,* the great Sanskrit epic composed between 300 BCE and 300 CE, in the Ganges Valley (though the central action takes place in the earlier Vedic world, up in the northwest of India and what is now Pakistan). The conflict and collusion between horses and snakes comes to symbolize the tension between good and evil both on the cosmic scale and on the political level, to which horses in India are always highly relevant.

Horses are built into the very structure of the *Mahabharata,* as it is narrated by Sutas, men who are both charioteers and bards. Each charioteer would have gone into battle with one warrior as a combination chauffeur and bodyguard. And then at night, when all the warriors retired from the field and took off their armor and nursed their wounds and sat around the campfire and relaxed with food and drink and women, the bards would tell the stories of their exploits. Later, traveling bards no longer participated in battle, or drove chariots at all, but still recited the great poems at sacrifices and festivals and night-long performances in villages.

Manu, to whom the most important of the ancient Sanskrit texts about caste is attributed, says that the caste of Sutas is descended from the illegal intermarriage of the first two of the four social classes: because they are bards their original father must have been a Brahmin (of the class from which priests are drawn), and because they are charioteers their mother had to be a Kshatriya (of the class of kings and soldiers).[1] (The other two classes are Vaishyas—farmers and merchants—and Shudras, servants.) But because of their connection with animals, as well as the forbidden miscegenation of classes, Sutas are very low caste, far below either Brahmins or Kshatriyas. Manu also tells us that the Sutas are in charge of chariots and horses, and that they are what he calls an excluded caste, very low (later to be called Untouchables and, still later, Dalits).[2] The dark hero of the *Mahabharata,* Karna, is despised because he is raised by Sutas whom he thinks are his parents; the Kshatriyas call him "Son of a Suta" to mock him, and only at the very end is he revealed to be not only of noble, Kshatriya, birth but another brother of the five royal Pandavas, the heroes. In fact, two of the five Pandava brothers—the twin sons of the twin Ashvins—are also closely associated with horses. Called Nakula (also the name of the author of a famous textbook about horses) and Sahadeva, they work closely with animals. When the five brothers take on disguises in their year in hiding, Nakula becomes the king's groom; he says, "I like that kind of work. I am good at training horses and curing them. I have always liked horses."[3] Even Krishna, an incarnate god, assumes the role of Suta for the hero Arjuna, narrating to him, as they stand in the chariot before the battle, not a tale of war but the *Bhagavad Gita.* This event is often illustrated in paintings of Krishna standing beside Arjuna on the chariot, holding the reins of several white horses. Clearly the Suta was a person of highly ambivalent status, like the horses that he drove.

HORSES AND SNAKES

Horses occupy an equivocal place in the symbolism of the *Mahabharata.* Horses and birds, who share the power of swift flight, represent the sun and are depicted flying in the brightness of the sky; both are often associated with fire or made of fire. In the *Rig Veda,* Agni (Fire) changes himself into a horse in order to deceive the anti-gods,[4] and his flames are his bay chargers.[5] The *Rig Veda* and, earlier, Indo-European mythology imagined horses, winged horses, in the sky. Horses and birds also share a common enemy: snakes, cold-blooded animals whose element is water, particularly dark, subterranean water. But Indian horses are also connected with the earth (their apparent natural habitat) and with the subterranean waters, from which they are often said to emerge. They are thus doubly amphibious, or tribious, mediating between birds and snakes, generally (though not always) in association with birds and in opposition to snakes.[6] Through the connection of birds with the gods, the sky, and the light, and the association of snakes with the anti-gods, the underworld, water, and darkness, we are led to the related tension in horses between the divine and the demonic (itself a most ambiguous ambiguity in Indian mythology). These ambivalent metaphorical and religious values complicate the use of horses as political symbols throughout Indian history.

Precisely how horses and snakes are related, and why, are questions that the

Mahabharata addresses in a complex cycle of myths, many of which associate the horse with the underworld. The snake mythology is dominated by Nagas—anthropomorphic above the waist, cobra from the waist down (often with a cobra hood spread over the anthropomorphic head)—and, more particularly, Naga women or Naginis. Nagas live in the underworld and often dispense valuable jewels to handsome heroes; many equestrian heroes win their princesses through the combined agency of a magic horse and a Naga or Nagini.

Snakes help and/or harm horses throughout the *Mahabharata*. On one occasion, the great serpents Nahusha, Karkotaka, and others become bands to bind the manes of Shiva's horses.[7] When King Nala rescues a tiny snake from a forest fire, the snake turns into Karkotaka, whose bite transforms Nala into a charioteer, peerless in his knowledge of horses.[8] But when Nahusha becomes king of heaven, usurping the place of Indra, his downfall occurs when he uses the wrong sorts of horses: he yokes sages instead of horses to his chariot, and when he goes so far as to whip the sage Agastya, Agastya curses him to become incarnate as a snake.[9] Another Naga, however, King Padmanabha, in another story, successfully takes the place of the horses that draw the chariot of the sun.[10] And the serpent who tries to save the snakes from a great forest fire is called Ashvasena ("Possessing an army of horses").[11]

The forest fires that endanger snakes in the *Mahabharata* are recurrent echoes of the great fire of the snake sacrifice attempted by the doomed King Janamejaya, a ritual that begins the *Mahabharata*, in the opening frame. Now, a horse sacrifice represents the culmination of the career of a royal Epic hero and the fulfillment of his righteous reign; King Yudhishthira, the eldest of the Pandava brothers, completes a successful horse sacrifice that is the central subject of one of the last books of the *Mahabharata* (Book 14). But a snake sacrifice is a tragic and broken inversion of a horse sacrifice. The horse is the right animal to sacrifice, the animal on which one rides triumphantly up to heaven; snakes, who drag one down to the watery hells beneath the earth, are the wrong animals to sacrifice. Vedic literature does tell us of a snake sacrifice, but it was a sacrifice *by* snakes, not *of* snakes; it was a sacrifice by which the snakes obtained immortality, by sloughing their skins. And two of the priests at that sacrifice were Takshaka, King of the Snakes, and a snake named Janamejaya.[12] In the *Mahabharata*, King Janamejaya attempts to destroy Takshaka and all the snakes in revenge for the death of his father, whom Takshaka had killed by biting him (in revenge for yet another snake disaster—it goes on and on, deeper and deeper into the past). Janamejaya fails; his snake sacrifice is interrupted (as was his horse sacrifice in the *Harivamsha*) and Takshaka

FIGURE 9. Krishna advising on the horse sacrifice. Probably from a picture-story series of the *Mahabharata*. From the Deccan, Karnataka or Andhra, nineteenth century. Opaque watercolor on paper. 11⅝ × 15¹¹⁄₁₆ in. (Philadelphia Museum of Art, Stella Kramrisch Collection, 1994–, 148-539a)

escapes, but only after hundreds of thousands of snakes have died in agony in the sacrificial fire.

Variants of the story of Janamejaya, told in Sanskrit and in the vernaculars, continue up to the present day. Near Varanasi, at Fort Chunar, people tell stories about a "Gun Major" (they use the English word); this name is a later British variant of the name of Janamejaya.[13] Here the *Mahabharata* lives on through the association with foreigners.

BETTING ON A WHITE HORSE WITH A BLACK TAIL

The saga of horses, birds, and snakes in the *Mahabharata* begins with one of the earliest attested examples of what we would call "fixing" (i.e., corrupting) a bet on a horse (though not the very earliest even in India; recall the "fixed" chariot race in the horse sacrifice in the Brahmanas):

> Kadru and Vinata, two sisters, were the wives of Kashyapa. Kadru gave birth to a thousand snakes, and Vinata gave birth to Garuda, king of the birds. One

day the two women saw the [white] stallion Ucchaihshravas. Vinata claimed that the horse was entirely white, but Kadru said he had a black tail. They made a wager, the loser to be the slave of the winner. Then Kadru ordered her sons to become like black hairs and to insert themselves in the horse's tail; at first they refused, and so she cursed them to be burnt in the fire at King Janamejaya's snake sacrifice; then they obeyed her. When Vinata saw what appeared to be the many black hairs in the horse's tail, she agreed to become the slave of Kadru.[14]

Though the horse in this myth is a stallion (like the Vedic horse, like all Indian sacrificial horses), it is surely significant that two females, two rival co-wives (the defining paradigm of enemies in ancient India, and sisters, to boot, as well as members of species hostile to one another) are the ones who make the trouble, causing one set of sons to be burned to death and the other set to be enslaved. Kadru and Vinata, the bad snake mother and the bad bird mother, carry on the tradition of Saranyu, the bad mare mother. The *Mahabharata* says, "Gandharvi gave birth to the horses; Surasa, the daughter of Kadru, gave birth to the snakes; and Kadru gave birth to the serpents."[15]

In a later Sanskrit version of the story of Kadru and Vinata, the two mothers dispute not the color of the tail of a single horse but the color of the entire body of each of the several horses of the sun (Kadru says they are black, Vinata that they are white), and the snakes spit venom on the horses to make them black.[16] In contemporary Tamil Nadu, they tell a version of the story in which Kadru and Vinata bet about the color of the tail of an *elephant,* not a horse; Tamil country is elephant country, not horse country, and since both are royal beasts, the substitution is easy enough. But the tail is still a matter of black-and-white, and the bet is still won dishonestly, and by the snakes: the great cobra Karkotaka raises his hood and casts a shadow on the elephant's tail, making it black.[17]

In the fifth book of the *Mahabharata,* there is another story about black-and-white horses:

> Vishvamitra told his pupil Galava to bring him eight hundred white horses, each with a black ear. (Along the way we discover that this is an impossibility: Originally Varuna, god of the ocean, had created a thousand of such horses, white with one black ear, at the Ford of the Horses, but four hundred of them were taken by a river as they were being led across, and only six hundred of the thousand survived). The great bird Garuda (son of Vinata) carried Galava to a

king who gave his daughter Madhavi to Galava. Galava sold Madhavi successively to three kings, each of whom gave him two hundred white horses (each with a black ear); each king also fathered an important son in Madhavi. Galava gave Vishvamitra the six hundred horses and (in place of the nonexistent remaining two hundred) gave him Madhavi for his wife, which satisfied him.[18]

The Garuda bird here, as usual, is the friend of horses and the enemy of snakes.

A BLACK HORSE WITH A WHITE TAIL IN THE UNDERWORLD

Another story in the first book of the *Mahabharata* involves snakes and a black horse with a white tail, the inverse of Ucchaihshravas, inverted perhaps because this story takes place in the underworld, where many things are reversed. In this tale, a sage named Uttanka, falling foul of the serpents, becomes the victim of a bizarre series of culinary challenges, including a bull's dung and the fiery farts of a magic horse:

Uttanka's teacher's wife asked Uttanka to bring her the earrings that belonged to King Paushya. Uttanka set out to do this, but on the way, he met a man mounted on an enormous bull. The man said, "Uttanka, eat the dung of my bull. Your teacher ate it in his day." Uttanka ate the bull's dung and drank the bull's urine and went on his way to Paushya's palace. When Uttanka asked Paushya's queen for her earrings, she gave them to him willingly, but she warned him that Takshaka, king of the snakes, wanted the earrings too. Uttanka assured her that Takshaka could not overpower him.

Uttanka set out with the earrings, but on the way, Takshaka stole the earrings from him and entered a chasm that had suddenly opened up in the ground. Uttanka followed him down into the realm of the snakes. There he saw two women weaving with black and white threads, and he saw a handsome man riding an enormous horse. He asked the man to help him overcome the snake. The man said, "Blow into the ass of this horse," and Uttanka did so. Then flames shot out from all the openings in the horse's body, and these flames smoked out the world of the snakes. Takshaka gave the earrings to Uttanka. The man gave the horse to Uttanka to ride back to his teacher's wife, and Uttanka arrived just in time to avoid her curse.

Then Uttanka asked his teacher the meaning of what he had seen, and his teacher told him that the two women were the fates, the handsome man on the horse was the god of rain and his horse was Agni, the god of fire; the bull was the king of snakes, and the man who rode him was Indra, king of the gods. It was because Uttanka had eaten the bull's dung, which was Soma, the elixir of immortality, that he had not been overcome in the land of the snakes. The teacher then dismissed Uttanka.[19]

The strange meals offered to Uttanka are part of the topsy-turvy world of the snake sacrifice. The purity or impurity of dung generally varies according to the nature of the creature that produces it: cow dung is a source of purification (when eaten as part of the *panchagavya* or five cow-products), but snake dung is highly impure: when the snakes hear of Janamejaya's intention to kill them in a sacrifice, some of them suggest that they dirty his sacrifice with their dung and urine, in order to defile all the food.[20] Indra's bull's dung is an unusual food, and disgusting, but probably more pure than impure; it was, moreover, we are told, eaten by Uttanka's teacher in previous times. In any case, a man capable of eating bullshit is surely capable of blowing into horses' asses. But Indra's remark is merely a twist on a statement often made to persuade someone to do something unusual: your teacher used to do it. And the dung turns out to be the best of all foods, the Soma, elixir of immortality. By blowing into the horse's ass, Uttanka inverts eating; more particularly, he inverts eating the bull's dung. And it is on this magic horse—who is the god of fire, Agni—that the hero rides away with his stolen treasure, the magic earrings.

Here, again, the horse is the enemy of the snakes. In light of the snake symbolism of the tail of the stallion Ucchaihshravas, it is not surprising that it should be the hind quarters of the horse that Uttanka must deal with in the world of snakes. This may be no more than an expression of the physical resemblance between a snake and a horse's tail, but it may mean something else as well: a reversal in keeping with the inversions generally characteristic of the underworld.

The black-and-white imagery also characterizes several pairs of women, who, like Kadru and Vinata, continue the contrast between good and bad women/ mothers. The two women weaving with black and white threads are the ambivalent fates, but we have also met both the greedy wife of Uttanka's guru, who makes the unreasonable demand to have the earrings, and the contrasting generous (and wise) queen in the underworld, who gives him the earrings.

The story of Uttanka is repeated, with variations, in the fourteenth book of the *Mahabharata* (the *Ashvamedhika Parvan*), the book that tells of Yudhishthira's successful horse sacrifice. This version of the Uttanka story is longer than the one in the first book and makes better sense of some of the incongruities of that version; it also introduces another episode of weird cuisine, involving a Chandala, a Dalit tribal hunter:

> Once when Uttanka was wandering in the desert, he saw a naked Chandala surrounded by dogs; the Chandala invited Uttanka to drink the copious fluids that were coming out of his penis. Horrified, Uttanka refused and the Chandala disappeared, whereupon Krishna appeared and told Uttanka that the Chandala was in fact Indra in disguise and that the fluid coming out of him was the Soma juice that would have made Uttanka immortal. In compensation for this lost opportunity, Krishna promised Uttanka that whenever he was thirsty, he could summon rain clouds, henceforth named Uttanka clouds.
>
> Now, Uttanka had been the pupil of the sage Gautama for many years, and when Uttanka grew very old, Gautama made him into a young man again and gave him his young daughter in marriage. Gautama's wife, Ahalya, asked Uttanka to bring her the earrings of Madayanti, the wife of the man-eating king Saudasa. Madayanti gave him the earrings, but the serpent Vasuki carried them down into an anthill, opening a way into the underworld, which Uttanka entered. There he saw a black horse with a white tail, who told Uttanka to blow into his ass. "Don't be disgusted; just do it," he said; "you used to do it all the time in Gautama's hermitage in the old days." Uttanka blew, and from the horse—who was Agni, the god of fire—came smoke, which pervaded the world of the snakes. Vasuki gave the earrings to Uttanka.[21]

In the first episode it is Indra, in disguise as usual (but with no bull beside him, let alone a snake disguised as a bull), who offers Uttanka the Soma (in the form of a liquid, far more appropriate than dung); with complementary economy, the horse in the underworld is riderless and speaks for himself. The masking of the sacrificially pure by the humanly disgusting here takes the form of the precious Soma, offered by Indra himself, masquerading as the urine not of a pure horse but of the most impure of humans, a Chandala, and this is the one thing that Uttanka refuses. In the second episode here, as in the earlier version, Uttanka blows into the horse's ass, and again the horse reminds him that this is an old habit long practiced in Gautama's hermitage (an expansion of the earlier statement that Uttanka's teacher used to do it, though now it is Uttanka himself who did it). But this time we learn more: the horse is fire, "your guru's guru," and so it is likely that Uttanka used to "blow" into it to fan its flames.

The guru's wife in this version is Ahalya, notorious for having deceived

Gautama with the god Indra, thus inventing adultery.[22] She is the paradigmatic evil woman, sending the innocent student on a dangerous and frivolous assignment, in contrast with Madayanti, who, though a cannibal's wife, is generous with her jewelry. Again we have these good-and-evil women.

THE HORSE IN THE OCEAN

There is an ancient connection between horses and the ocean. The *Rig Veda* refers to the winged horse "born from the ocean." The *Brihadaranyaka Upanishad* says that the sea is the womb of the sacrificial horse. And in the *Mahabharata,* the great horse Ucchaihshravas is born from the ocean, when the gods and anti-gods churn it to obtain the elixir of immortality.[23]

The connection between horses and the ocean is the central theme of the myth of Sagara, a story that is told in the *Ramayana.* When prince Rama was growing up, the sage who was educating him told him the story of Sagara:

King Sagara had two wives. In order to have sons, he generated ascetic heat [*tapas*] for a hundred years; then he propitiated a great sage, who blessed him so that one of his wives gave birth to sixty thousand sons and the other bore just one son, Asamanja. But Asamanja took pleasure in seizing children and throwing them into the waters of the Sarayu river, laughing as he watched them drown. His father banished him. Eventually Asamanja had a son, Amshuman, whom the people loved, as he was always kind.

After some time, King Sagara performed a horse sacrifice, but Indra took the form of an ogre (*rakshasa*) and stole the horse. The priests advised Sagara to find the thief, kill him, and bring back the horse. The king sent his sixty thousand sons to search for the horse; they dug down into the earth with spades, digging down sixty thousand leagues, destroying many living creatures, who screamed as they died. The sons reached down into the underworld. Then the gods and anti-gods and serpents, deeply distressed, complained, "The sons of Sagara are digging up the whole earth! They shout, 'He has carried off the horse! He has ruined our sacrifice!' and then they slaughter everyone." The sons continued to dig up the entire earth. Eventually they came upon the sage Kapila, with the horse grazing near him. They ran at Kapila in fury, but he, too, became furious, and he burnt them all to ashes.

Then the king sent his grandson, Amshuman, to find the horse. Amshuman found the ashes of the sons, and the horse grazing nearby. He brought the horse back to Sagara, who completed the sacrifice. Eventually, Amshuman's

FIGURE 10. The sons of Sagara discover the stolen sacrificial horse grazing near the sage Kapila. Mughal dynasty, reign of Akbar, 1597–1605 CE. Artist: Syama Sundara; patron: Abd al-Rahim. (Freer Gallery of Art, Smithsonian Institution, Washington, D.C., F1907.271.1, folio 45 recto)

FIGURE 11. Amshuman finds the horse and the ashes of his sixty thousand uncles. His maternal uncle Garuda advises him to return with the horse in order to complete the sacrifice. From a manuscript of the *Ramayana* originally produced in Udaipur, 1712. (© The British Library Board, Add. 15295, f. 117)

grandson, Bhagiratha, brought the Milky Way down from heaven to earth, where it became the river Ganges. He brought the Ganges to the ocean [*sic*] and it entered the hole in the earth where the sixty thousand sons had been burnt to ashes. The river flowed over the ashes and purified the sons so that they were able to go to heaven, and the waters of the ocean remained in the world.[24]

The bad river Sarayu at the start, the river into which the evil son throws children to kill them, is contrasted with the good river, the Ganges, which revives rather than kills those whom it touches, just as the evil son is contrasted with his own good son. The Sarayu, a river known to the *Rig Veda*,[25] echoes the name of Saranyu, the bad mother in the Vedic myth. Here, instead of helping the hero with horses in the underworld, as he helps Uttanka, Indra interrupts the horse sacrifice, as he did when he seduced Janamejaya's wife. In many ways, the river in these variants replaces the horse as the means of moving people. The Vedic sacrificial horse rode to heaven, often taking the sacrificer with him; now the river carries the sons to heaven. And where only a consecrated king could ride the Vedic horse to heaven, now ordinary people—even sinners—could bathe in the Ganges and be carried to heaven.[26]

The sacrificial horse goes underground (a practice more natural to rivers than to horses), as we have seen him do before, but at first this deep excavation is a dry place, where a horse can graze. Only when the Ganges comes down from heaven does the great hole in the earth fill with water and become the ocean (though the text already refers to it, proleptically, as the ocean even when Bhagiratha comes to it and is *about* to fill it with water). Some texts helpfully remark that the horse did enter the ocean, but that the ocean at that time was empty of water. And indeed, the ocean is called, in Sanskrit, "Sagara's" (*sAgara*), after the king whose horse sacrifice started the chain of events that finally created the watery ocean. The main purpose of this story is to tell how the ocean became the ocean, how it got its water. Only at the end of the story, therefore, does the underground horse become an underwater horse.

The twisted connection between horses and fire, snakes, rivers, the ocean, and the underworld, a connection that begins in the Vedas and blossoms in the *Mahabharata* and the *Ramayana,* continues to color stories about horses throughout later Indian history.[27] Often these symbolic aspects of horses take on moral, religious, or political values, as different groups harness them to serve different ends.

5 ❂ Horses in the Ocean in the Sanskrit Puranas

400 to 1400 CE

THE BIRTH OF THE FIERY UNDERWATER HORSE

The Puranas, Sanskrit texts composed from about 400 CE to the early modern period, are encyclopedias that cover all sorts of miscellaneous topics, including medical knowledge, how to build a temple, how to perform a ritual, and everything they think you need to know about elephants and horses. They also have a great deal to say about history and mythology, particularly about the connection between horses and human sexuality, and about the role of horses in the eternal war between the powers of good and evil.

The Puranas built upon earlier stories about horses, particularly underwater horses. In one Brahmana, Prajapati takes the form of a white horse to seek Agni when he hides from the gods, in water; when Prajapati enters the water in this form, Agni burns the horse's mouth.[1] The *Brihadaranyaka Upanishad* says that the fire that all men share is the open mouth of the sacrificial horse in the sea, and the sea is his womb.[2] The Puranas tell many stories about a horse (in early texts a stallion, then a mare) who lives in the watery underground or in the ocean and who is the source of fire, either because the whole horse is made of fire or because fire comes out of the horse's mouth. The fire in the mouth of the underwater horse drinks the waters of the ocean and lets them out again; the fire keeps the waters of the ocean from breaching the shore and flooding the earth, while the water keeps the fire from escaping and burning the earth. Eventually, when it is time for doomsday at the end of the aeon, the supreme deity will whistle to the fiery horse, who will gallop up out of the ocean and burn the universe, and the newly unrestrained waters of the ocean will then also escape and flood the universe. The story is told in many different ways in many different texts.

The *Mahabharata* associates the story of the underwater fire with the sage Aurva and with the Fathers, the dead male ancestors:

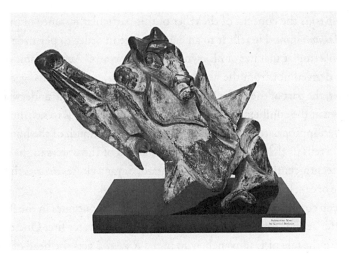

FIGURE 12. *The Submarine Mare.* Sculpture by Carmel Berkson, 2019. 17 × 10 × 15 in. (Collection of Wendy Doniger)

A group of Kshatriyas went through the land killing all the children in the womb. The women fled to the Himalayas, but one woman with beautiful thighs hid her child in her thigh. The Kshatriyas found her, but the child split open his mother's thigh and blazed so brightly that he blinded the Kshatriyas. They begged the child's mother to forgive them and restore their sight. But the child, named Aurva because he was born from his mother's left thigh (*uru*), blazed with anger toward the Kshatriya class. He generated *tapas* (ascetic heat) in order to destroy the world and its people, and that great heat heated all the gods. When the Fathers begged him to be merciful and to control his anger, Aurva said, "My vow of anger cannot be in vain, or I could not live. If I were to restrain my anger, undispersed, it would burn me as fire burns a forest." The Fathers said, "Release it into the waters if you like, and, since the waters are the people, this will fulfill your vow to burn the people." So Aurva placed the fire in the ocean, and it became the fiery horse head [*haya-shiras*], which vomits fire from its mouth and drinks the waters of the ocean.[3]

Since Aurva cannot restrain his excessive ascetic heat, it must be placed in the one situation in which it can do no harm: under water, like a controlled nuclear reaction. It becomes an underwater volcano; Jvala-Mukhi, "Mouth of Fire," the name of the underwater horse, is also the word for a volcano in several Indian languages.

The problem of the dispersal of destructive power (particularly fiery ascetic power, *tapas*) is the concern of the teller of this particular instance of the myth in the *Mahabharata*. He tells it to an enraged sage in order to persuade him to dispose in a similar manner of his own destructive wrath.[4] Aurva's name may actually be derived not from the word for "thigh" (*uru*), as this text suggests, but from *urva*, the part of the ocean into which many rivers flow; the underwater fire often arises at the confluence of a river and the ocean, which is to say, the mouth of the river, appropriate for the fire that appears in the mouth of the horse. One Brahmana tells us that Agni is the *urva*, the mouth of the waters in the ocean.[5] The fourteenth-century CE Vedic commentator Sayana glosses *urva* as the mare-fire in the ocean, like the fire of lightning inside a cloud.[6]

The deep connection between horses and the ocean continues in the Puranas, which offer several different genealogies for the underwater fire. One of them relates it to the tale of Dadhyanch, who in the *Rig Veda* gets the head of a horse from the Ashvins. But the *Rig Veda* also tells us that Dadhyanch gave up the bones of his head to be made into weapons for the gods: "Indra with the bones of Dadhyanch slew nine times ninety (or ninety-nine) enemies; as he sought the head of the horse, which was hidden in the mountains, he found it in Lake Sharyanavat."[7] Or, as Sayana explains, "When Dadhyanch died, he left behind the horse's head. The gods sought it and found it in Lake Sharyanavat, a lake in Kurukshetra. With the bones of this head, Indra slew the demons."[8]

The *Skanda Purana*, which calls the man not Dadhyanch but Dadhichi, develops the story in other directions:

> The gods placed their weapons in the hermitage of Dadhichi for safekeeping, and Dadhichi made them into a liquid and drank their essence. One day Subhadra, his wife, put on his loincloth for a menstrual cloth, and she became pregnant with the seed that was on the cloth. When she brought forth a child, she cursed the unknown father, in ignorance, saying, "I swear by my chastity: let the man who engendered this child die." At this time the gods returned to take back their weapons; and Dadhichi abandoned his body so that the gods could make their weapons of his bones.
>
> When Subhadra learned that Dadhichi was the father of her child, she rejoiced; but the child, named Pippalada, wished to kill the gods who had killed his father. He went to the Himalayas and generated great ascetic heat to propitiate Shiva; he churned his left thigh with his left hand and from it a mare appeared, followed by a stallion. The stallion covered the mare, who brought forth a foal and disappeared. Pippalada then told the foal to devour the gods.

The gods sought help from Vishnu, who tricked the foal into eating the gods one by one, beginning with the waters. The foal, haloed in flames, asked to be brought to the waters, but no one but the river Sarasvati could bear the fiery foal.

As Sarasvati carried the foal to the waters, a mountain saw her and asked her to marry him; she refused, and he threatened to rape her. She then agreed to marry him if he would hold the fiery foal while she bathed; he did so and was burnt to ashes. She took up the foal and set out again for the ocean. When they reached the ocean, the foal was full of joy and offered Sarasvati a boon. Sarasvati said, "Promise that you will drink the waters through a mouth no larger than a needle." Then she threw the fire into the ocean, and this is the story of the birth of the Aurva fire.[9]

Dadhyanch's horse head, submerged in the Vedas, surfaces here to explain the form of the foal born of Dadhyanch's son, a foal (of indeterminate gender) that in turn explains the equine form of the fire in the ocean. Although the story refers to the Aurva fire, Aurva does not appear. But in place of Aurva's chaste ascetic powers, this text introduces the theme of female chastity: the mother of Pippalada swears by her chastity, and Sarasvati's steadfast chastity enables her to fulfill her role and dispose of the fire. Sarasvati's place in the myth is clear: as a river she is, like the ocean, a viable watery receptacle for the fire. The fire is tricked first into drinking the waters instead of the gods (a gimmick first used in a *Mahabharata* version of the story) and then into reducing the size of its mouth to a needle (which, with Vishnu's gift to the ocean of inexhaustible waters, results in the eternal balance of food [water] and eater [fire]). This image is reminiscent of the hungry ghosts of Buddhism, with their enormous bellies and needle mouths, another metaphor for the control of dangerous appetites. Pippalada, literally, "eater of figs," is the name of a famous Vedic sage.[10] But the word also comes to designate someone addicted to sensual pleasures,[11] a contradiction to what we are told about Pippalada in this version but an overtone not irrelevant to the myth's broader concern with the chaste control of sensuality.

CONTROLLING THE UNDERWATER MARE

Aurva's chastity plays a more central role in the *Matsya Purana* version of the story of the underwater fire, which begins when the gods persuade Aurva to abandon his ascetic vow and to place his *tejas* (i.e., his fiery power, but also his seed) where it will cease to generate heat—in water:

The sage Urva was generating ascetic heat; the gods asked him to stop and to begin family life. He replied: "This is the eternal dharma of sages, to live in the forest in a hermitage, in chastity. I will not take a wife, but I will create a son nevertheless." Then by his ascetic heat Urva placed his thigh in the fire and churned it; a halo of flames broke out of his thigh and became a son, named Aurva.

Aurva blazed so fiercely that he terrified the universe; he said, "Hunger binds me: I will eat the universe." He grew great, burning all creatures, until Brahma said to Urva, "Restrain your son's fiery power, for the good of all people. I will give him a dwelling-place and a food like Soma; he will dwell in the mouth of the mare in the ocean, and he will live upon an oblation of water. This water-eating fire will burn all creatures at the end of the aeon." "So be it," said Urva, and he threw the fire into the ocean.[12]

Aurva's blaze of hunger is derived from the combined ascetic heat of his father's chastity and his own, a force that becomes dangerous in this text only when Aurva is made to abandon his celibacy.

And here, briefly but significantly, the underwater fire is associated not with a stallion but with a mare, who is already in the ocean, presumably waiting for Urva to place the fire in her mouth. This mare has a history of her own. One brief passage in the *Mahabharata* specifies that the fire born of Aurva is not itself equine but lives in the mouth of the underwater mare: "A sage named Aurva will be born, blazing like a fire, and he will create a fire of anger to destroy the three worlds and reduce the earth to ashes. After some time he will extinguish the fire, throwing it into the mouth of the mare in the ocean."[13] The *Mahabharata* also refers casually to the underwater mare-fire on other occasions. When Kadru and Vinata go to view the stallion Ucchaihshravas to settle their bet, they see the underwater fire in the mare's mouth (*vadava-mukha*).[14]

There is also a Vedic precedent for the idea of a fiery mare subdued with water. One Brahmana text speaks of the taming of a wild horse that it refers to as "she." The verb used to represent her taming is the same as the term for extinguishing a fire or a passion (*sham/shanti*), and the priest who tames her prepares the waters of tranquillity and sprinkles them over her; flames shoot forth from her every limb, and she is henceforth perfectly tame.[15] Sayana remarks that the underwater mare-fire is a metaphor for unsated desire.[16] All the negative connotations of mares that we have seen in the tradition beginning with Saranyu determine the ultimate gender of this destructive fire, which most subsequent texts refer to as a mare.

The *Brahma Purana* tells a version of the story of Pippalada and Dadhicha (*sic*) which offers a more blatant rationalization for the presence of the mare in the story:

> Pippalada the son of Dadhicha generated great ascetic heat in order to kill the slayers of his father, and Shiva gave him the power to kill the gods. The *pippala* (fig) trees said, "Your mother was said to be a mare," and when Pippalada heard this he became angry, and from his eye an evil spirit came forth blazing in the form of a mare with a deadly tongue; she had the form of a mare because he had been thinking of a mare. He told her to eat the gods, but she began to eat him, since he had been made by the gods. In terror, Pippalada fled to Shiva, who told the mare not to eat any creature within the distance of a league from that place.
>
> Then the mare set out full of fire to burn the universe, terrifying the gods, who sought refuge with Pippalada; but Pippalada could not restrain the mare. As she came to the Ganges, the gods begged her to begin with the waters of the ocean and then to devour everything. The mare-fire said, "How can I reach the ocean? Let a virtuous maiden place me in a golden pot and lead me there." The gods asked the maiden Sarasvati to do this, and she asked them to join her with four other rivers, the Yamuna, Ganges, Narmada, and Tapati. The five rivers put the fire in a golden pot and brought it to the ocean; they threw it into the ocean and it began to drink the waters little by little.[17]

The theme of chastity plays a part here in the slur against Pippalada's mother — a mare, as usual, used as a metaphor for an oversexed woman. But the myth then leans over backward to establish the chastity of the mare-fire, making explicit the purity and power of Sarasvati.

SHIVA AND KAMA AND THE UNDERWATER MARE

The god Shiva often participates peripherally in the myth of the mare, both in symbolic forms and anthropomorphically. In the *Shiva Purana* version, Shiva makes possible the birth of the fire-foal, and Pippalada appears elsewhere as an incarnation of Shiva.[18] But in many Puranic myths, Shiva is at the center of the action.

Heat in Indian symbolism sometimes takes two mutually opposed forms: *kama,* the heat of sexual desire, and *tapas,* the heat generated by ascetic practices, particularly by chastity.[19] These two forces meet and interact in the Shaiva version of the myth of the underwater mare:

Kama, the god of desire, once attempted to shoot an arrow of desire at Shiva, the god of ascetic heat, the great yogi. He deluded Shiva, arousing him, but when Shiva realized that Kama was attacking him he released a fire from his third eye, burning Kama to ashes. This resulted in a fire composed of two sparks: the erotic fire that Kama had kindled in Shiva and the ascetic fire from the third eye in Shiva's forehead. The fire, having come from Shiva's eye, could never return to Shiva; moreover, Brahma had paralyzed the fire in a vain attempt to shield Kama.

When Shiva had vanished, the combined fire began to burn the gods and all the universe. The gods sought refuge with Brahma, who made the fire of Shiva's anger into a mare with gentle, ambrosial flames issuing from her mouth. Then Brahma took the mare to the ocean and said, "This mare is the fire of Shiva's anger; it has burnt Kama, and now it wishes to burn the whole universe. I gave it the form of a mare; now you must bear it until the final deluge, at which time I will come here and lead it away from you. It will devour your water, and you must make a great effort to bear it." The ocean agreed to this, and the fire entered and was held in check, burning quietly with its halo of flames. At doomsday, the mare will emerge from the ocean, and the flame from her mouth will burn the universe to ashes, and then the ocean, released from the imprisoning fire, will flood the universe.[20]

In many tellings of this myth, Kama's widow, Rati, the goddess of sexual pleasure, persuades Shiva to revive her husband, who remains bodiless but incarnate in such things as moonlight and the arched brows of beautiful women. Rati herself is often portrayed riding on a mare composed of beautiful women.

Many Shaiva texts speak of the underwater mare fire. One text states that a river named the Vadava ("Mare") was given to Death as a wife; in gratitude to Shiva for this gift, Death established a great Shiva linga known as the Mahanala (the Great Fire) at the mouth of the Vadava river.[21] The mouth of the river, or of the horse, is, as usual, the site of fire—or, in this case, death. In Nath versions of Kundalini yoga, the underwater mare is said to be the doomsday fire at the base of the spine, homologized with the Kundalini serpent[22]—horses and snakes again. The fire of Shiva's anger, the Aurva fire, and the fire of Kama combine in a verse that a lovesick king addresses to Kama:

Surely the fire of Shiva's anger still burns in you today,
like the fire of Aurva in the ocean;

Ratheedary - a Hindoo Goddess - Horse formed by Women

FIGURE 13. Rati riding a horse made of women. Trichinopoly, 1850. Gouache on mica.
(© Victoria and Albert Museum, London, 4663:16/[IS])

> otherwise, Kama, how could you be so hot
> as to reduce people like me to ashes?[23]

The mare, deep in the ocean, with fire in her mouth, is frequently used as a meta-phor for a voracious or insatiable energy: "Not by anything can the fire of enmity be assuaged; it is inextinguishable, like the underwater fire."[24] The mare-fire is considered a particularly apt metaphor for the insatiable appetites of a flirtatious woman;[25] but it stands equally well for the emotions of a man: a character in a medieval Sanskrit play boasts that he has crossed the ocean of passion, escaped from the whirlpool of affection, and dispelled the mare-fire of anger.[26]

A connection between the horse sacrifice and the mare-fire appears in the belief that the underwater fire devours the offerings of the horse sacrifice.[27] The Vedic stallion and the Epic and Puranic mare are thus joined at last.

VISHNU AS THE HORSE-HEADED HAYAGRIVA

The mythology of an underwater equine fire (in this instance generally male rather than female) colors a highly ambivalent line of equine mythology involving Vishnu. In one text, Saranyu and the Sun in their equine forms give birth to yet another child (in addition to Manu and Yama/Yami, and right after the Ashvins): "As the seed stopped flowing [*retaso'nte*], a son named Revanta was born, mounted on a horse."[28] This Revanta later makes trouble between the god Vishnu and his wife Lakshmi:

> Vishnu cursed his wife Lakshmi to become a mare because she had lusted for Revanta when he was mounted on the marvelous horse Ucchaihshravas. Vishnu promised that Lakshmi would be released from the curse when she had a son. Lakshmi, who was the daughter of the ocean, went to the very place where Saranyu had wandered as a mare, generating ascetic heat, at the confluence of the Kalindi and Tamasa rivers. Lakshmi took the form of a mare, meditated upon Shiva, and generated ascetic heat for a thousand years. Then Shiva came to her and promised that Vishnu would appear to her in the form of a stallion and beget a son upon her. Shiva vanished and sent Vishnu to Lakshmi; Vishnu begat a son upon her, stallion mounting mare; then they resumed their normal forms and returned home, giving the son to a king who had generated ascetic heat to obtain him.[29]

This text invokes the Vedic mare Saranyu as a precedent for a goddess who becomes a mare to bear a son, but now Saranyu draws in the later, Puranic motif of the mare that generates ascetic heat at the confluence of the ocean and rivers.

Vedic and Epic equine themes thus feed into the Puranic mythology of Vishnu, which also has its own Vedic roots. From the time of the Brahmanas there are references to a horse-headed Vishnu, Hayagriva, "Horse-Neck" (or Hayashiras, "Horse-Head"). Hayagriva in iconography sometimes holds a serpent; according to some texts, his left foot should rest on the cosmic serpent Adi-Shesha.[30] In one Brahmana story, Vishnu is accidentally beheaded (when ants gnaw through his bowstring as he sleeps), and the Ashvins replace his head with the head of a horse,[31] as they had done for Dadhyanch.

In the *Mahabharata,* Vishnu purposely takes on a horse head to enter the ocean:

> When the anti-gods Madhu and Kaitabha stole the Vedas and carried them down into the waters, Brahma became blind, for the Vedas were his eyes. He prayed to Vishnu, who took on a marvelous horse-headed form (Hayashiras): his mane was made of the rays of the sun, the sun and moon were his two eyes, lightning his tongue, and the night of doomsday was his neck. When Vishnu had taken on this horse-headed form, he vanished into the waters. He recovered the Vedas and gave them back to Brahma, who became whole again; then Vishnu placed the horse head in the Northeastern region of the ocean.[32]

In earlier stories in which anti-gods carry the Vedas down to the bottom of the ocean, marine Vaishnava avatars such as the fish or the aquatic boar retrieve the Vedas.[33] Here, perhaps through the influence of the myth of the underwater mare, Vishnu takes on an equine form to enter the water.

The *Mahabharata* connects these anti-gods, Madhu and Kaitabha, with the idea that the underwater fire devours the offerings of the horse sacrifice:

> The anti-gods Madhu and Kaitabha stole the Vedas and took them to the world beneath the great ocean. Brahma told Vishnu what had happened, and Vishnu took a horse-headed form and entered the underwater world. He took the Vedas back to Brahma and then he resumed his own form, leaving the horse head in the ocean as the dwelling of the Vedas. Then he killed Madhu and Kaitabha. Vishnu himself is the horse head that lives in the ocean, devouring oblations.[34]

The horse head that Vishnu assumes in this myth becomes simultaneously the underwater horse head—the thing that "devours oblations"—and the place of the restored Vedas. But some Puranic retellings of this story no longer mention the Vedas, merely saying that when Vishnu resumed his own form and left the horse head in the ocean, it became the head of the underwater mare, now devouring oblations instead of water.[35]

A Tamil text makes Hayagriva a horse-headed human sage; when a princess laughs at his horse head, he curses her to be reborn horse-headed herself; she is indeed reborn that way, but after bathing in a particular shrine, she loses her horse face and gets a face like the flawless moon.[36] More often, Hayagriva is an anti-god, still closely associated with Vishnu. In a discussion of anti-gods killed by Vishnu, the *Mahabharata* says: "When Vishnu was lying in the ocean, he killed the two anti-gods Madhu and Kaitabha; and then, in another birth, he killed Hayagriva."[37] One Purana connects the anti-god Hayagriva with the Vedic theme of the beheaded Vishnu, and casts in the role of savior Vishvakarman, also known as Tvashtri, the Vedic blacksmith and father of Saranyu:

> Once, when Vishnu was in a deep sleep, the gods snapped his bowstring to wake him, and it cut off Vishnu's head, which fell they knew not where. At this, the world was plunged into darkness. The gods propitiated the Goddess, who told them why Vishnu had been beheaded:
>
> "Once, Vishnu laughed when he saw the face of his wife, Lakshmi. Fearing that he thought her face ugly or that he had taken a more beautiful woman as her co-wife, she cursed him to have his head fall off, because she thought that being a widow would be less painful for her than having a co-wife. For false-hood, trickery, stupidity, rashness, excessive greediness, impurity, and cruelty are the faults that every woman is born with by her nature. Because of that curse, Vishnu's head fell into the ocean of salt. I will put it back on, and this is how and why: Once upon a time, an anti-god named Hayagriva propitiated me and asked me to promise that he could be killed only by someone who was horse-headed like him. Now he must be killed. As Vishnu has been acciden-tally beheaded, let Vishvakarman fix a horse head onto Vishnu's headless body so that, as Hayagriva, he can slay the wicked anti-god."
>
> Vishvakarman took an axe and beheaded a horse and gave the head to Vishnu, who became Hayagriva and slew the anti-god Hayagriva.[38]

The character assassination of women in this text takes the place of the exagger-ated praise of their chastity that pervades other stories about submerged fires that we have considered; they are two sides of the same coin. A similar diatribe against the wickedness of women colors another text in which Lakshmi, in fury at a pretty girl who was presented to Vishnu as a potential co-wife, curses not Vishnu but the girl to be reborn with a horse head.[39]

The schizophrenia of Hayagriva the god and the anti-god continues to shadow the Puranic mythology of Hayagriva, who is sometimes horse-headed, sometimes a horse, sometimes an ogre, sometimes an ogre slayer. One bemused scholar re-marked that since Vishnu is both horse-headed and kills horse-headed demons, terms like Hayagriva and Ashvagriva indicate "a demoniac as well as a divine form."[40] Like that of horses themselves.

VISHNU AS KESHAVA AND KALKI

Vishnu's ambiguous identity as Hayagriva and as the enemy of Hayagriva continues in Vishnu's relationship with another equine character, Keshi (or Keshin), "Long-maned," who is explicitly related to Hayagriva. The *Mahabharata* tells us that Keshi was an anti-god who carried off the daughters of Prajapati and was defeated by Indra.[41] But elsewhere, the *Mahabharata* tells us that, after Vishnu had killed Hayagriva, Hayagriva took the form of a horse named Keshi, who was killed not by Indra but by Krishna.[42] And the *Harivamsha,* the appendix to the *Mahabharata,* further complicates the relationship by stating that Hayagriva was killed not by Indra or Krishna but by a horse, and that it was the horse, rather than Hayagriva, who was then reborn as Keshi: "A flesh-eating ogre who oppressed people with his demonic heart was killed by a horse, and so the ogre was reborn as Hayagriva. The horse was reborn as Keshi, an evil horse who had a long mane and a shrill whinny, who lived alone in the forest and ate human flesh."[43] Here both the ogre and the vicious horse are reborn in equine or quasi-equine forms.

In the *Bhagavata Purana,* Keshi appears as a huge horse and attacks Krishna with his feet, kicking him; Krishna thrusts his arm into Keshi's mouth, suffocating him to death.[44] Significantly, where the horse uses his feet as his weapons, just as a real horse would, Krishna kills Keshi by wounding him in the mouth, the site of mythological equine fire.

The *Vishnu Purana* tells us more:

> The evil king Kamsa sent Keshi, in the form of a horse, to kill Krishna, but Krishna vowed to knock Keshi's teeth down his throat. Keshi attacked Krishna; his mouth, vast as a cavern, was wide open in rage. Krishna thrust his arm into that mouth, like a serpent entering a hole, knocking out Keshi's teeth, and began to expand until Keshi was split in two pieces, each having two legs, half a back, half a tail, one ear, one eye, and one nostril. Krishna threw him down, like the Garuda bird throwing down a serpent.[45]

The physical bisection of Keshi mirrors the moral bisection of Hayagriva, half god, half anti-god. A Gupta image depicts a young Krishna kicking a horse, presumably the anti-god Keshi, in the stomach and jamming his elbow into the horse's mouth.

Keshi's name appears, already with equine overtones, in the Vedas: Keshi is the

FIGURE 14. Krishna killing the demonic horse Keshi. Gupta, fifth century CE, Uttar Pradesh. Terra-cotta. 21 × 16 × 4 in. (Metropolitan Museum of Art, New York, 1991.300, Purchase, Florence and Herbert Irving Gift, 1991)

long-haired (or long-maned) sage who rides the wind and is called "the stallion of the wind." But the *Mahabharata* also calls Krishna Keshava ("Long-haired") and says that he is the killer of Keshi. And the *Bhagavata Purana,* after narrating Krishna's killing of Keshi, says that that is why Krishna is called Keshava.[46] Keshi is thus, like Hayagriva, an anti-god identified with his own Vaishnava killer.

And then there is the equally ambivalent equine form of Vishnu, the inverted centaur, Kalki (or Kalkin), the last of Vishnu's ten avatars. Kalki is the only Hindu god who rides a horse. Though all of the gods have vehicles (the Sanskrit term, *vahana,* is cognate with our English word "vehicle")—the bandicoot for Ganesha, the bull for Shiva, the peacock for Skanda, the lion for the Goddess, and so on—significantly, none of the *vahanas* are animals that people actually

FIGURE 15. A groom is presenting the horse Kalki to Krishna. Punjab Hills, Guler, c. 1760–70. Page from a dispersed manuscript. Ink and opaque watercolor on paper. 6¼ × 8⅜ in. (Metropolitan Museum of Art, New York, 1975.412)

ride. And none of the ancient Hindu gods rides a horse as a *vahana,* though Indra and the sun god drive horses in their chariots. In fact, the gods don't usually ride on their *vahanas;* some do—the Goddess sometimes rides her lion into battle, and Vishnu often sails through the skies on Garuda—but more often they are awkwardly depicted in sculptures and paintings as just sitting sideways on the animal as if on a bench or a sofa. Yet the point is that the god is somehow present wherever the animal is present, in much the sense that we say a certain play is a "vehicle" for a particular actor. Kalki is the only god who rides a horse, astride—but he exists only in the future.

Kalki is first depicted (in the *Mahabharata*) with only one equine referent: he will give the earth back to the Brahmins (the twice-born) at a great horse sacrifice. The rest of the text simply states that Kalki, a part of Vishnu, will be born into a Brahmin family at the end of the Kali Age (the present, evil period of invasions by defiling foreigners) to uproot the barbarians and usher in a new Golden Age.[47] By the Gupta period, Kalki is depicted, both in sculptures and in the texts of the Puranas, as a rider on a horse. "The gods will give him a swift horse to ride on,"[48] says the tenth-century *Bhagavata Purana*. Still later he is depicted as a horse (sometimes a winged horse) or as a man with a horse's head.[49] Iconographical texts dictate that the image of Kalki should have the face of a horse and the body of a man with four arms, or that he should ride on a horse.[50] When the Muslim sect of the Imam Shahis reworked the stories of the avatars, Kalki, the tenth avatar, became the Imam, who rides on a horse.[51]

The irony is that the concept and image of the rider who comes with a sword to destroy the barbarians may well have been imported into India from European millennialism by those very barbarians,[52] the Scythians, Parthians, Greeks, and Kushanas (the people whose empires occupied what is now Iran, Iraq, and Armenia), who came to India in the first centuries of the Christian era, at a time when millennial ideas were rampant in Europe. Kalki himself has the form of an invader; like them, he comes riding on a white horse. But his purpose is to destroy the invaders, to raze the wicked cities that had been polluted by foreign kings—foreign horsemen—and drive them out of India. His very name is ambiguous: Kalki is one who has *kalka*—filth, dregs, sediment, impurity, and deceit. He "has" the dregs of the Kali Age in one way or another, as the barbarian who is impurity incarnate, or as the god who destroys that impurity. Like the underwater mare, he ushers in doomsday. Thus Kalki is both the invader, the foreigner on the horse, and the Indian horseman who repels the invaders, fighting fire with fire—or horses with horses.

6 | ✿ | *Ashvashastra,* the Science of Horses

200 BCE to 1200 CE

The Sanskrit word *shastra* designates a knowledge system or a text that contains such knowledge. So *ashvashastra* in general means the science of breeding and training horses, while an *ashvashastra* attributed to a particular author is a textbook about the breeding and training of horses. This chapter will consider the science of horses in the broader sense, and so will include discussions of passages in this genre that appear in texts other than the actual textbooks called *ashvashastras,* as well as some passages from the textbooks themselves. Textbooks about the science of horses tell us as much about the ways that ancient Indians imagined horses as they do about their actual treatment.

THE SCIENCE OF HORSES IN THE TEXTBOOK OF POLITICS (*ARTHASHASTRA*)

The textbook of politics, the *Arthashastra,* attributed to Kautilya, was probably composed in the first centuries of the Common Era. It deals in great detail with all the subjects that a king would need to know in order to govern a kingdom, and one of these subjects is the care and feeding of horses. This is treated in a chapter detailing the tasks of the man in charge of all the king's horses, which begins, like many chapters of this very practical administrative text, with a concern for the source and value of the objects of interest, in this case, horses:

> The Superintendent of Horses should get the total number of horses recorded in writing—those received as gifts, those acquired by purchase, those gained by war, those born to the herd, those procured in return for assistance, those pledged in a treaty, and those borrowed temporarily—according to their ancestry, age, color, marks, class, and provenance. He should report those that

are defective, lame, or sick. The horse keeper should take care of them, collecting the monthly allotment from the treasury and the storehouse.[1]

There follows the description of a very well-designed stable:

> The Superintendent of Horses should have a stable constructed, a stable whose length corresponds to the number of horses, whose width is twice a horse's length, with four doors and a central area for rolling on the ground, as well as an entrance hall, and planks for seating near the main door. It should have many monkeys, peacocks, spotted deer, mongooses, partridges, parrots, and myna birds. He should have a stall facing east or north constructed for each horse, a stall that is square in shape, with each side the length of a horse and with a floor made of smooth planks, equipped with a hamper for feed and an outlet for urine and dung. Or he may adjust the direction in accordance with the requirements of the stable. The stalls for mares, stallions, and foals should be separated from one another.[2]

The mongooses and birds are for protection against snakes; the deer may be for company. The stipulation of "a central area for rolling on the ground" demonstrates an endearing affection and appreciation for the actual behavior and pleasures of horses.

The text then goes on to prescribe the feeding of the horses, much of which makes good sense, with the exception of ghee, clarified butter, which is a staple of a good Indian diet but, as we have seen, not likely to be very good for horses:

> A mare that has just given birth should be given *ghee* to drink for three nights, and afterwards, for ten nights, barley meal and a stimulating drink of fat and medicine, and thereafter porridge, green fodder, and food appropriate for the season. After the first ten days, a foal's food should consist of barley meal, ghee and milk until it is six months old. Thereafter, its food is barley, until it is four years old. After that time, when it is four or five years old, it has reached its full size and is capable of working.[3]
>
> The finest type of horse is one whose length is five times its face and whose height is four times its shank.[4] The ration for the finest type of horse is rice, barley, or panic grain, half dry or half cooked, or a porridge of beans; fat, salt, meat, juice or curd to moisten the lumps; and a stimulating drink made with sugar or milk. In order to make them eat, horses that are tired after a long jour-

ney or after pulling a heavy load should be given fat as an enema, fat for the nose, green fodder and grass. A chariot-horse gets the same ration as the finest type of horse; one quarter less than that is the ration for mares and mules; and half of the latter for foals. Those who cook the rations, those who hold the reins, and the doctors are obliged to taste the food.[5]

This last stipulation about tasting the food is probably to ensure that the food is not poisoned, a perennial danger for ancient Indian kings and, apparently, ancient Indian horses. (In our day, too, valuable racehorses are carefully guarded so that they will not be "nobbled" by someone slipping something bad into their food or water.)

The author goes on to distinguish between different conditions and dispositions of horses:

> Horses unable to work due to war, sickness, or old age should receive sufficient food to maintain themselves. Those that are unfit for battle should be employed as stallions to service mares for the benefit of people in the cities and the countryside. Of those fit for battle, the best are those bred in Kamboja, Sindh, Aratta, and Vanayu; the middling are those bred in Bahlika, Papeya, Sauvara, and Titala; the rest are the lowest. According to whether their dispositions are ardent, gentle, or sluggish, he should assign them to activities relating to the military or to transportation.[6]

"Ardent, gentle, or sluggish" refers to the three types of horses that we will soon see set out in detail in an *Ashvashastra*. Arguments about which parts of India are the best for breeding horses continue through the ages. The *Ramayana* specifies that the great kingdom of Ayodhya "was filled with the finest horses, bred in the regions of Bahlika, Vanayu, Kamboja and Sindh,"[7] areas also favored by the *Arthashastra*.

Next comes the description of a horse's gaits:

> Gallop, canter, leap, trot, and dressage movements are the gaits of a riding horse. The gallop when the head and ears remain unaffected is the canter. The types of leaping are monkey-leap, frog-leap, one-leap, one-foot-leap, cuckoo-gait, chest-motion, and crane-gait. The types of trotting are heron-gait, heron-gait on water, peacock-gait, half-peacock-gait, mongoose-gait, half-mongoose-gait, boar-gait, and half-boar-gait. Dressage is acting in accordance to cues.[8]

These movements (other than gallop, trot, and dressage) are difficult to correlate with the sort of gaits that we know, tolting and pacing, passage and piaffe, and so forth, but something very similar to our special gaits was evidently cultivated in ancient India.

There follows a rather miscellaneous set of stipulations about working horses:

> The distance that a chariot-horse would travel in a day is thirty, forty-five, or sixty miles, while that of a riding horse is twenty-five, thirty-five, or fifty miles.[9] The training masters should give directions concerning the fastenings and equipment of chariot-horses, and the charioteers concerning their military trappings. Horse veterinarians should provide remedies for the decrease or increase in body weight and food appropriate for each season. Those who hold the horses' reins, tie them, give green fodder, cook their rations, guard their stalls, and groom their hair, as well as experts in the cure of poisons, should take care of the horses according to their respective tasks. And if any of them neglects his tasks, he should lose a day's wages. If someone rides a horse kept locked up for the rite of lustration [for war horses] or on the orders of the veterinarian, he is to be fined. If a sickness becomes worse because treatment or medicine was delayed, the fine is twice the amount spent for the cure. If the horse dies because of their fault, the fine is the price of the animal.[10]

And the chapter on horses concludes (like most of the chapters in this text) with two short verses, in a religious register that has not appeared in the rest of the chapter (and that was probably not part of the original text):[11]

> He should have the horses bathed twice a day
> and given perfume and garlands.
> On new-moon days, offerings to spirits should be made,
> and on full-moon days, blessings should be proclaimed;
> and the lustration rite at the beginning or end
> of an expedition, or during an illness.[12]

Throughout, the *Arthashastra* deals with horses in remarkably realistic terms that agree, in many particulars, with the traditions followed in good stables to this day. But the *Arthashastra* is, as we will see, almost unique in the *ashvashastra* tradition in its practical details and, even more, in its almost complete absence of supernatural concerns.[13]

HORSES IN AN *ASHVASHASTRA*

Many *ashvashastras* have been preserved in Indian libraries, in large part because rich and royal patrons often had them copied for their private libraries, prizing them particularly but not only for their gorgeous illustrations. One of the most famous of the *ashvashastras* is the text attributed to Nakula,[14] one of the twin brothers in the *Mahabharata* who are the incarnation of the Ashvins, the children of the mare Saranyu. No reliable date has been established for this text, though it probably reached something like its present form between the eight and twelfth centuries CE. B. C. Law reasons that the fact that the *ashvashastras* refer to Persian and Arabian horses means that they cannot be earlier than the seventh century CE, when Persian horses first began to be imported into India; he also argues that these texts may reflect the concern of Hindu kings from 800 to 1300 CE to provide "such manuals for the care of their cavalry with a view to combating such cavalries as the one used by Shiab-ud-din against Prithiviraja of Ajmer in A. D. 1191."[15]

The *Ashvashastra* is a mix of what we would regard as practical information, derived from the observation of horses, and magical/religious/mythological beliefs about omens, most of which ultimately concern not the horses but the humans who depend upon them, their riders and others in the equestrian community. (This tradition may owe something to the widespread belief that, as one contemporary Muslim remarked of the horse in the Karbala ritual, "The animal's ability to recognize truth is greater than man's.")[16] The text begins with invocations of various gods and sings the praise of horses, particularly in battle. Then it tells the tale of how the horses lost their wings, which we have already encountered. There follows a hymn to Raivata (a variant of Revanta), "the divine master of horses, the son of the Sun and the Shadow,"[17] connecting the origin of horses with the tale of Saranyu. After these prefaces, the text of the *Ashvashastra* proper begins. Here is a summary of the main topics covered in the rest of the text, with selected details of particular interest:

Anatomy of horses;

Good and bad physical characteristics of various parts of their bodies;

Avartas (what we would call cowlicks, more properly here horse-licks): An *avarta* is a whorl, a twist of hair that curls in a direction against the grain, invested with great meaning according to its position on the horse. There are 123. The ten permanent *avartas* are invariably good; a horse without them will be

FIGURE 16. *Ashvashastra*, Nepal. *A Treatise on Horses (hippology)*, Nepal. (The Royal Library, National Library of Denmark and Copenhagen University Library, Shelfmark Nepal.122)

short-lived, unlucky, and possess bad qualities. They should twist to the right and be situated two on the chest, two on the head, two on the sheath, two on the phallus, one in the middle of the forehead, and one on the upper lip. Of the 113 impermanent forms, there are thirty-seven good ones found in twenty good places, and seventy-six bad ones in seventy-six bad places;

Horses of multiple colors;

Neighing: When horses neigh at the sight of a Brahmin or flowers it is a good omen; when it sounds like the sound made by a crow, pig, jackal, ass or camel, it is a bad omen; and so forth;

Smell: A horse should smell like a lotus, sandalwood, or honey, and should not smell like a "dog-eating" Dalit (*shva-pacha*), a tortoise, or bugs, or like the urine and feces of an ass, camel, pig, or owl;

Shadows (*chaya*): A shadow is a kind of overcoat of hair, something like what we would call "roan" (though we generally recognize only bay, chestnut, or black mixed with white, and the ancient Indians had five roan colors), which is said to come over a horse's body like clouds covering the rising sun (recall the "Shadow" who takes the place of Saranyu, wife of the sun). These are seen when the horse is has just bathed, or is drinking water, grazing, or just waking up. The shadows of earth, water (clear as crystal, like a cloud full of water) and fire (ruby-red, like the rising sun) are good; the shadows of wind (harsh and broken) and sky (thin and coarse) are wild and unsteady;

Character: Horses are divided (as humans are) into three basic categories—gentle (*sattva*), ardent (*rajas*), and sluggish (*tamas*); but horses are further subdivided into subcategories (named after various gods or supernatural creatures):

Gentle (*sattva*):

    The Creator (Brahma): without passion or forgetfulness;

    Sage (*rishi*): without desire, hatred, deceit, or lust;

    King of the Gods (Indra): strong and noble;

    God of the Dead (Yama): without treachery;

    God of Wealth (Kubera): with visible joy, anger, memory and passion;

    God of the Waters (Varuna): fond of pleasure, playful, heroic;

    Gandharva: fond of music and singing and worship (*puja*).

Ardent (*rajas*):

    Anti-God (Asura): fierce and angry;

    Ogre (Rakshasa): priapic and gluttonous;

    Ghoul (Pishacha): gluttonous and timid;

    Cobra (Naga): excitable, nervous, and clean;

    Father (Ancestor, Pitri): bad-tempered and unresponsive to good treatment;

    Vulture (Shakuna): greedy for food, lustful, and inclined to frown.

Sluggish (*tamas*):

    Cattle (Pashu): hungry, dull, timid and lazy;

    Fish (Matsya): greedy for food and water, and cowardly;

    Hostile god (Viruddha): sleepy, moody, and lazy.

Defects to be avoided: black or broken teeth, bad limbs, extra limbs or missing limbs, etc.;

Family line (*kula*, what we would call "blood stock");

Age: how to determine it, mostly by the teeth;

Colors of the coat (the equivalent of our bay, chestnut, and so forth): white, red, black, yellow, and a variety of multi-colors. Great emphasis was placed on the colors of horses, here and in the mythological and historical texts as well. The *Faras-nama* of Hashmi, based in part on a translation of Shalihotra's *Ashvashastra*, divided horses according to their color,[18] as indeed riders and breeders everywhere often do to this day.

Horses suitable to different riders (gods, chaplains, kings) and occasions (coronation, warfare, riding), determined not by the character or physique of the horse but by the color of the coat and various auspicious signs on the horse;

Lifespan (*ayur*), mainly the signs of a horse that will live long;

Signs of potential disaster on the body of the horse, such as: If a healthy horse refuses food or sheds tears without any cause, it portends evil; if a horse weaves his head back and forth and licks his lips, it portends victory; if a horse strikes the earth with his left leg, it is a bad omen; if a horse looks at his owner on the right side as he mounts, it portends victory; if a horse loses his teeth for no accountable reason, it is an occasion for fear; if a horse swishes his tail on its left side, it portends a journey; on the right side, victory;

Training: Again the horses are divided into classes, this time of four types, named after the four classes of Indian society. The anti-Brahmin, and pro-Kshatriya, bias makes sense considering that the patrons of *ashvashastras* were most likely to have been kings and nobles:

> Brahmins (the class from which priests are drawn): the horses tend to be timid, appetitive, and ravenous, and should be trained by the use of force, before dawn;
>
> Kshatriyas (kings and soldiers): bold and spirited, these horses should be trained by gentle persuasion, in the morning;
>
> Vaishyas (merchants): evil, cunning, and brutal, these horses should be trained with a whip and by sounds, in the evening;
>
> Shudras (servants): coarse, cowardly, and cruel, these horses should be trained with a whip, at night.

Training horses in general: Irascible or thoughtless people, who have unsteady seats or deal out punishment for no good reason, will not succeed in training a horse, nor will those who tremble when they mount a horse. The trainer should sit tight, understand the horse's mind and character, and be vigilant, patient, hopeful, and strong.

Riding: The rider must maintain good posture and stay calm and must not swing to left or right or bend down or look at the ground. He must keep his eye on the top of the horse's head between the ears. His back must be straight but he should not sit stiffly. He should mount from the right. When he first rides a horse, he should bathe and put on red clothes and red flowers and pray to the horse, in the horse's right ear. Later, when he has bathed, fasted, and dressed in white garments, he should whisper this prayer in the horse's right ear in the morning:

"Horse, you are the king of Gandharvas; listen to my speech. You were born in the family of the Gandharvas; don't disgrace your family. . . . Remember how you were born when the gods and the anti-gods churned the milky ocean.[19] You were born in the family of the gods; keep your true word, fulfil your promise. You were born in the family of horses; be my constant friend always. Long ago, when the gods mounted your back, they conquered the antigods; now let me mount you and conquer the army of my enemies."

And with this final reference to Ucchaihshravas, the horse who emerged from the churning of the ocean and fought against the anti-gods, the *Ashvashastra* returns from the world of practical advice to the world of mythology with which it began.

HORSES IN THE *AGNI PURANA*

The Sanskrit Puranas incorporate a great deal of shastric material on various topics, including horses. The *Agni Purana* puts its rich discussion of horses in the mouth of Dhanvantari, the divine physician who is said to have emerged, along with the horse Ucchaihshravas, when the gods churned the ocean:

Dhanvantari said, "I will proclaim the essence of riding horses, and the art of curing horses. When the moon is in certain favorable constellations, that is a time recommended for riding a horse for the first time. Winter, the cool month, and spring are for riding horses; in summer, autumn, and the rains, the riding or harnessing of horses is forbidden. Do not strike the horse with sharp or inconsistent blows, nor hurt him in his mouth. Do not ride on ground that is strewn with sharp pieces of wood or bones, nor on uneven ground, or ground that is thorny, or covered with sand or mud, or spoilt by ditches or holes. A professional master of horses or an expert equestrian player can ride a horse better without a stirrup or bridle.

A person who rides without knowing the mind of horses, and without the proper methods, is carried along by the horse, stuck on its back. But the wise and accomplished rider, whoever he is, can communicate his wish, and rides by his own ability, by practice and application, without book-learning.

With a series of chants ending with Om, harness the gods in the body of a horse that has been bathed and faces east: harness Brahma in the mind, Vishnu in the horse's strength, Garuda in his courage, the Rudras in his sides, Brihaspati in his intelligence, and all the gods in his vital spots; harness in the horse's eyes the moon and sun, that revolve within the sphere of vision; and the Ashvins in his ears. Agni in his stomach, Svadha in his sweat, speech in his tongue, and wind in his speed; the vault of heaven on his back, and all the mountains in the tips of his hooves. The stars in the pores of his hairs, and the quarters of the moon in his heart; Agni in his energy, Rati in his loins, and the lord of the universe in his forehead. The planets in his whinny, and Vasuki in his breast.[20]

After fasting, the rider should worship the horse and whisper this prayer in his right ear: [There follows the same prayer that ends the *Ashvashastra*]. Having whispered in his ear and thus confounded his enemies, the rider should lead the horse around and ride him to victory as he goes into battle.

The flaws that generally appear in the bodies of horses may be overcome, with great effort, by the best of riders, and appear as good points. And these good points that actually result from the skill of the rider appear to be innate. But other sorts of riders destroy the good points that are there, even when they are actually innate. One person knows the good points of horses, and another knows their flaws; the wise and fortunate person knows both the flaws and the good points of a horse, but the fool knows neither. A rider who does not know the proper movements, nor the proper methods, who is impatient and quick to anger, who is fond of using the whip to get his way, who is inconsistent—such a rider does not learn even after he has been taught. But the rider who knows the methods and knows the mind of the horse, who is calm, able to eradicate the flaws of the horse, intent upon bringing out the horse's good points, is always nimble in all the movements.

The horse that is to be ridden should be grasped by the halter and led into the riding arena by a good rider and should be handled both from the left and from the right. A fine horse should not be mounted suddenly nor struck, for from being struck fear arises, and from fear, panic. In the morning, the rider should make the horse move with the leaping pace of capering, loosening the reins; at the end of the day, the rider should go slowly slowly, holding in the reins. The equivalents of the political methods of conciliation and giving gifts [according to the *Arthashastra*],[21] when applied to the handling of horses, are talking nicely and soothing; the equivalent of using armed force is striking with the whip and so forth; and the equivalent of bribery is forbearing for a while or allowing the horse to rest.

As soon as each lesson is learned, proceed to the next. You should place the bit on a riding horse without touching the surface of the tongue and tighten it at the corners of the mouth. Gradually loosen it, to make the horse forget that he is being ridden. Loosen the string that ties down the horse's tongue, but do not let go of the mouth. A horse that holds its head high by nature should have a tightened breast-plate.[22] An excellent rider should ride with grace and elegance, and should control the horse's left fore-leg by the left rein, and the left hind leg with the right rein. The horse that goes on the left with a bent head should be controlled by the left rein....

Soft on the shoulder, light in the mouth, loose in all joints—to control the horse the rider should collect him.[23]

And, as he is a physician, Dhanvantari also deals in some detail with ways of curing sick horses, which included bloodletting.

Like the *Ashvashastra* we have just seen, on which it draws in several places, the *Agni Purana* is a strange mix of mythology and quite clear-headed advice on the training and riding of horses, though neither of these texts aspires to the level of practical detail that we saw in Kautilya's *Arthashastra*.

A PERSIAN *ASHVASHASTRA*

Sanskrit works on horses, above all the *Ashvashastra* of Shalihotra, were often translated into Persian at Indian courts in the fifteenth, sixteenth, and seventeenth centuries, and a seventeenth-century Persian translation of the Shalihotra text was translated into English in the eighteenth century.[24] Under the Mughals, horses were categorized in muster rolls in ways that made use of Persian (ultimately Sanskrit) *ashvashastras*. For example, in a book on how to describe horses, by the Delhi-based Khatri litterateur Anand Ram Mukhlis (c. 1697–1750), the terminology for recording horses' colors is defined with many combinations of colors and patterns: dark red, streaked with grey lines or brindle, reddish or chestnut, red and black mixed or bay, or greenish brown stripes or grullo. Specific terms for unique patterns on the animal's forehead signified particular kinds of horses: "If the forehead is black and has stripes of red with some white..., record it as *nil*. And, if the forehead is white and all four legs are also white (stockings up the leg), write down *pechakliyan*."[25]

Information from Indian texts about horses was also incorporated into earlier Persian texts, such as the eleventh-century *Qabus Nama,* or *Mirror for Princes,* by Kai Ka'us Ibn Iskandar. Here is part of chapter 25 of that text, "Buying Horses,"

FIGURE 17. Bloodletting on a horse. From an eighteenth-century CE Hindi text. (Wellcome Library Collection, CC BY, https://wellcomecollection.org/works/p7b4d2bb)

in which, having described the virtues of a good horse, the author considers the flaws in a bad horse:

Of the defects in a horse, one is silence: the silent horse has very little value. The sign of this is that when he sees a mare, although he may erect the penis, he fails to neigh. Then there is the half-blind horse, which is night-blind. The sign of this is that he has no fear at night of those things which horses usually fear; and he will not shy but will venture on to any ground which you ride to, however bad. A deaf horse is also bad. The sign of this is that the horse does not hear the neighing of other horses and never answers, although he always has his ears forward and open. A "left-legged" horse is also bad, constantly stumbling. The sign of this is that when you lead the horse into a passageway, he puts forward his left fore-leg first. Moreover, he cannot swim. The purblind horse is bad because he cannot see in the daytime. The sign of this is that the pupil of the eye is black verging on green, and he keeps his eye always open so that the lids never touch. This may occur in one eye or in both. Although this defect may appear to be a bad one, both Arabs and non-Arabs are agreed that it is well-omened. The "stockinged" horse has a white fore- or hind-leg; if the left fore- and hind-legs are white it is ill-omened.

If the horse is blue in both eyes, that may pass; but if he is blue in one only, then the horse is defective, particularly if it is the left eye. The wall-eyed horse is bad, that is, the horse that has a white eye; and the blue roan is bad, too; so is the long-necked horse, that is, the one that has its neck stretched out straight. No regard should be paid to a horse of that description. The "crab" horse is bad because both of his hind legs are crooked; in Persian it is called "bow-legged." He frequently falls down. The hair-ringed horse similarly is bad because he has hair around his legs and under his hoofs. It is worst if the hair grows on both sides, but it is bad if the hair is around the legs above the hoof on the inner side. If it is on the outer side, it is tolerable.

The horse with distorted hoofs is bad also, that is, one that has the hoofs turned inwards. (It is also called *ahnaf*.) Bad also is the horse that has an overlong fore- or hind-leg, whether in descent or ascent. (It is called *afraq*, i.e., "That which has one haunch higher than the other.") The crooked-tailed horse (called *a'zal* or *akshaf*) is bad; his genital organs are open to view. So also is the dog-tailed horse and one whose [hind-]legs are set wide apart in such fashion that they cannot follow in the traces of the fore-legs. It is called *afran*, if the infirmity is in the hind-legs; and that is equally bad. Bad also are the horses which refuse harness, bore, bite, neigh frequently, break wind, kick, are slow to eject their droppings, or maintain the penis erect. . . .

The worst defect of all is old age; one may contrive with any of the other disabilities to have some work done, but with old age it is impossible.[26]

The topics chosen for discussion in this text, the organization of the subject matter, and much of the data are familiar to us from the Indian texts. But the absence of an aura of magic or a consistent system of classification, and a greater interest in the peculiarities of real horses, distinguish this text from the Sanskrit *ashvashastra* tradition.

EQUINE LEXICOLOGY AND MORE EQUINE LEXICOLOGY

Many Sanskrit terms for parts of the horse (such as *vidu* or *palihasta*) do not appear in the principal extant Sanskrit dictionaries. Other terms appear in the standard dictionary by Sir Monier Monier-Williams but are unhelpfully glossed, such as "a particular part of the head of a horse" (for the *stuva*, or poll). He defines the *randhra*, or sheath, with vague euphemisms about being situated somewhere under the belly. Still other terms are given definitions that apply only to the human body or that have quite a different meaning when applied to a horse, such as *manya* (top of the poll) as "the nape of the neck," and *sthura* (hock) as "the ankle or buttock." The problem is that one needs to translate not just from Sanskrit to English but from horsey Sanskrit to horsey English, and Monier-Williams was evidently not horsey. Often the translation depends entirely on the context; here, as so often, it is necessary to take the Sanskrit from the meaning rather than the meaning from the Sanskrit (to paraphrase Dr. Johnson's notorious slur on the Latin of his colleague David Garrick).

In 1978 I decided to remedy this situation, at the same time hoping to get the *Journal of the American Oriental Society,* a proudly pedantic publication (whose clientele are the rough equivalent of the ancient Indian clientele of *shastras*), to publish a satire on a typical *JAOS* article, "Contributions to an Equine Lexicology, wih Special Reference to Frogs." I therefore constructed a list of obscure Sanskrit equine terms with their equally obscure (to non-horsey scholars) English equine equivalents, basing them primarily on the *Ashvashastra* of Nakula and the *Ashvavaidyaka* of Jayanta Suri.[27] I positioned the Sanskrit terms on a sketch of a horse taken from one of the books that horsey English children were given to learn about "the points of the horse."

I also pointed out several terms that were used in a special sense in Sanskrit equestrian parlance: thus *nirmansa* (literally, "without flesh") would be translated as "dry" when referring to a leg or a head, and *kurca-vrana* ("scar on the back tendon") would be a "curb." One curious point arises regarding the word for the elastic horny substance growing in the middle of the sole of a horse's foot. The Sanskrit word for this is "frog" (*manduki* or *manduka*), and so it is in English.

Other ancient and modern Indo-European languages have other words for it; the ancient Greeks called it the "swallow" (*chelidon*). In the late Byzantine period, however, it was called the "little frog" (*batrachos*), and the late Latin word for it was also "little frog" (*ranula*). Our use of the term in English, I concluded, might derive from these Latin and/or Greek sources, skipping over the different medieval terminology, but it could also derive from the ancient Sanskrit usage.

When I made this suggestion, tongue in cheek, in the pages of the *JAOS,* one scholar (that I know of) got the joke: Richard W. Lariviere, then a professor of Sanskrit at the University of Texas at Austin.[28] He responded with a "Brief Communication" entitled, "More Equine Lexicography: The Hamstring Is Not Connected to the Nose," and the *JAOS* obligingly printed that one, too. Professor Lariviere began by remarking that I had evidently, "with an eye peeled for lurking philistines, felt the compulsion to justify this manifestly helpful contribution" with examples of ways that modern scholars might tumble over the technical vocabulary. Riding to my rescue, he therefore wished both to support my assertion and to add that modern scholars are often misled by commentaries even within the Sanskrit tradition. The example he chose, taking off from my own remark that *sthura* (hock) was often wrongly translated as the ankle or buttock (the latter being *payu* in Sanskrit), was one in which the most famous of all Sanskrit commentators, Sayana, had glossed *sthura* as "a particular part of the flesh found near the anus." Professor Lariviere, pointing out that the *sthura* is "the closest thing a horse has to an elbow," therefore concluded that "Sayana, in this case at least, did not know his *payu* from his *sthura.*" He went on to adduce dozens of other examples of commentarial confusions over *sthura,* and he concluded that the commentators "did not have the necessary familiarity with the lexicography of large animal anatomy." And so he thanked me for my contribution. I, of course, have always been grateful to him for joining me in a bit of high-spirited academic horseplay.

WHO KNEW THE *ASHVASHASTRAS?*

Though the knowledge of Sanskrit was limited to a privileged few in ancient India, primarily men, and among them primarily Brahmins and some kings and wealthy merchants, the information in the *ashvashastras* was widely diffused, as we know from its citation in vernacular texts and from the many illustrations of horses of various colors and conformations, corresponding to lists in the textbooks, that appear in paintings and sketches, on palm-leaf pages, ivory, walls, and, throughout India, in any place where there is room for an image of a horse.

The ideas of Sanskrit texts have always been well known in India, even among people who did not read. They listened. The third-century CE *Kamasutra,* in arguing for this general point in the context of women's access to the *Kamasutra,* specifically mentions the science of horses. It begins with a challenge from "scholars," a term that in this text designates pedants who are usually wrong:

> Scholars say: "Since females cannot grasp texts, it is useless to teach women this text [the *Kamasutra*]." Vatsyayana [the author of the *Kamasutra*] says: But women understand the practice, and the practice is based on the text. This applies beyond this specific subject of the *Kamasutra,* for throughout the world, in all subjects, there are only a few people who know the text, but the practice is within the range of everyone. And a text, however far removed, is the ultimate source of the practice. "Grammar is a science," people say. Yet the sacrificial priests, who are no grammarians, know how to gloss the words in the sacrificial prayers. "Astronomy is a science," they say. But ordinary people perform the rituals on the days when the skies are auspicious. And people know how to ride horses and elephants without studying the texts about horses and elephants. In the same way, even citizens far away from the king do not step across the moral line that he sets. The case of women learning the *Kamasutra* is like those examples.[29]

The question of the specific people, or groups of people, who were aware of the horsey oral traditions—stable boys, grooms, riding masters, the owners of horses—is one to which we will return. But we have already seen the *Agni Purana* declare that "the wise and accomplished rider, whoever he is, can communicate his wish, and rides by his own ability, by practice and application, without book-learning." Or, to put it differently, as the Rajput saying goes, to this day, "A man who reads doesn't ride."[30]

The persistent canard that Indians who owned horses did not know how to care for them has been bolstered by two other false beliefs: that the *ashvashastras,* which, admittedly, do incorporate much magical and mythical material, contained *no* useful knowledge about horses; and that, as the *Agni Purana* and the Rajput saying agree, people who worked with horses didn't read about horses. (These two wrongs might of course cancel one another out and make a right: that Indians were not aware of the bad advice of the *ashvashastras* and therefore devised their own more practical ways of caring for horses.) But we will see how the knowledge of the *ashvashastras* was in fact part of a rich textual and oral appreciation of horses in India.

7 | ✿ | Buddhist Horses

500 BCE to 500 CE

Buddhism shares with Hinduism many stories and images of horses, as well as the tendency to dichotomize equines in the Vedic manner, contrasting the good stallion with the evil mare. For the good stallion, we will here consider a fundamental Buddhist myth, the story of the faithful horse that carried the future Buddha out of his life as a prince and into his life as the Buddha. For the evil mare, we will sample a range of stories about voracious horse-headed female creatures who bedevil Buddhist men.

Stories about Buddhist horses are inevitably colored by Buddhist ideas about the meaning of life, which differ in many significant ways from their Hindu equivalents. So, from now on, and more and more as we continue to move into Mughal and British and tribal worlds, we will be stretching and qualifying some of the basic paradigms that we have carved out of the Sanskrit corpus. In the field of visual art, too, Buddhism changed the course of the history of representations of horses in India. The emperor Ashoka, in the third century BCE, who did much to promote Buddhism in India and beyond, put a galloping stallion (together with a bull, a lion, and an elephant) on the great Lion Pillar that he had built in Sarnath to proclaim his reign. The style of that horse, seeming to burst with breath from within, became the particular genius of Indian sculptural representations of animals ever after.[1]

The *Jatakas,* tales of the former lives of the Buddha, preserve quite a lot of information about horses. They tell us that horse dealers from northern districts used to bring horses to Varanasi for sale; Sindh horses were especially valued and were used in royal ceremonies.[2] Moreover:

> Sindh horses are milk white (*Jatakas* #22, 23, 160, 211, 529, 547, 538), ... white as lilies, swift as the wind and well trained (#266, 544, 547). Horses

FIGURE 18. Horse on the Sarnath column abacus. Sarnath, Varanasi Dt., Uttar Pradesh, c. 250 BCE. Beige sandstone. (Courtesy of the John C. and Susan L. Huntington Photographic Archive of Buddhist and Asian Art; photo by John C. Huntington)

like to eat pears (#176) . . . [and] are fed on parched rice drippings, broken meats and grass and red rice-powder (#254). Horses are fierce (#115). When they become rogue, they bite quiet horses, but when two rogues meet they lick each other's bodies (#156). Horses can also imitate men. A horse watching its lame trainer as he tramped on and on in front imitated him and limped too (#184). A well-bred war-horse will not bathe in the same place where an ordinary horse took its bath (#25). Horses were employed for drawing state-chariots (#22) and cars (#211). Well-bred Sindh horses sheathed in mail were used for war (#23, 547). . . . There was a trade in horses (#4, 5). There were valuers employed by kings to fix the proper price of horses, elephants, and the like (#5). Good horses used to fetch high prices.[3]

In addition to this more or less practical information, the *Jatakas* also know about magical horses:

A high-bred foal was sold at Varanasi at a high price; a separate price was paid for the foal's four feet, for its tail, for its head—six purses of a thousand pieces of money, one for each part. This horse could run so fast that nobody could see it at all. It could run over a pond without getting its hoofs wet, and gallop over lotus leaves without even pushing one of them under water.[4]

This is a fine Buddhist variation on the theme of the winged horse.

In one *Jataka* (#23, the *Bhojajaniya Jataka*), the future Buddha himself actually becomes incarnate as a "thoroughbred Sindh horse" who becomes King Brahmadatta's best warhorse. The horse saves Brahmadatta from seven powerful attacking kings, fighting on though he is mortally wounded. As he lies dying, he makes Brahmadatta promise not to kill the captured kings but to bind them with an oath and set them free; he also reminds Brahmadatta to rule with charity, righteousness, and justice. And as they are taking off the horse's armor piece by piece, he dies.

KANTHAKA, THE FUTURE BUDDHA'S HORSE

One of the most famous horses in Indian history is Kanthaka,[5] the white stallion that Prince Siddhartha (also called Gautama Shakyamuni), the future Buddha (or Bodhisattva/Bodhisatta), rode before he achieved Enlightenment.

Kanthaka plays an important part in one of the best-known versions of the story of the Buddha, Ashvaghosha's *Buddhacharita* or "Life of the Buddha," a Sanskrit poem composed in the first or second century CE. Here is a summary of what Ashvaghosha says about Kanthaka in his poem:

> One day, Prince Siddhartha set out from the palace on his fine horse Kanthaka, with golden bells swinging from the horse's bridle. After a while, the prince dismounted and eventually encountered several gods who had come to earth in disguise to meet him. Then he who had conquered the horses of the senses mounted his horse and returned to the city.
>
> After some time, the prince decided to leave the palace forever. In the night, he awakened his charioteer, Chandaka, and told him to bring Kanthaka to him quickly. Kanthaka had strength, heart, speed and breeding; he had a golden bit in his mouth and a soft cloth on his back. His back, rump and fetlocks were long, his hair, tail and ears short and erect, his back low, his belly and flanks rounded, his nostrils, forehead, hips and chest wide. The prince embraced the horse and caressed him, speaking sweetly to him, as if to a friend, saying, "Best of all horses, you often carried the king when he conquered his enemies; now you must help me to conquer death. Use your speed and courage, for your own welfare and for that of the world." The white horse carried him without

FIGURE 19. Prince Siddhartha's horse Kanthaka with an empty saddle leaves the palace via an elaborate gate (*torana*). The Bodhisattva is represented by an umbrella held over the horse by a servant. Inscribed. Dome-slab carved in limestone ("Palnad marble") with the Great Departure. Amaravati, second century CE. 123 × 86 × 11 cm. (© The Trustees of the British Museum, 1880, 0709.51)

making a sound that might cause alarm in the night, stifling his neighing and walking with careful steps. Then demigods (Yakshas) bent low to cup the tips of their hands under the horse's hooves. . . .

After riding for a while, the prince entered a grove of trees and, dismounting from his horse and stroking him, told Chandaka to return with the horse to the palace. But Kanthaka licked the prince's feet with his tongue and began to shed warm tears. The prince stroked the horse gently with his hand and spoke to him like a companion, saying, "Please do not weep, Kanthaka. You've proven what a good horse you are; bear with me now." And so, though Kanthaka was a powerful horse, he walked on in low spirits, turning back and looking into the grove of trees, neighing loudly again and again, piteously. Though he was hungry, he did not touch the grass or water that he used to enjoy along the path.

When they arrived back at the city, the women of the city rushed out to see them, but when they saw that the horse had no one in the saddle, they turned back. Chandaka took Kanthaka deep inside the palace. The horse looked around with tears in his eyes and neighed loudly, as if to tell everyone how unhappy he was, but the horses stabled near him, thinking that his neighing meant that the prince had returned, neighed in reply. So, too, people in the palace near there thought, "Since the horse Kanthaka is neighing, surely the prince must be entering the palace." But when the women saw that it was just the horse, they wept.

Yashodhara, Gautama's wife, said, "This horse, Kanthaka, seems to want to destroy me, for, like a jewel-thief, he has carried away the one who is everything to me. Since he could bear the lash of arrows, he could certainly bear the lash of the whip. Why then did he fear the whip so much that he stole my fortune and my heart? Now, after doing such terrible things, he neighs loudly, filling the king's house. But the wretched horse stayed silent enough when he carried away my beloved. If he had neighed to wake people up, or made noise with his hooves on the ground, I would not have to bear this terrible grief."

Chandaka replied, "Don't blame Kanthaka, or me. We are blameless, for we did not act of our own wills. The prince was a god among men, and he went away with the gods, like a god. This fine horse never even touched the ground as he galloped, for the tips of his hooves seemed somehow suspended; and his mouth was sealed shut as if by some divine force, and that's why Kanthaka didn't neigh."

When the king learned all this, he fell to the ground, and, looking up at the horse, he said, "You did me so many favors in battle, Kanthaka, but now you have done me great harm. Either take me today to where he is, or gallop there fast and bring him back again."[6]

But Kanthaka did neither, and the future Buddha continued on his spiritual journey.

Kanthaka in this text carries the prince on two separate crucial occasions. Before the episode we have just considered, Kanthaka had carried the prince, by day, out of the palace, where he had been sheltered from the experience of human suffering, into an open place where he encountered the four signs—an old man, a sick man, a dead man, and a renouncer—that inspired his ultimate decision to renounce. We learn very little about the horse on this occasion, though the prince himself is described with the familiar Indian equine metaphor, for he is said to have "conquered the horses of the senses [*jitendriyashva*]." In a Tibetan version of this text, a mendicant says to the Buddha, "The senses of others are restless like horses, but yours have been tamed. Other beings are passionate, but your passions have ceased."[7]

On the second outing from the palace, at night, the horse is described as having the qualities sought in the best horses, according to the *ashvashastras*—long back, wide chest, and so forth. We also hear hints, in the lament of the prince's wife, that Kanthaka had been subjected to the sort of painful treatment that ordinary warhorses endure: "Since he could bear the lash of arrows, he certainly could bear the lash of the whip." Up to this point, Kanthaka is apparently a superior but not supernatural horse. He shows a fine but not unnatural sensitivity later on when he neighs in sorrow, both when he learns that he must leave the prince and, later, when he returns to the palace without the prince. And he demonstrates a fine, but still not miraculous, intelligence when he understands enough human speech to know that he must not make a sound and allows the demigods to cup their hands under his hooves. But it is the moment when he weeps warm tears in sorrow as he is parted from his beloved rider, unlike any natural horse (though we have seen mythical horses weep in other Indian texts), that makes him famous throughout Buddhist literature. The *Ashvashastra* tells us that if a horse sheds tears for no apparent cause, it is a bad omen;[8] here, however, there is a real cause. It is this image of the horse who grieves for his rider that marks this text as belonging to a genre that we will soon encounter, that of the horse who loves his rider with a love that seems human—or, indeed, more than human.

Stories about Kanthaka in later Buddhist literature embroider upon the basic themes: It is said that Kanthaka was eighteen hands high;[9] that he was born on the same day as the Buddha; that he neighed with joy when he realized that he was being saddled for the Great Departure, but the gods silenced his neighing; that he jumped over the great city gate when it was locked against them.[10] Other texts tell us that Kanthaka didn't merely weep when Siddhartha renounced his life as a prince but died of a broken heart; or that he died later, when he had endured the brunt of the emotional reactions and bitter attacks of the people in the palace who grieved for the departed Bodhisattva; or that he starved himself to death and was reborn as a deity in heaven.[11] Finally, Kanthaka has been seen as a scapegoat for the Bodhisattva, dying for him, sacrificing himself for him, so that the narrative of the Great Departure as a whole makes use of a sacrificial idiom—involving kingship and the idea that horses sacrifice themselves for us[12]—that might allow us to see Kanthaka as a reincarnation of the Vedic sacrificial horse. Kanthaka's fame leaps over national boundaries: a successful American racehorse named Kanthaka, a chestnut colt, was foaled on January 28, 2015, by Jimmy Creed out of Sliced Bread.

THE GREAT DEPARTURE AT SANCHI

One of the most famous of the early sculptural images of the Buddha is the carving at Sanchi, from the first century BCE, illustrating the future Buddha's departure from the palace, the episode that we have just seen represented in Ashvaghosha's poem. In fact, it is *not* an image of the Buddha himself, for he is not actually represented here but is assumed to be invisibly present on the visible horse, Kanthaka. Thus Kanthaka is the "vehicle" of the Buddha not only in the conventional way (the future Buddha, who is regarded as a human, rides a horse, as humans do) but also in the sense in which, as we have seen, various animals serve as the "vehicles" of the Hindu gods, "carrying" the gods invisibly. For in the Sanchi carving, wherever we see Kanthaka we understand that the future Buddha is invisibly riding on him—until the two last images, when the Buddha has finally departed and is no longer present (though invisible) on the horse but is still "carried" by him in the more metaphysical sense that the Hindu gods' *vahanas* carry them. In fact, the Buddha is seldom shown in visual art forms; he is usually represented symbolically—sometimes by the *bodhi* tree, or a stupa, or a parasol, or his footprint, or, as here in one frame, his sandals, and so forth. But here the sculptors chose to represent him as a horse, a living creature, more precisely a *vahana*.

The frieze depicts five images of the same horse, Kanthaka, moving from left to right and then, in the fifth scene, from right to left. In the first image, the demigods are holding up his legs to muffle the sound of his hooves on the marble floors of the palace. In the second and third scenes, Kanthaka continues to carry the invisible Buddha away from the palace. At the extreme right, on the top, when the (invisible) Buddha has dismounted, and the previously only apparently riderless horse is now actually riderless, his groom Chandaka kneels at the feet of the invisible Buddha (here represented by his sandals) first to beg him not to depart and then to bid him farewell. And finally, in the lower image on the far right, turning back to the left, the riderless horse returns to the palace, led by Chandaka.

FIGURE 20. The Great Departure. Sanchi, Madhya Pradesh, second half of the first century BCE. Carved in sandstone on the East Gate of the Great Stupa. (Photo by Anna Lise Seastrand, 2011)

HALF-HORSE CREATURES: ASHVAMUKHAS AND KIMPURUSHAS

In contrast with this exemplary stallion, Buddhist texts depict horse-headed females, familiar Indian nighttime bogeywomen, who carry men off for dastardly purposes. Indian tradition includes them in the more general mythology of mares, regarding them as beautiful but sexually voracious. Horse-headed demigods in general, especially the females of the species, are sometimes martial or ascetic but, at the same time, fatally attractive.[13] The poet Kalidasa, probably in the fifth century CE, describes beautiful horse-headed women who walk slowly, weighed down by their heavy hips and breasts.[14]

The Ashvamukha/Ashvamukhi (fem.) ("Horse Head" or "Horse Face")[15] is an anthropomorphic figure with the head (sometimes just the face) of a horse, a kind of Horse-human, often a kind of Horse-god. The Kimpurusha or Kinnara (What?-man) or Kinnari (What?-woman) may be the same as the Ashvamukha but is sometimes the reverse, with the body of a horse and the head or, often, the whole upper torso, of a human, like a Greek centaur.[16] The two sets of terms are used rather loosely. A passage in a seventh- or eighth-century CE Sanskrit poem says that a Kimpurusha is a demigod with a horse's head and a human body, while the Kinnara has a human head and a horse's body.[17] The horse head (on an anthropomorphic body) is the ritual figure: it conjures up ceremonies in which humans wear masks of the heads of animals, with implications of superhuman powers. Post-Vedic texts and paintings often depict the four Vedas as anthropomorphic creatures with animal heads: the *Rig Veda* has a donkey's head, the *Yajur Veda* a goat's head, the *Sama Veda* a horse's head, and the *Atharva Veda* a monkey's head.[18] The centaur, by contrast, is the mythical figure: it conjures up the image of the rider astride a horse, often idealized as an image of flying, or sex.

A seventeenth-century Telugu poem from Andhra, mocking the god Vishnu for his apparent lack of martial aggression, invokes the double image of the horse-head figure and the centaur:

Why this weakness of yours?
Shouldn't a god be strong?
Aren't you known as the 'scourge of enemies'?
If even a Brahmin like me
had a weapon like the discus that you hold in your hand,
I would carve up all the Turks,
put a horse's head on a soldier's body
and a horse's body on a warrior's head—
I would cut them, hack away at them,
pursue them, chopping them to pieces![19]

The violence in this poem is directed against the "Turks" as the usual placeholders for any foreigners, particularly foreign horsemen.

DANGEROUS BUDDHIST HORSE-HEADED WOMEN

Ancient Buddhist monuments depict horse-headed women,[20] and ancient Buddhist texts describe them in lurid detail. A second-century BCE carving at Sanchi depicts horse-headed women carrying off men (and, sometimes, women), and an eleventh-century carving from Barha Kotra represents horse-headed Yoginis (supernatural female magicians) trampling men under their feet. Buddhist sculptures from the second century BCE to the fifth century CE also depict men happily mounted on creatures with the heads of women and the bodies of mares, as well as women happily mounted on creatures with the heads of men and the bodies of stallions.

The *Mahavamsa,* the ancient Pali history of Sri Lanka, tells us that King Pandukabhaya pursued a Buddhist demoness (Yakshi or Yakshini in Sanskrit; Yakkhi or Yakkhini in Pali), who appeared as a beautiful mare named Vadavamukhi ("Mare's Head" or "Mare's Mouth"), with a white body and red feet; when she plunged into a pond, he grasped her mane, subdued her, and rode her into battle.[21] The motifs of dangerous beauty and flight into water are, as we have seen, typical of mare mythology, and the name of this mare is also the name of the underwater doomsday fire in Hindu mythology.

One Pali story of the Buddha's former birth tells of a Yakkhi[22] who is, significantly, the reincarnation of an unfaithful and shameless wife. When she was then

FIGURE 21. Horse-headed Yakshini holding a woman. Vedika, northwest quadrant, inner face, pillar, central medallion. Sanchi, Uttar Pradesh, 199–100 BCE. (Photo: American Institute of Indian Studies)

reborn as the Yakkhi, though unfortunately addicted to both seducing and eating men, she was also capable of unselfish love both for her lover and for her son, the future Buddha or Bodhisatta:

> Once upon a time, when Brahmadatta reigned as king of Varanasi, his queen was unfaithful to him, and when the king questioned her, she swore, "If I have sinned against you, I will be reborn as a horse-headed Yakkhi." She died and was reborn as a horse-headed Yakkhi, who lived in a rock-cave in a great forest at the foot of a mountain. She used to catch and eat the men who travelled on the road there.

FIGURE 22. Horse-headed Yogini trampling on a man. Barha Kotra, Banda, Uttar Pradesh, 1000–1099 CE. Sandstone. 62 × 39 cm. In the State Museum, Lucknow. (Photo: American Institute of Indian Studies)

One day a rich, healthy, young Brahmin was traveling on that road with his entourage. When the Yakkhi saw him, she laughed out loud and rushed at him, and all his attendants fled. She seized him and carried him on her back into her cave. But under the influence of passion she fell in love with him, and instead of eating him she married him, and they lived happily together. And from then on, whenever she captured men, she took their clothes and rice and oil and so forth for him, and cooked delicious food for him, while she continued to eat the men. But whenever she went away, she shut the mouth of her cave with a huge stone to keep him from escaping.

Now, while they were living happily in this way, the Brahmin impregnated the Yakkhi, and she gave birth to the Bodhisatta. Filled with love for them both, she fed them, and as the boy grew up she shut him up in the cave with his father. One day, the Bodhisatta asked his father, "Why is your head different from my mother's?" And his father replied, "Well, my son, your mother is a Yakkhi and lives by eating men, but you and I are men." "If that is so," said the boy, "why do we live here? Let's go to the places where men live." "My son," replied his father, "if we try to escape, your mother will kill us both." But the Bodhisatta said, "Don't worry, father. I'll make sure that you will return to the place where men live."

The next day, when the Yakkhi had left, the Bodhisatta took his father and fled. When she returned and found them gone, she ran with the speed of the wind and caught them and said to the Brahmin, "Why are you running away? Do you lack anything here?" and he replied, "My dear, don't be angry. Your son took me away with him." Because of her love for her child, she didn't say a word, but brought them back to her home. Then the Bodhisatta realized that her powers extended only over a certain area, and after a few days he carried his father on his shoulders beyond the river that was the limit of her land. She ran after them and called to them from her bank of the river, begging them to return, but her son replied, "Mother, we are men and you are a Yakkhi. We will never return to you." And so, though she was overwhelmed by great sorrow, she loved her son so much that she gave him a magic stone. And then her great sorrow for her son broke her heart, and she fell down dead on the spot.

The Bodhisatta burned her body on a funeral pile, made offerings of flowers, wept, sobbed, and returned with his father to Varanasi. There he used his magic stone to expose the wickedness of the reigning king, and the people made him king.[23]

The telltale horse head is the only thing that tips the human boy off to the fact that his mother is not a human. Though her story begins in unchastity and continues through murder and quasi cannibalism, she is redeemed by her love first for her lover and then for her son. The mare's head is the one sign of her evil, and that (well, that and her unfortunate track record of serial murders) is enough to justify her death. But her love for her son, which breaks her heart, might remind us of Kanthaka dying for his love of the Bodhisatta, who is also echoed in the son's decision to leave home as Gautama did.

A much retold Jataka tale[24] tells of an entire band of man-eating ogresses:

> Five hundred merchants were shipwrecked on Sinhala Island near a city of man-eating ogresses (*rakshasis*), who transformed themselves into gorgeous women and approached the merchants, bearing food and carrying children. They seduced the merchants, but when they captured new bands of men, they secretly threw the older group one by one into a house of torment and ate them. The head merchant finally realized that his wife was an ogress and urged the others to flee with him. Half of them refused to leave, but the others prayed to the Bodhisatta, who took the form of a magical flying white horse, beaked like a crow, with hair like *munja* grass, who came from the Himalayas and flew the ones who wanted to leave back to their homes, thus saving them from this fate worse than death (and from death).[25]

The *rakshasis* in this variant are not said to have horse heads, but they behave just like the horse-headed Yakkhis, not only eating humans (as most Yakkhis do) but seducing them. The equine imagery is transferred, instead, to the Bodhisatta Avalokiteshvara, who is sometimes called "the white winged steed of salvation,"[26] and whose salvific character may have been inspired by that of the Bodhisatta who became the wise, brave, and articulate Sindh warhorse, or even by Kanthaka, the noble Buddhist horse.

8 ❖ Arabian Horses and Muslim Horsemen

500 to 1800 CE

EQUESTRIAN RULERS AND THEIR HORSES

Intimacy with, and mastery of, horses is a hallmark of the Turkic peoples of Central Asia.[1] Turkic and Arabian merchants and storytellers and seekers and mercenary soldiers brought Arabian horses to India from early in the Common Era, both by sea and over the Northwest passes. In subsequent centuries, the horse trade continued to bring Arabians (both human and equine) to India. Other groups also rode in on horseback, now including conquerors, most notably the Turkic peoples of the Delhi Sultanate (1206–1526) and the Central Asian Mongols who became the Mughals (1526–1857). Indians tended to call all of these political groups—including Persians (many of whom had entered India centuries before the Arabs), Arabs, Mongols, and Turks—"Turks." And they usually called their horses Arabians, even when they were really Turkish or Persian. In fact, one of the great qualities of Arabian horses is what breeders call "prepotency": the ability to transmit their characteristics to their offspring. And so each Arabian horse may have had a disproportionate influence on other breeds, so that those "Turkish" or "Persian" horses may indeed have been, to a significant degree, Arabian.

Mahmud of Ghazni (r. 999–1030) had the advantage of having his forces mounted on Central Asian horses; the most an Indian could hope for in an encounter with them was "perhaps a fleeter horse."[2] When Muhammad bin Tughluq (r. 1325–51) recruited men from Western and Central Asia, he made them submit to a test of equestrian skill before he signed them on.[3] The Turkish conquerors were probably the ones who introduced polo into India,[4] which was so well established there by the early twelfth century CE that the Western Chalukya king Someshvara, in his great encyclopedic Sanskrit work, devoted an entire chapter to "Indian polo."[5] Qutb al-Din Aibak, ruler of the Delhi Sultanate from 1206 to 1210, died when his polo pony fell on him in the course of the game.[6]

Under the Delhi Sultanate and the Mughal Empire, practical information and imaginative mythologies about horses crossed the invisible borders between the cultures in both directions. We have noted the influence of Sanskrit *ashvashastras* on the Persian and Arabic sciences of horses. There are also extensive Persian records about horses under the Delhi Sultanate and the Mughal Empire. The founding Mughal emperor, Babur (r. 1526–30), a brilliant and passionate horseman, seems to have spent more time in the saddle than on the ground, and his memoir delights in the pleasures he took in his horses, recording many of his wild rides, often under the influence of wine or drugs. On one occasion, he notes, he was "roaring drunk" but got on his horse and, "reeling first to one side and then the other, let the horse gallop, free-reined, along the river-bank, all the way to the camp."[7] A painting from c. 1589 depicts this scene.[8] The historian Abu'l Fazl (1551–1602), in his record of the reign of the Mughal emperor Akbar (r. 1556–1605), the *A'in-i Akbari*, describes Akbar's stables in great detail.[9] Akbar had luminous polo balls ("balls of fire") made so that he could play night games,[10] and the Mughal emperor Jahangir (r. 1605–1726), too, was fond of playing polo.

IMPORTING HORSES INTO INDIA

The literature of the Delhi Sultanate and the Mughal Empire deals at great length both with the crucial importance of importing horses into India and with the use of native-bred, or country-bred, horses. Vast numbers of horses were necessary to maintain the military machine of the Delhi Sultanate, most of them, and probably the best of them, imported.[11] Abu'l Fazl notes that horses were constantly being imported: "Merchants bring to court good horses from Iraq, Turkey, Turkestan ... Kirghiz, Tibet, Kashmir, and other countries. Droves after droves arrive from Turan and Iran, and there are now twelve thousand in the stables of His Majesty."[12] Akbar had 150,000 to 200,000 cavalry men, plus the emperor's own crack regiment of another seven thousand.[13]

Akbar used imported horses primarily for cavalry, but also for strategic political gifts.[14] The Sultan Muhammad bin Tughluq, too, was said to have distributed to his retinue every year "ten thousand Arab horses and countless others."[15] Jahangir in his memoir notes such a gift of a Persian horse:

> On the fifteenth of the same month I presented my best horse by way of favour to Raja Man Singh. Shah 'Abbas had sent this horse with some other

FIGURE 23. Jahangir on a white horse, playing polo with his three sons: Parviz on the bay horse, Mirza Abu'l-Hasan on the dun, and Khurram (later Shahjahan) on the black. From the *Dīvān* of Ḥāfiẓ, 1582–83. (© The British Library Board, Or.7573, f. 194v)

horses and fitting gifts by Minuchihr, one of his confidential slaves, to the late king Akbar. From being presented with this horse the Raja was so delighted that if I had given him a kingdom I do not think he would have shown such joy. At the time they brought the horse it was three or four years old. It grew up in Hindustan. The whole of the servants of the Court, Moghul and Rajput together, represented that no horse like this had ever come from Iraq to Hindustan.[16]

Though the horse "grew up in Hindustan," it was presumably born in Persia, or sired by an imported Persian stallion. Elsewhere, Jahangir said, of another Persian horse, "In truth a horse of this great size and beauty has hardly come to Hindustan."[17] The Hindus, too, preferred to use imported horses as gifts: in a Punjabi tale, the kings gave gifts and cows to the Brahmins, "and to the bards and genealogists they [gave] Turkish and Arab horses as alms."[18]

The rulers of the Delhi Sultanate regarded the so-called country-bred horses as inferior to the horses imported by sea from the Persian Gulf, Arabia, Central Asia, or the highlands of Afghanistan.[19] They did not consider the ordinary Indian country-bred horse suitable either as a gift horse or for service as a warhorse,[20] and Ziya-al-Din Barani (1285–1357), an early historian of the Delhi Sultanate, notes that "dealers selling horses to mounted archers passed off Hindi or Baladasti (Afghan or central Asian) horses as Arabs or Gulf Persians."[21]

THE FOREIGN APPRECIATION OF INDIAN HORSES

Yet the Delhi Sultans regarded *some* of the country-bred horses from the Northwest and the western coast of India as useful warhorses, even before those horses were improved by being crossbred with imported bloodstock.[22] (It's worth noting how early the idea of crossbreeding enters the argument, and the belief that imported bloodstock was needed to improve the breed.) Some horses were bred successfully in North India long before the Turkish invasions, and they continued to be bred under the Mughals. Abu'l Fazl remarked, "In this country, horses commonly live to the age of thirty years,"[23] quite a respectable age.

In the Punjab, especially between the Indus and the Jhelum, they bred horses called *sanujis,* which resembled Iraqi horses.[24] In the northern mountainous district of India, they bred small but strong horses, called *gut,* while in Bengal they bred another kind of horse, strong and powerful, called *tanghan* (or *tangana*).[25] The seventh-century CE poet Bana had remarked, "Old people sang the praises of the tall *tangana* horses, which by the steady motion of their quick footfalls provided a comfortable seat."[26] The *tangana* and *gut* horses, bred in the mountains to carry goods and people, were famous for their endurance.[27] The Indo-Persian poet Amir Khusrau Dehlavi (1253–1325) praises both the some twenty thousand mountain horses (*kohi*) and the sea-borne, imported horses (*bahri*) that were captured in 1310: "The sea-borne horse flies like the wind on the surface of water, without even its feet becoming wet. And when the mountain horse steps on a hill, the hill trembles like a Hindi sword."[28] Jean-Baptiste Tavernier, a French merchant who traveled to Persia and India between 1630 and 1668, wrote that the indigenous horses of Gorakhpur "are by nature so small that when a man is upon them his feet touch the ground, but they are otherwise strong, and go at an amble, doing up to twenty leagues at a stretch, and eating and drinking but little."[29]

Barani notes that "serviceable war-horses . . . fine Hindi horses" had been bred in the eastern Punjab before the Muslim conquest, and cheap, too, so that there was no need to bring horses from the lands of the Mongols. He adds that the horses of the Punjab and its adjacent hills "were among the best bred in India," and that one could raise "very superior horses . . . wherever there was enough food to maintain them."[30] Abu'l Fazl insists that the best horses of all were bred in India, particularly in the Punjab, Mewar, Ajmer, and Bengal near Bihar. He continues: "Skillful, experienced men have paid much attention to the breeding of this sensible animal, many of whose habits resemble those of man; and after a short time, Hindustan ranked higher in this respect than Arabia, whilst many Indian horses cannot be distinguished from Arabs or from the Iraqi breed. There are fine horses bred in every part of the country, but those of Kutch excel, being equal to Arabs."[31] This, then, is one solution to the quandary: Indian horses (or, rather, some Indian horses) are Arabian horses, and so there is no contest. The general foreign consensus, from the time of the Persian and Turkish presence in India, was that Kathiawar and Marwar horses are good for long distances in the desert but, being slightly built, are not big or fast or strong enough for military or parade use. The country-bred horses had much to recommend them. Each type of horse had its place and its virtues suited for that place.

Yet there was usually a clear hierarchy. A notable feature of the attitude to horses among the Delhi Sultans and the Mughals, and one that continued under the British Raj, was a kind of equine caste system. We saw the early stirrings of this way of thinking in the *ashvashastras*' ranking of horses according to the four classes (or *varnas*) of Indian society. The *Arthashastra* had a different hierarchy: "Of horses fit for battle, the best are those bred in Kamboja, Sindh, Aratta, and Vanayu; the middling are those bred in Bahlika, Papeya, Sauvara, and Titala; the rest are the lowest."[32] Someshvara listed thirty-eight breeds of horses, which he divided into best, middle, and inferior breeds.[33] And Abu'l Fazl had his own way of ranking the horses in India: the first are "either Arab bred, or resemble them in gracefulness and prowess. . . . The second class are horses bred in Persia, or such as resemble Persian horses in shape and bearing." The third are Turki or Persian geldings, strong and well-formed, but not as good as the best Persian horses. The fourth are horses imported from Turin, strong and well-formed, but not as good as the third-rate Persian horses. The fifth class (*yabus*) are bred in India, and lack strength and size, nor do they generally perform well: "They are the offspring of Turki horses with an inferior breed. . . . The last two classes are mostly Indian bred."[34]

The categorization of horses among Indian rulers, native or foreign, boiled down to a general belief that imported horses were ultimately of higher quality, and suitable for higher people, than the so-called country-breds. Barani notes that, in fourteenth-century Delhi, "Muslim kings not only allow but are pleased with the fact that infidels, polytheists, idol-worshippers and cow-dung worshippers build houses like palaces, wear clothes of brocade and ride Arab horses caparisoned with gold and silver ornaments."[35] Clearly, non-Muslim Indians who could afford to ride Arabian horses did so. Despite, as we have seen, several important dissident voices that praised the qualities of the native breeds in particular parts of India, and for particular tasks, the prevailing attitude was that Arabian horses were the best, and the rest nowhere (to borrow the famous call on the victory of the great racehorse Eclipse).

THE INDIAN APPRECIATION OF FOREIGN HORSES

Turning now from the foreigners' attitudes to native Indian horses, let us consider Indian attitudes to the foreigners and their horses. For horses not only affected the practical relationship between Indians and the people they generally called "Turks" but also functioned, in art and literature, as a symbolic gauge of shifting attitudes within those relationships. Many Hindu rituals and myths involve Arabian horses and/or Muslim riders. Despite or because of the political domination of the Delhi Sultanate and the Mughal Empire, the Indian stories from this period generally depict both Arabian horses and their Muslim riders in a favorable light. For Muslims had lived in India for many centuries by the time these stories were composed, and were no longer always associated with dominant political groups, and many Hindus welcomed Muslims as the bearers of the gift of horses.

Arabian horse lore strongly influenced Indian horse lore, and there are many Indian stories about heroic "Turkish" horses and horsemen. One of the most interesting examples of a Muslim equine hero in Indian folklore is Muttal Ravuttan, who is worshipped in Hindu temples in the southern districts of Tamil Nadu. As Alf Hiltebeitel tells us, "The name Muttal Ravuttan derives its second element from a term meaning Muslim cavalier, horseman, or trooper. The term clearly evokes its common and traditional association of the Muslim warrior on horseback, a Sufi warrior leading his band of followers or the leader of an imperial army of conquest."[36] Hindu worshippers make vegetarian offerings to an image of Muttal Ravuttan as a horse-rider (a *ravuttan*) sculpted in relief on a stone plaque.[37] Sometimes Muttal Ravuttan rides the horse within his temple; often a clay horse or horses await him outside the shrine. The horse is canonically white and is said to be able to fly through the air. At Chinna Salem, Muttal Ravuttan receives marijuana, opium, and cigars for himself, and horse gram [*kollu*] for his horse.[38] His religious affiliations are complex indeed: "The hero Muttal Ravuttan is both 'rajputized' and 'afghanized': at one temple, he may be 'Muttala Raja,' at another 'Muhammed Khan.'"[39]

VATAVURAR AND THE HORSES THAT WERE JACKALS

A trace of mystery, perhaps also of resentment and glamor, hedges one of the best-known South Indian stories about Arabian horses, the story of the devotee of the god Shiva who spent on the worship of the god the money meant to buy horses. This story is often retold in Tamil, Telugu, and other Dravidian languages, as well as in Sanskrit.[40] The *Basava Purana*, a thirteenth-century Telugu epic poem about *jangamas*, saints of the sect of Virashaivas, tells it quite simply, and tells it about Basava, the founder of the sect:

> The Pandya king of Madurai gave his minister, Basava, a large amount of money and asked him to buy horses with it. Because of his excessive devotion, the minister spent all of the money on worshipping *jangamas*. When the money was gone, there was nothing left with which to buy horses. Then, without the slightest hesitation, the minister rounded up all the foxes in the fields, brought them there, and showed them to the Pandya king. The god in his great compassion turned all the foxes into fine horses. Then the king gave fine clothing and precious ornaments to Basava. Very lovingly and devotedly, while everyone listened, the king said, "If anyone slanders my treasurer again, I'll have that person's tongue cut out; I'll have lime smeared on the wound; I'll have hot sand poured into his mouth." With that he took leave of the lionlike Basava.[41]

In this telling, no violence is committed against Basava, nor against the king's horses (who are not yet said to be of foreign origin), but Basava is likened to a lion, and the king, though said to act "lovingly and devotedly," conjures up considerable violence for any future slanderer.

The horses (now foreign) play a far more active, and violent, role, in a fifteenth-century Tamil text, the *Tiruvatavurar Puranam* of Kadavul Mamunivar, which tells a story about the South Indian saint Vatavurar (also known as Manikkavacakan):

> The Pandyan king made Vatavurar his prime minister. When news arrived in Madurai that foreign merchants with fine horses had landed on the coast at Perunturai, the king gave Vatavurar a huge sum of money and sent him, with a large retinue, to the east, to the port of Perunturai, to buy the horses.
>
> Shiva took on the form of a guru in Perunturai. Vatavurar became Shiva's devotee and surrendered to the guru all his belongings, including the funds that had been given to him to purchase horses. Vatavurar dressed as a Shaiva ascetic and forgot about everything else. His aids, thinking he had lost his mind, went back to Madurai and told the king what had happened.
>
> When Vatavurar failed to bring the horses, the King became furious and sent a letter, beginning, "You left here with a huge treasure. Without purchasing the horses you put on a loincloth . . ." The king ordered Vatavurar to return to Madurai. Vatavurar took the letter to the divine teacher and asked him to listen to its contents. When the guru heard the letter, he smiled. He said that he himself would bring horses to Madurai at midday on the first day of the month of Avani [August–September]. Meanwhile Vatavurar should return to the king and inform him of the promised arrival of the horses.
>
> Vatavurar returned, and the king made him stand in the hot sun, to force him to return the misappropriated funds. Vatavurar prayed to Shiva, who answered his prayers by arriving in Madurai disguised as a horse-groom, leading a herd of beautiful horses, which he had produced by transforming all the jackals in the region into horses. The king was delighted and restored Vatavurar to his former status. The day, of course, was the first of Avani. When the Pandyan king presented the horseman with a beautiful piece of silk, Shiva smiled, caught it with his horsewhip, and simply left. This disrespectful behavior angered the king, but Vatavurar mollified him by attributing the horseman's strange manner to foreign customs. The king had the horses examined by experts, who determined that these excellent animals were worth eight times the sum he had sent with Vatavurar to Perunturai.
>
> On the following morning, Madurai awakened to the howling of jackals, for the horses had reverted to their former nature, gobbled up all the horses of the king, and returned to the forests, like lions, their mouths smeared all over

with blood. The grooms reported the evil deeds that the horses had committed. The jackals' clamor struck terror in the hearts of the population, causing
people to question the righteousness of their king. The Pandyan was beside
himself with rage. Again he tortured Vatavurar in the hot sun. Again Vatavurar
prayed to Shiva, who caused the river Vaikai to flood, and the king released
Vatavurar, forgiving him for the misappropriation of royal funds.[42]

Where, in the Virashaiva text, Basava was like a lion in his controlled power, here
the horses are like lions in their carnivorous mayhem. The transformation into
jackals might be regarded as a transformation from tame to wild, jackals being
the untamed form of dogs; or from pure to impure, jackals, like other scavengers,
being polluted and polluting, in contrast with the ritually pure horse; the sound
of a jackal howling strikes terror into the heart of anyone performing a religious
ceremony. Both of these categories would make the jackals inversions of horses.

The false horses eat the other horses, as jackals would; but since they appear
to be horses, they seem to be cannibals. Such incidents identify this as a myth
told by people who do not know horses, and who fear the horse's mouth, with its
big teeth. This is a dangerous misconception, for, as anyone who has been bitten
by a horse will testify, a horse's teeth are relatively dull, so that getting bitten by
a horse is like getting your hand caught in a door but not cut by a knife. It's the
other end of the horse that poses the real danger—the back hooves; it's much
worse to get kicked by a horse than to get bitten. And horses are, in any case, by
nature strict vegetarians (*pace* the recurrent allegation that Indian owners fed
their horses meat). The devouring equine mouth is a projection onto the horse of
the violence that *we* inflict upon *it* in taming it, through the use of the bit in the
mouth. (Recall that Krishna kills the demonic horse Keshi by thrusting his arm
into Keshi's mouth.) This is a horse myth told by people who do not have horses.

An early sixteenth-century Sanskrit text from South India, Mandalakavi's
Pandyakulodaya, adds some details to the central event: "Shiva took the form of
a supreme horseman and chose a horse that was swifter than the speed of light,
a horse that split open the earth with his hoof in order to adorn the form of
Shiva with snakes. The horse reared up, as if to drink cool water from the clouds.
Shiva brandished his sword and made all the horses dance before the king, raising a storm of dust. The hissing of the snakes that he wore in his hair blew away
the dust from his face."[43] These verses turn upon the tradition that the god Shiva
wears snakes all over his body; the horse digs into the earth, in order to make an
opening for snakes from the netherworld to emerge and adorn Shiva. The pas-

sage also reflects the broader theme of the battle between the solar horse and the underworld snake.

The story of Shiva as the foreign horseman is represented in the temple of Avadayarkoil in Pudukottai District in several ways. There is a large, frequently worshipped image of Shiva mounted on a leaping horse. The pavilion where this image stands is called Kutirai Mantapam ("Horse Hall"), and the god in this form is known as Pariviran ("Horse Hero") or Parimel Alakan ("the Beautiful One on a Horse").[44] On the first day of Avani in Madurai and Tiruvatavur, they enact the episode of the horses and the jackals.[45]

The story emphasizes the foreignness of the horseman who brings the horses. The horse traders in this cluster of stories may well have been Arabs. A ninth-century CE Tamil version of the story refers this incident to the "western region" (*kutanatu*).[46] In a recent retelling of the Vatavurar story, the temple *otuvar* (who sings and recites the ritual texts) said that a thousand years ago there was an Arab fort in Perunturai and that Arabs traded horses there.[47] Moreover, the name used at the Tirumarainatacuvami Temple in Tiruvatavur for Shiva as the horse groom, viz., Cokka Ravuttar, in recent times at least is a Muslim name (recall Muttal Ravuttan with his marijuana), another clue that the horse traders were Arabs.[48] Though there is no indication in the text of the Vatavurar story that the author ever met or had even heard of Arabs,[49] yet he did know that foreigners of some sort were the ones who brought splendid, if ultimately devastating, horses to South India.

THE HORSE OF KARBALA

Shiva is depicted as an Arab in the tale of Vatavurar and the jackals. But the Arabs in that myth are there only as *objects* of the myth, not as a subjective part of it. That is, this is an Indian story *about Arabs,* not an Indian story borrowed from the Arabs or other Muslims (who, like all great horse people, had their own horse myths) or an Indian story that shows the influence of Muslim stories about horses (which we will consider in the next chapter).

But before considering horse lore among Muslims in India, we should pause for a moment and veer only slightly aside to consider, briefly, horses in Pakistan, where the population is overwhelmingly Muslim. There the land is in general more hospitable to horses than it is in India; and there, for the many centuries when the area was regarded as the northwest part of India, before the creation of Pakistan in 1947, many of the best horses in India were bred. Some of the Hindu and Parsi breeders whom I consulted in 1996 complained that, at Partition,

Pakistan got the best grazing land,[50] a statement that has a lot of truth in it, as well as resentment. But in Pakistan today, as in India, horses are seldom used for any work but the pulling of tongas, equestrian sports, police patrols, weddings, and casual hacking by farmers who may maintain just one horse for that purpose. There are a number of distinct native breeds, as well as Arabians and Thoroughbreds (though, as in India, the absence of formal criteria for individual breeds tends to blur definitive breed characteristics).[51] And there are equestrian competitions and games, such as polo, and race tracks that attract international entries, notably in Karachi and Lahore.

Muslims in India and Pakistan maintain many of their own equine myths and rituals. One of the most popular of these is the ritual of the horse of Karbala. Each year, during the first ten days of Muharram (late August/September), the first month in the Islamic calendar, but particularly on the tenth day, known as the Day of Ashura, Shia Muslim communities in India and Pakistan (as elsewhere in the Muslim world) celebrate the festival of Muharram. At this time they mourn the Imam Husain, the Prophet Muhammad's grandson, who was martyred in a battle in 680 CE in Karbala, in the Iraqi desert. Central to this celebration is Husain's battle stallion, Zuljenah (in Urdu; Dhu al-Janah in Arabic), "the winged one," the "Horse of Karbala," who is said to have returned, wounded and riderless, after Husain was killed. The horse is sometimes called "the Buraq of Karbala,"[52] after the winged horse said to have carried Mohammed to heaven.

In some villages in Bihar, during this celebration a horseshoe said to come from Zuljenah is carried to all the Sufi tombs in the village, touching each tomb.[53] Elsewhere in India, wherever there are significant Muslim populations, such as Hyderabad, Darjeeling, and Ladakh, a horse representing Zuljenah is decorated and led riderless through the streets. The horse's mane and flanks are streaked with red paint to represent his wounds, and his mane, colored red, is said to be stained with Husain's blood. Worshippers make images of the horse, riderless, pierced by arrows, his chest streaming blood.[54] Sometimes they attach an open copy of the Qur'an to Zuljenah's saddle; sometimes they attach two doves, who are also said to have announced the Imam's martyrdom. The doves and the horse are regarded as messengers (143). An Urdu poem about Zuljenah laments,

> This horse struck its head
> against the earth and spoke:
> "I have lost my rider;
> my rider is dead." (115)

One worshipper explained the importance of Zuljenah: "We have faith that Husain was on Zuljenah, that Zuljenah was alone with Husain on the battlefield, was a witness to his death and was the last creature to see him alive. Also Zuljenah brought the news of Husain's death to Zaynab (Husain's sister). When Zuljenah comes back with an empty saddle, we know that Husain is dead" (119). All the marchers are male (145), but mothers bring their children (usually infants or toddlers) up to the stallion, to press the child against the horse's flank or to pass the child under the horse's belly. They pray to the horse for their children's health (146), as Zuljenah himself, incarnate in the village horse, is said to have the power to ward off diseases and satanic influences (197).

The crowds on the street weep over him (122). But the horse is also said to weep. It is said that Zuljenah lowered his head, and teardrops fell from his eyes (124). Informants insist that the horse chosen to represent Zuljenah in the annual procession understands the meaning of the tragedy he helps to commemorate. That is why the horse sometimes weeps during the procession, "not because of its own distress at being led through agitated crowds and ranks of bloody flagellants . . . but out of sympathetic solidarity with the Karbala martyrs." Some contemporary paintings of Zuljenah show the horse standing on the battlefield, pierced by arrows, with tears of grief streaming from his eyes (124–25).

We have encountered the idea of the suffering horse, the compassionate horse who weeps for his dead or absent master, in stories about Kanthaka, the horse who shed tears at parting from the future Buddha. The wounds of Zuljenah evoke compassion for the horse as well as for his dead rider, but the tears shed by Zuljenah express the belief that the horse is compassionate for his wounded/dead rider. According to one text, "The animal's ability to recognize truth is greater than man's. At Karbala, Zuljenah's conduct is exemplary" (126). The fact that it is the Shias who celebrate the horse of Karbala—the Sunnis generally celebrate Muhurram merely by fasting—allows the pageant to represent, on another level, the persecution of Shias by Sunnis. But Karbala may also represent, in India, the persecution of Muslims by Indian Hindus. Zuljenah may be weeping for them, too.

KHANDOBA, THE EQUESTRIAN GOD OF HINDUS AND MUSLIMS

Most Indian equine myths and rituals stem from a time long before the partition of Pakistan from India, and many of them involve both Hindus and Muslims. Hindus as well as Muslims worship at the shrines of Muslim horse saints such as Alam Sayyid of Baroda, known as Ghore Ka Pir, or the horse saint: "His horse was bur-

FIGURE 24. The god Khāndoba and his wife. Brass statue, twentieth century. (© Ethnologisches Museum zu Berlin, Stiftung Preußischer Kulturbesitz, ID-Nr.: IC 48764 a-c)

ied near him, and Hindus hang images of the animal on trees round his tomb."[55] In Bengal, Hindus offer clay horses to deified Muslim saints like Satyapir.[56]

Khandoba is an important god among both Hindus and Muslims in Maharashtra. The Emperor Aurangzeb (r. 1658 to 1707), who is said to have been forced to flee from Khandoba's power (i.e., from Marathi armies), is also said to have given Khandoba the name of Mallu Khan or Ajmat Khan, by which some people still call him.[57] The Muslim equestrians of Maharashtra are often followers of Khandoba.[58] Yet Khandoba is an equestrian manifestation of the Hindu god Shiva.

A Muslim leads the horse in the Khandoba festival in Maharashtra, and a Muslim family traditionally keeps the horses of the god in Jejuri, an important center of Khandoba's worship. During the festival of Dussehra at Devatagudda (Karnataka), and at the Somvati Amavasya festival in Jejuri, devotees possessed by the power of Khandoba gallop like horses, whipping themselves with horsewhips, running like horses in front of the palanquin.[59] Shiva as Khandoba, together with other gods on horses, is depicted as a horseman throughout Maharashtra, in temples as well as in family shrines in houses, sometimes on silver plaques or metal statues or small plaques used as charms tied around the neck. Murals on temples and old glass paintings often depict the myth of the battle of the god, always on horseback, against the anti-gods.[60] The god is said to enter the devotee in the form of a wind whose name is related to the word *varu*, which means "warhorse" or "charger."[61]

A rich mythology accounts for the origin of the horse that Khandoba/Shiva rides. The Dhangars of Maharashtra say that the horse was hidden in a mountain cave in the form of wind, until Khandoba brought it out to ride it.[62] Sometimes it is said that Khandoba got the horse from the demons Mani and Malla, who owned it before him.[63] Or it is said that Mani took the form of a horse-faced demon seated on a white horse, and neighed so fiercely that he agitated the whole world; but Khandoba knocked him from his horse, and Mani and the horse fell into a water tank.[64] Or Shiva ordered the moon to become a horse and, seated on it, cut off the head of the demon; ever since then, the horse has been the beloved mount of the god.[65] Often both the horse and the chariot are said to derive from the demon.[66] Some images depict Khandoba's white horse holding the heads of the demons down on the ground or trampling the demon under his hooves, while Khandoba approaches to apply the coup de grâce.[67] The horse, originally a demon's horse, is now tamed and divine.

Many of the stories involve Shiva's bull, Nandi, his usual *vahana* or "vehicle." It is said that Shiva stopped riding Nandi and mounted the horse in order to fight the demons Mani and Malla, and that after Khandoba cut off Mani's head, Mani became "horse-headed" (*hayamukha*) and started neighing.[68] Or that one day, when the demon Mani was on horseback, his horse tripped and fell into the water, and so Mani was captured. Then Mani asked Khandoba to take his horse, and Khandoba took the horse and used him instead of Nandi.[69] Or that Nandi turned into a horse (*turanga, haya*).[70] The image of Nandi stands at the bottom of the hill at the shrine of Khandoba; the horse of Khandoba stands at the top, and is regarded as an avatar of Nandi,[71] just as Khandoba is an avatar of Shiva. Nandi and the horse are waiting for Shiva and Khandoba to mount them.[72]

Khandoba is not a horse; he is a god who *rides* a horse, which is, in this context, the very opposite of *being* a horse. In the myth, he rides a demonic horse; in the ritual, he rides his human worshippers. Khandoba is the subduer of horses, the tamer of horses. He makes demonic horses, like his worshippers, into divine horses. Icons of the myth of the battle of the equestrian god against the demons[73] depict the victory over the demon not merely in the obvious way—by demonstrating how the god on his horse kills the demon—but also, indirectly, by demonstrating how the god harnessed the evil horse for the good of his worshippers.

This story assimilates demonic horses to the Muslim enemies of the Marathi warriors. But even here, the horse of the enemy, the demon, the conqueror, becomes the horse of the hero, the Indian, the Hindu worshipper. Khandoba is the ruler who turns demonic enemies into willing devotees, domesticated horses. The image of the demon under the hooves of Khandoba's horse owes something to the Indo-European dragon-slaying motif, something to the Indian tradition of equestrian rulers, and something yet again to the assimilative imagination of Indian folklore.

It is therefore particularly tragic to note that though Khandoba used to be worshipped widely in Maharashtra by all castes, and by Muslims and Hindus together, this has changed in recent years. Now, at celebrations of the Khandoba rituals in some parts of India, Hindus have taken over the Khandoba festival and excluded Muslims. The Horse of Karbala would surely weep for them.

9 | ✿ | Equestrian Epics and Mythic Mares

600 to 2000 CE

Many horse stories are told by Indians from traditions that have long regarded horses as native to their people and an integral part of their very nature. Chief among these are the Rajputs, the aristocracy for whom the riding of horses long remained a privilege.[1] The word "Rajput" (from the Sanskrit *raja-putra,* "son of a king") stands for a cluster of various castes and geographical groups tradition-ally known as brave equestrian warriors. The Rajput population and the former Rajput states are found primarily in Rajasthan, Maharashtra, Gujarat, Punjab, Madhya Pradesh, and Bihar. Though they came to symbolize the proud resis-tance of native Indian warriors to the Mughals and the British, the Rajputs often intermarried with these foreigners, shared power with them, and rode the horses that they brought into India. To cite just one of many instances, in the Battle of Haldighati, in 1576, Haakim Sur, a Muslim noble, joined Rana Pratap against the Mughals, while the Rajput Raja Man Singh led the army of the Mughals.

The origins of the Rajputs have been linked with foreigners such as the Scyth-ians and the Huns, who were assimilated into the Kshatriya class of kings and warriors during the sixth and seventh centuries. Though Indian nationalist his-torians often insist that the Rajputs are descendants of the ancient Vedic people, it is most likely that they came from a variety of ethnic and geographical groups, castes, tribes, and nomads who eventually became landed aristocrats and were transformed into the ruling class, assuming the title "Rajput" as part of their claim to higher social positions and ranks. That term acquired its present mean-ing only in the sixteenth and seventeenth centuries, when membership in this class became largely hereditary rather than acquired through military achieve-ments. Historians then fabricated genealogies linking the Rajput families to the ancient Kshatriya dynasties, and the Rajputs employed bards to chronicle their exploits in songs and myths about heroic horses and the brave men and women who rode them.

Rajputs have long been celebrated for their skill as equestrian warriors, and there is substantial evidence for the highly skilled horsemanship of Indian troops—Rajputs and others—at this period. Stirrups on horses are shown in Indian stone sculptures from around the first century BCE to the first century CE in Sanchi, Bhaja, Pitalkhora, and Mathura.[2] Iron stirrups, concave saddles, and horseshoes came into general use in the armies of Indian rulers after the seventh century CE, and stirrups are depicted at Khajuraho in Madhya Pradesh (c. 950 CE) and at Belur in Karnataka and Konarak in Orissa (twelfth century). This contradicts the widespread assertion that the Delhi Sultans, who had learned about stirrups and horseshoes from the Persians and Central Asian Turks in the twelfth century, introduced them into India.[3]

In Hardwar, in the Mughal period, the great spring horse fair coincided, not by coincidence, with a famous religious festival that drew thousands of pilgrims to the banks of the Ganges each year. This combination of trade and pilgrimage was widespread; the Maharashtrian and Sikh generals and their troops came to the fairs to pay their devotion at the holy place in the morning and secure a supply of warhorses in the afternoon.[4] Yet the Rajputs were slow to develop a strong cavalry. As Simon Digby put it: "[It] is not that the Rajput was a worse horseman than the Turk, but rather that, after the initial establishment of Muslim power, he had access to fewer war-horses."[5]

Rajputs even in the modern period still consider good horsemanship a noble talent.[6] "We are warriors," a man says in a Rajasthani story. "Our proper place is on horseback, not in the warmth and comfort of the home."[7] The Rajputs increased their power through their monopolization of horses in the land that became Rajasthan. All across Central and North India, horses were used as an instrument of social mobility; people who came from low backgrounds managed to rise in the social scale through the use of horses. Horsemanship conferred a higher status; a warrior who had his own horse to ride into battle grew in importance. Horses were valuable booty, given to the king. As late as the nineteenth century, the great Sikh leader Ranjit Singh (1780–1832) in his empire-building battles would immediately appropriate all enemy horses, to build up a massive equine population.

Rajput princes and princesses were often depicted on horseback, which may or may not reflect an actual tradition of women riding; the *ashvashastras* say nothing about this. The tradition of equestrian artistic representations contin-

FIGURE 25. Chand Bibi (d. 1599, wife of 'Ali 'Adil Shah I of Bijapur) out hawking on a white horse, moving across a field in the direction of four flying cranes. A hawk is about to be released from her right hand. A girl attendant stands on the left with a second bird. Inscribed on reverse in Persian: Portrait of Chand Bibi. Originally published/produced in Hyderabad, c. 1800. Gouache with gold. 156 × 201 mm. (© The British Library Board, Add.Or.3849)

ued through the Mughal and British periods, to include such different heroes as the great Marathi warrior Shivaji (1630–80) and the notorious Marxist Subhas Chandra Bose (1897–1945).[8] The love affair between the sixteenth-century Sultan Baz Bahadur of Malwa (r. 1555–62) and his Hindu mistress Rupamati is often depicted in later Mughal paintings of the lovers riding together. Lakshmibai, Rani of Jhansi, was famous for riding her favorite horses, named Sarangi, Pavan, and Baadal. Legend has it that she rode Baadal in her escape from the fort at Jhansi under attack from the British in 1858; the horse jumped to safety (though to his own death) with her on his back (and with the Rani carrying her adopted son Damodar Rao on her back).[9]

EQUESTRIAN EPICS

The local hero on a horse was not always a Rajput. Some successful farmers kept a horse or two, for symbolic status as well as a useful aid in dealing with cattle raids

FIGURE 26. Baz Bahadur and Rupamati. Kulu, c. 1720. (© Ashmolean Museum, University of Oxford)

carried out by horsemen, which seems to have been a recurrent problem. The Ahir cowherds of the Delhi area have an extensive knowledge of horses, and some scholars trace their origins back to Central Asia.[10] But horses are also omnipresent in the folk myths and rituals of the Deccan and western India, where the Rajputs built upon an already well-established lore of the hero and his horse, the symbol of the castes of royal warriors.[11]

Some aspects of the vernacular equestrian epics—cycles of stories about heroic horsemen, told in languages other than Sanskrit—derive from survivals of the Vedic horse sacrifice or the *Mahabharata* horse sacrifice, and some from other traditions. It is often hard to separate the Vedic from the Epic, since the *Mahabharata* tales of horse sacrifices are themselves retellings of the Vedic tales of horse sacrifice, though some of the incidents of the *Mahabharata* that do not derive from Vedic texts are also recapitulated in folklore, and the charioteers of the *Mahabharata* are replaced by mounted warriors in the vernacular epics. It

FIGURE 27. Lakshmibai, Rani of Jhansi. Crowned female figure with a sword riding on a white horse, c. 1890. Calcutta, Kalighat school. 430 × 280 mm. (© The British Library Board, Add.Or.1896)

makes better sense to regard the Vedic and Epic traditions as parallel to one another, rather than chronologically sequential, and, indeed, to regard both of them
as parallel to, rather than chronologically prior to, other Indian traditions. The
regional epics embellish the trope of the end of an era, from the *Mahabharata,*
with sad stories of deaths of the last Hindu kings. The bittersweet Pyrrhic victory
of the *Mahabharata* heroes here becomes transformed into a corpus of tragic
tales of the heroic culture and martial resistance of the protagonists and their cultural triumph, despite their inevitable martial defeat. As Alf Hiltebeitel puts it,
"A *Mahabharata* heroic age is thus mapped onto a microheroic age."[12] The Sanskrit epic supplied a pool of symbols,[13] a sea of tropes, characters, and situations
that form a kind of "underground pan-Indian folk *Mahabharata,* feeding into a
system of texts animated by a combination of Hinduism and Islam."[14]

The resulting epics were nurtured by a culture that combined Afghan and
Rajput traditions[15] and much more. The long struggle and eventual fall of the
Rajput kingdoms under the onslaught of Sultanate and Mughal armies gave
rise to a genre of regional, vernacular epics that evolved out of oral narratives
in this period, taking up themes from the Sanskrit epics, the *Mahabharata* and
Ramayana, but transforming them by infusing them with new egalitarian or plu-
ralist themes, such as the figure of the hero's low-caste or Muslim sidekick. The
vernacular equestrian epics first moved from northwestern and central regions
to southern ones and then carried southern religious, martial, and literary tropes
back north. The irony is that Islamic culture contributed greatly to these grand
heroic poems composed in response to what the authors perceived as the fall of a
great Hindu civilization at the hands of Muslims.

WHY COCONUTS ARE OFFERED TO THE GODDESS

Stories that reflect these medieval interactions are still prevalent in twentieth-
century oral traditions. A story of a human and an equine beheading is told in
the greater Punjab area (Punjab, Haryana, Himachal Pradesh, and Delhi), where
horses have remained important throughout Indian history. This story, which
was also published in popular bazaar pamphlets in Hindi and Punjabi, is the tale
of Dhyanu Bhagat (or, "Why Coconuts Are Offered to the Goddess"):

> There was once a devotee of the Goddess named Dhyanu Bhagat, who lived
> at the same time as the Mughal Emperor Akbar. Once he was leading a group
> of pilgrims to the temple of Jvala Mukhi, where the Goddess appears in the
> form of a flame. As the group was passing through Delhi, Akbar summoned

Dhyanu to the court, demanding to know who this goddess was and why he worshipped her. Dhyanu replied that she is the all-powerful Goddess who grants wishes to her devotees. In order to test Dhyanu, Akbar ordered the head of Dhyanu's horse to be cut off and told Dhyanu to have his goddess join the horse's head back to the body.

Dhyanu went to Jvala Mukhi, where he prayed day and night to the Goddess, but he got no answer. Finally, in desperation, he cut off his own head and offered it to the Goddess. At that point, the Goddess appeared before him in full splendor, seated on her lion. She joined his head back on his body and also joined the horse's head back onto his body. Then she offered Dhyanu a boon. He asked that in the future, devotees not be required to go to such extreme lengths to prove their devotion. She granted him the boon that from then on, she would accept the offering of a coconut as equal to that of a head. And that is why people offer coconuts to the Goddess.[16]

The devouring goddess appears not merely in the deity who demands blood sacrifices; she appears at the very start of the story, in her equine form, as Jvala Mukhi, the holy place (in Kangra, Himachal Pradesh) where she takes the form of a flame. For Jvala Mukhi (literally "Mouth of Fire," a common term for a volcano) is the name of the underwater mare with the doomsday fire in her mouth, known to us from Epic and Puranic sources.

This story offers us at least one good clue to the fact that it is a myth about human sacrifice—perhaps a local myth—that has been adapted to take account of the more "Sanskritic" tradition of the horse sacrifice. This clue is the coconut, an essential part of a *puja* (the most widespread Hindu ritual, a simple ceremony usually offering flowers or fruit to a deity), just as animals are an essential part of a blood sacrifice (*yajna* or *medha*). Now, a coconut closely resembles a human head (a resemblance that is often explicitly alluded to in *pujas*) but does not at all resemble a horse's head. We might read this text as a meditation on the historical transition from human sacrifice to Vedic horse sacrifice to contemporary vegetarian *puja* (a coconut sacrifice), subversively incorporating the Vedic myth of Dadhyanch (now called Dhyanu), whose head was temporarily replaced by a horse's head. In fact, coconuts do not grow in the Punjab; the rituals specify that one must use *dry* coconuts for all offerings, presumably because they have traveled all the way from Gujarat, a long distance. Since these coconuts must be imported, they may, therefore, represent either the adoption of a myth that is "foreign" (i.e., from another part of India, or connected with the "foreign" ruler

Akbar) or a local tradition about a "foreign" ritual that requires *imported* coconuts, appropriate to a ritual whose myth involves (imported) horses.

THE TESTING OF HARISHCHANDRA

A myth collected in Chandigarh (the capital of Punjab and Haryana) similarly imagines the simultaneous sacrifice of a horse and a human, but this text has a closer source in the well-known Puranic myth of King Harishchandra, whose son (rather than his horse) was killed in order to test Harishchandra and was eventually restored to him.[17] Both son and horse are at stake in the Chandigarh story:

> Queen Tara told her husband, King Harichand, of a miracle that the goddess had performed, involving snakes. The king asked, "How can I get a direct vision (*pratyaksh darshan*) of the Mother? I will do anything." Tara told him that it wasn't easy and that he would have to sacrifice his favorite blue horse. He took out his sword and killed his horse. Then she ordered him to sacrifice his beloved son. He then killed his son. Next she told him to cut up the horse and the boy, place them in a cauldron, and cook them. He did this as well. Finally, she told him to dish out the food on five plates: one for Mata [the mother goddess], one for himself, one for the horse, one for the son, and one for her, Tara. When he complied, she told him to start eating his share. The king, bound to his word, started to eat, but tears welled up in his eyes. The horse and the son both came back to life. The goddess granted him her *darshan,* appearing before him on her lion. King Harichand worshipped her and begged for forgiveness. Mata forgave him and then disappeared.[18]

The imagined double sacrifice is carried out but then reversed, as the goddess relents.[19] The Vedic gods, generally male, had not been so merciful to the sacrificial stallion, though they did, on one occasion, pull a man back from the brink of the sacrifice of his son.[20]

REVIVING THE GOD'S HORSE

A corpus of myths from Maharashtra combines the Vedic theme of the dismemberment and resurrection of the sacrificial horse, the Epic theme of the equestrian journey to the underworld of the serpents, and the later theme of possession by a horse god in a trance. The story concerns Kalbhairi, a local god who protects people from snakes; Yelamma, a goddess; Bhola, a form of Shiva; and Shiva's wife, Parvati:

The Goddess Yelamma did not want to let the gods into the continent of Bengal. She sprinkled magical ashes (*vibhut*), and the gods' horses fell down. Thus she drove away the horses of the three hundred and fifty gods. Kalbhairi left and came to Bhola and his wife Parvati. Bhola opened the doors of the house and showed Kalbhairi the rooms that were filled over and over again with *ganja* (marijuana). "Look, Baba," said Parvati. "Smoke as much *ganja* as you want." Kalbhairi dedicated himself to his vice, crushed the *ganja,* and smoked it until he fell into a state of intoxication.

Then he looked around. He came to an underground hole where a wind was blowing. He asked, "What is blowing there?" Parvati said, "That is Bhola's wind." "Give it to me!" "If you want it, take it." He took it. It was a horse, dark black, white on the forehead, with a white tail, and a reddish-brown back. He saddled the horse, fastened the silver saddle straps and the golden stirrups, and mounted it. The Divali festival was approaching. Bhola said, "Kalbhairi should be sent to the land where the three hundred and fifty gods are to be found." So Kalbhairi set off to search. When he had traversed the nine continents, and Kashi [Varanasi], the tenth, he came to the eleventh, that is, to the land of Bengal. There Yelamma stood in his path. When Kalbhairi saw her from far off, he jumped down from heaven with the horse. Yelamma let him come. She sprinkled ashes, and the horse fell down. He lifted the horse high, and again she threw him to the ground. A third time he lifted the horse up violently. Again she threw him down. When the horse had fallen to the ground, Kalbhairi dismounted.

There was a pond there. As Kalbhairi was addicted to *ganja,* he crushed *ganja* and took water to help him, and he smoked it. And then he went to set the horse upright. He grabbed him by the tail, and the tail broke off. "Bhola's horse," he said, "is no good." He grabbed him by the ear, and the ear broke off. "Bhola's horse," he said, "is no good." He grabbed him by the neck, and the neck broke off. "Bhola's horse," he said, "is no good." Then he grabbed the horse by the leg, and the leg broke off. "The god's horse," he said, "is worthless."

Only the body was left. "How can I ride back now?" he thought. Kalbhairi reached into the bag, and, calling out the name of Bhola, he sprinkled ashes; and the horse stood there again, saddled and bridled. The horse neighed and danced. Kalbhairi cracked the whip. The horse was highly spirited; it flew up to heaven. Then Yelamma said, "The horse may not pass through." Kalbhairi attacked her with his trident (*trishul*), put her in his bag, and found the gods. The skeletons of the three hundred and fifty horses lay there. Then he said,

"Gather the skeletons together!" So they gathered the skeletons and joined them piece by piece. Kalbhairi sprinkled the elixir of immortality (*amrit*) on the horses, and—calling out the name of Bhola—brought the horses to life. Then he brought the procession of gods to Bhola.[21]

Shiva's notorious marijuana, *ganja,* is here used by Kalbhairi, a servant of Shiva, to give him the strength to win through his ordeal. Traditional counterparts to that drug appear in two forms: first as the magic ash that revives Bhola's horse (the ashes of Yelamma having originally killed the gods' horses and knocked down Bhola's horse) and then as the *amrit* (elixir of immortality, obtained we know not how) that revives the gods and their horses.

There are loud echoes here of the *Mahabharata* story of Uttanka. Kalbhairi, like Uttanka, goes to the underworld (in a trance) and encounters a black horse with a white tail. Uttanka blows into the anus of the horse; Kalbhairi breaks off the tail of the horse that is itself a wind that blows. Horses are naturally associated with the wind through the metaphor of swift flight; in Arabic mythology, the wind is said to have begotten the first Arabian horse, impregnating a mare who stood with her hindquarters to the wind. Here the wind magically becomes the horse that Kalbhairi needs in order to revive the horses of the gods.

MYTHIC MARES

One strong hint that much of medieval Indian horse lore comes from Arabs is the gender of the horses. Arab horsemen (and Turks and Mongols) generally rode mares, regarding them as more intelligent, sensitive, and, above all, loyal and affectionate than stallions. They told stories about Muhammad's magic horse Buraq, often said to be a mare and/or to have a woman's face, and about his five faithful foundation mares. John Lockwood Kipling remarked, in 1891, "Among the Biloch [an Afghan tribe], who have strong Arab characteristics, . . . only mares are ridden, colts being killed as soon as they are born—a practice which may be expected to die out"[22] (as indeed it would, if strictly followed).

One argument for the Arab preference for mares was that, in raids that required silence, mares would be less inclined than stallions to whinny and give away the position of the riders, particularly if the enemy, with malicious intent, happened to bring along one or two mares in heat. This would of course apply equally well to Indian cavalries, but their practical concerns were apparently overridden by the mythology of the early Indian texts, the Vedas and Epics and Puranas, which are all about stallions, with their positive symbolism kept entire (virility, fertility, aggressive volatility). These Sanskrit texts code the females of the species, the mares, as evil, as wild animals never really tamed, the familiars of wild, sexually voracious women who deceive their husbands and abandon their children. And so Indians before the Sultanate period generally preferred stallions. (The British, too, preferred stallions to mares or geldings in their Indian cavalry, though not back in England.)[23]

But, in opposition to the enduring anti-mare bias (and misogyny) of the Sanskrit texts, a dramatic change takes place in the vernacular Indian equestrian epics, which abound in benevolent mares. The heroes whose stories we are about to encounter—Pabuji, Devnarayan, Desinghu/Teja, and Gugga, even Peddanna—all ride highly cooperative magic mares. And where the stallions of the earlier tradition were usually white (with the occasional black ear or tail), the mares are often black. Clearly the authors of these stories are either ignorant of the Vedic and Puranic bias against mares (which seems unlikely) or chose to ignore it in favor of an imported Arabic pro-mare tradition. Here we encounter a narrative pattern of considerable detail repeated in many different stories, suggesting that, once the tradition of good mares took root, it was diffused throughout this area, rather than arising independently everywhere where people rode mares.

PABUJI AND HIS BLACK MARE

Pabuji was a minor Rajput chief of the fourteenth century, subsequently deified by the local people. His story is often illustrated in Rajasthan on twenty-foot-long scroll paintings, called *pars*. The story is particularly told among the Charans, a caste of Sutas (bards), and there is even a contemporary version of it available on YouTube.[24] Here is one telling of the story:

> Pabuji was born in the desert area of western Rajasthan, from the union of a Rajput chief and a water nymph (Apsaras or Pari). At his niece's wedding he promised her, as dowry, a gift of reddish-brown she-camels, which no one there had ever seen. Deval Bai, an old lady, lent Pabuji her magical black mare, named Kesar Kalmi. With the help of his companions, Pabuji captured the camels and delivered them to his niece and returned the mare to Deval Bai.
>
> Then Pabuji's marriage to a princess in Umarkot was arranged. As it was the local custom for the bridegroom to prove his worth in a horse race, Pabuji again borrowed the magic mare, promising Deval Bai that he would come to her aid immediately if she needed him. He won the race, and when the wedding ceremony was almost over, the mare became restless, and a bird told Pabuji

FIGURE 28. Pabuji ki Phad, detail. Rajasthan, twentieth century. (Given to the University of Chicago Library by Kali Charan Bahl)

that Deval Bai's brother-in-law, Jind Rao Khici, had rustled her cattle, and that Pabuji was urgently needed. Pabuji went to Deval Bai's assistance without completing the wedding ceremony. He saved the cattle but was killed.[25]

Another version of the tale of Pabuji adds several details about the mare:

Pabuji Rathore, who lived in the fourteenth century, died at the age of twenty-five. The beautiful Deval Devi rode on a splendid black mare, Kalimi, while tending her cattle in the desert of Marwar. Deval was an incarnation of the Great Goddess. Jind Raj, a baron of Jayal, saw and coveted the splendid black mare Kesar Kalimi, but Deval would part from her only at the price of his head. Fearing for her safety after this incident, Deval gave her black mare to Pabuji, who promised to protect Deval and her cattle at the cost of his life. A beautiful princess fell in love with Pabuji on his beautiful mare, and wanted Pabuji to marry her; he agreed, but told her that he had pledged his life to protect Deval and her cattle.

Meanwhile, Jind Raj took away Deval's cattle. Deval took the form of a bird and told Pabuji to keep his word; he left his bride during the wedding rites. With seven men he rode on Kalimi, the black mare, against Jind Raj and his thousand soldiers. He rescued the cattle, but he and the mare were mortally wounded and died. His bride immolated herself as a Sati and joined Pabuji in heaven.[26]

Now the old lady Deval has become young and beautiful (like Pabuji's bride), but it is still her black mare (also beautiful) that is Pabuji's true love.

Another version of the birth of Pabuji tells us more about his mother:

Pabuji's father saw a flock of nymphs bathing; he stole their clothes and forced one of them to marry him. She did so, on condition that he never enter her room without first warning her of his approach (by clearing his throat). She was Kesar Pari, the saffron nymph. In time, Pabuji was born. One day, Pabuji's father forgot to warn Kesar, and entering the room he saw her suckling the child, but she had the form of a tigress. She left him forever, but first she promised the baby that she would return when he was grown, in the form of a mare for him to ride.[27]

The flock of bathing nymphs, the broken contract, and the wife's secret animal nature are survivals of the widespread myth of the animal wife, who takes the form of a seal or silkie (in Scotland), a snake (Melusine, in France), a fox (in Japan), a swan (in the ballet *Swan Lake*), and so forth. The swan maiden first appears in India in the Vedic myth of Urvasi.[28] The animal wife, captured by a human man who steals her wings or fur pelt or scaly skin, marries him on condition that he promise not to see her naked; eventually he breaks his promise and discovers that she is really an animal, and she leaves him.[29]

The animal wife in the Pabuji story also takes another form, that of a tigress, closely related to the lion that is the Goddess's vehicle; and indeed, in another telling, when Pabuji's father deliberately spied on the nymphs, "what did he see but a lioness giving suck to her cub." The lioness turned back into the nymph, the cub turned back into Pabuji, and the nymph disappeared into the sky.[30] This animal wife lets Pabuji ride her when he comes of age; the verb *ram,* used here in the sense of "to ride, or to sport with," often has sexual connotations.

In another telling, we learn in more detail how Pabuji got his magic mare from Deval:

Pabuji noted that he and his chieftain had travelled round the four borders of the earth but had not found a horse for him to ride. Deval, however, had been to the far shore of the seven seas and brought back horses of great price. Pabuji said that he had dreamt that he had sported [*ram*] with Deval's mare Kesar Kalami. And so they saddled their five horses and went to become Deval's beloved guests. He told her of his dream and asked to have the mare Kesar Kalami to ride. She told him that if he took the mare, Khici would attack. But Pabuji's chieftain held the stirrup for Pabuji's foot, and Pabuji put his hand on the mare's black mane and his other hand on the saddle, and he mounted the mare. The other horses raced, their hooves beating on the earth; Kesar Kalami shone in the sky.[31]

Yet another version of the advent of Pabuji's magical mare tells us that the Charans had taken a mare with them to load a cargo by the sea. As they halted by the edge of the sea, a glorious (*tejala*) horse came out of the sea and mounted the mare. She gave birth to the filly Kalami/Kalavi. (As a related text puts it, Pabuji's "Kalavi mare had been born to the Kachela Charanas by a mare fecundated by a marine horse.")[32] Both Khici and Pabuji asked for the filly, but the Charans would not give her to Khici; they gave her to Pabuji, and they said, "If we ever have need, come to our aid." And he promised and took the filly.[33]

The name Kesar (in Kesar Pari and Kesar Kalami/Kalmi/Kalimi) means saffron, a rare and precious substance, golden and solar and, significantly, imported, like horses. Pabuji goes to get saffron to dye his wedding clothes.[34] But "Kesar" is also related to the Sanskrit word *kesha* or *keshara*, which may designate the mane of a horse (recall the equine anti-god Keshi whom Krishna kills) or, significantly, the ruff of a lion. The second half of the name, Kalami/Kalmi/Kalimi, designating "a mare of a dark color" (Sanskrit *kala*, "black"), is used especially for Pabuji's mare, who also appears in Marwari folksongs as "the mare with the black mane."[35] So "Kesar" may carry these two meanings. This rare mare could be obtained, according to one telling, only by someone who "had been to the far shore of the seven seas and brought back horses of great price," as, in fact, the generous older woman is said to have done. That is, the mare was imported, like the expensive horses cherished by Indians throughout history.

The Pabuji story also tells of an interrupted wedding, a widespread theme in equestrian folktales and folk epics. In paintings and actual wedding processions, all over India, the bridegroom rides to the wedding on a horse to whom a kind of *puja* is offered. This horse is preferably white, a more auspicious color than black, and is usually a mare, for reasons that we will consider in a later chapter. The real-life weddings are generally completed, unlike the weddings in these folktales. We might, therefore, see the black mare in the folktale as a kind of mythic shadow, or even a subversion, of the auspicious white mare in the real weddings. The inter-rupted wedding is a variant of a broader Indian theme of interrupted rituals that we know from texts about two ancient sacrifices: the Vedic ceremony of conse-cration, which was "interrupted" by a chariot race as well as by a game of dice,[36] and the interrupted horse (or snake) sacrifice in the *Mahabharata*. The Vedic horse sacrifice is simultaneously a marriage and a slaughter; ideally, both are con-summated. In the Pabuji epics, the marriage is interrupted first by a horse race and then by the slaughter of both the horse and the bridegroom. The incomplete marriage is consummated by a completed sacrifice; the horse—now a mare—is the "new bride," who must die as the Vedic sacrificial stallion died.

DEVNARAYAN AND HIS MARE

Devnarayan (affectionately known as Dev or Devji or Dev Maharaj) was a leg-endary Gurjar warrior from Rajasthan who is worshipped as a folk deity with a magic mare, mostly in Rajasthan and northwestern Madhya Pradesh. The oral epic of Devnarayan consists of a number of episodes that the Bhopas, tradi-tional storytellers, sing in all-night performances in the villages of Rajasthan and Malwa.

One version of the story, recorded from an oral narrative recited in Rajasthan,[37] is a long text for which we have space here only for a summary (laced with quotes from the translation) of the parts of the story that deal with Devnarayan's mare (Lila or Lilagar, "Magic" or "Magical Horse"):

> Devnarayan's mare, Lilagar, was born at the same time as Devnarayan. Sadu Mata was his mother. As Dev was an incarnate god (Bhagavan), his mother was his devotee. Lilagar was the foal of Sadu Mata's mare Kalavi.[38] When Dev Maharaj became incarnate, Lila, the horse, became incarnate at the same time. Then Lila and Dev Maharaj made a promise. He said, "Listen, Horse! You take to the teat of this Kalavi Mare, and I'll take to the breast of this Gurjar Mother." The filly Lilagar started suckling the teats of the mare Kalavi.[39] Horse and rider were inseparable, seamlessly connected. On another occasion, Dev suckled a lioness, while Lilagar suckled her mother, the mare Kalavi.

The theme of the simultaneous birth of the hero and his horse is Indo-European in its provenance.[40] Here it is expanded with the competitive suckling by animals, reminiscent of the tales of Romulus and Remus—and, closer to home, to the tale of Pabuji suckled by a tigress.

The story continues:

> When Dev set out on his equestrian adventures, he saw the good omen of a snake on his right hand. He then rode Lilagar down to the netherworld, where he defeated the Naga king Basag in a gambling match and married Basag's daughter.[41]
>
> Dev refused to pay taxes to the evil king of Ajmer, who told his servant, the Bhat, "Go and collect either the tax or Lilagar, the horse that Dev Maharaj rides."[42] The Bhat had all the doors and windows sealed but for one narrow window. Then Dev said, "My horse and I will enter through the window." He pulled the mare's reins back at that spot. The mare stepped back, stepped back, stepped back until she stopped at a distance of five miles. At that place, Dev, lord of the three worlds, tightened her saddle, lifted up her reins, and sprang over the door. The Lilagar mare galloped one and a half arm-lengths above Mother Earth. The saddle stayed one and a half arm-lengths above the mare, and Bhagavan sat half an arm-length above the saddle. After that, the Bhat sang a song of praise of Dev for the king of Ajmer: "Through the blow of Lila's hooves a surge of cold water arose from the underworld and split open the hill." The king said, "The horse has been ridden back and forth superbly."
>
> Then the king asked Dev to "ride in" his speckled pony, who was known to be extremely difficult to train. Dev Narayan agreed. He removed Lilagar's bridle. As soon as he went there he gave the horse a slap. The horse was immediately prepared to be ridden. Dev mounted the horse and he began to move with a gait even better than Lilagar's gait. He rode the horse for a while and then he gave him a kick with his heels and sent him down into the thirteenth underworld. He said, "I gave the earth the offering of a horse." The king said, "Hey, he reduced my horse to ashes. He finished off that horse that was worth one and a half lakhs." And he said that Dev Narayan didn't have to pay any taxes.[43]

The poem, so far, is a mix of metaphysics, storytelling, and horse lore. The opening episode draws on the *Mahabharata* mythology of horses and Nagas below the earth, which is echoed in the final episode when a horse is reduced to ashes in what Dev calls a sacrifice to the earth. The details of the saddle and the reins tell of the poet's knowledge of horses, as does the episode in which Dev tames the notoriously unridable horse, which the king asks him to "ride in," that is, to break in, to train.

But the poet also incorporates a broader mythology. In another episode, Shiva's wife Parvati calls his attention to Dev's supernatural qualities:[44] "The goddess Parvati saw Dev Narayan's horse and told Shiva, 'Look, traveling above the ground! Look at what a vehicle Dev is traveling by. Hey, it's moving above the ground.'"[45] Dev's divinity is manifested more dramatically in the final episode of the poem:

> Dev Narayan wanted to leave, but his mother wanted him to stay. Dev sat on Lila, but his mother held the mare's reins. He told her to let go of the reins, but she held on tightly. Lila stamped her hooves. Dev threw down Lila's whip and looked around and said, "O Mother, see, the horse's whip has fallen down." She would not let go of the reins, but, holding them firmly, she bent down to pick up the whip with the other hand. As she looked away, Dev shouted out, and the sound made a hundred Devs and a hundred Lilas appear. When his mother lunged for the whip, the rein slipped out of her hand. One of the Devs said, "O Mother, give me the whip," and another said, "O Mother, give me the whip. Keep your Devji now! The other Devjis will go.... Hold onto your Devji, and take him back!" His mother could not tell which was her own son among the hundred horses and hundred riders. But she refused to give him back the whip unless the real horse and the real rider alone appeared. He told her to turn around, and in that moment Dev stood there sitting on his mare alone. Then his mother gave him permission to go.[46]

As Dev is a form of Vishnu, like Krishna, he can multiply himself (as Krishna so famously does when he dances with the cowherd women)[47] and reveal his divinity to his own mother (as Krishna also does)[48]—though Dev also multiplies his horse.

Another variant of the story of the simultaneous births of the prince and the foal was recorded in India at the beginning of the twentieth century:

> A queen wanted to have a child and asked a yogi for his blessing. Her co-wife (who was also her twin sister) tricked her, appearing to the yogi in her place and receiving the blessing that she would have two children. The real

queen then appeared, and the yogi gave her an apple, of which she was to eat three quarters and give the remainder to her favorite mare. A miraculous child was born, with the power to suck the head of a cobra unhurt. When he grew up, he had a mare named Leilah, "a foal of the mare that had been favored with a bit of the yogi's apple."[49]

The cobra is our old friend the Naga, ambivalent ally of the equestrian hero, who recurs throughout this corpus, as does the name of the mare, Leilah, a variant of the "Lila" mares of other heroes of this genre.

TEJA/DESINGU RAJA AND HIS MARE

The hero called Teja or Tej Singh or Desingh in North India (Tecinku or Desingu Raja in South India) rides several great horses, one of which is a mare named Lila. The many stories about Teja are loosely based upon a historical figure, a Raja, the son of the commander of the fort of Senji (also called Gingee) in the reign of the Mughal emperor Aurangzeb (r. 1658 to 1707). The story goes that when Tej refused to obey a summons from the Nawab of Arcot, the deputy of Aurangzeb, the Nawab waged war against him, in the course of which Tej rode his horse at the head of the Nawab's elephant; the horse reared and drummed his hooves on the forehead of the elephant, blunting the Mughal advance. A soldier sliced the hocks of Tej's horse, unseating Tej, who died in the battle, as did his best friend, the Muslim Mahabat Khan.[50] His queen, a beautiful woman aged sixteen or seventeen, "having embraced her husband, ordered with an incredible serenity that the pyre be lit, which was at once done, and she too was burned alive with him."[51]

(The story of Tej's horse and the elephant found its way into a suspiciously similar legend, this one about the battle of Haldighati [1576], in which Chetak, a gray stallion, is said to have reared up and drummed his hooves on the forehead of the war elephant of the Mughal imperial commander, helping his rider, Rana Pratap — the last Rajput to succumb to the Mughals — to kill the elephant's driver. Even with one of his hind legs hacked off above the hoof, Chetak carried Rana Pratap away to safety. The horse's name has been immortalized in a line of Chetak motor scooters produced by India's Bajaj Auto Ltd.)[52]

Stories of Hindu equestrian heroes often depict them in complex relationships with Muslims. In Tamil and Telugu legend, Tecinku was a devout Vaishnava, and his best friend was a Muslim.[53] Yet this is not a simple story of communal harmony. Tecinku's Muslim companion is a very Vaishnava sort of Muslim, who prays to both Rama and Allah on several occasions and goes to Vishnu's heaven when he dies.[54] Vaishnavism here encompasses Islam.

But Tej/Desingu is also celebrated in fable for conquering a celestial horse that a fakir (a Muslim holy man, usually a Sufi) presented to the Mughal emperor. Here is the way one Tamil version of the story goes:

> A celestial horse named Barasari lost his way from the heavens and came to the earth. The fakir who bought him presented him to the Mughal emperor and departed. But no one there was able to mount the horse. Dharani Singh tried and failed and was put in jail with other rajas; meanwhile Dharani's wife gave birth to a boy at Senji.
>
> The boy, Desingu, grew up and tamed the horse; the emperor offered him his daughter's hand, but Desingu refused; he set free his father and the other rajas, and in due time married. He ruled for twelve years. Then the Nawab attacked the Senji fort. Desingu sent for his friend Mahaboob Khan, who was about to be married. Mahaboob mounted his famous steed Nilaveni and came to the battle. Desingu's horse, Barasari, had a premonition of the end of the battle and displayed signs of fear. But Desingu comforted him and went to the temple of Ranganatha to take his leave. Mahaboob was killed, and his horse reached Desingu's side. Mahaboob Khan's noble horse no longer wanted to live, and, out of compassion, Desingu killed the horse. Desingu fought until they cut the legs of his horse under him. Not wishing to live after his friend and his horse had fallen, he threw his sword high up into the air and received it on his breast and died on the sword in the traditional way of Rajput warriors. The queen gave up her life on his funeral pyre.[55]

As M. Arunacalam remarks about this epic, "The chief attraction is the exploits of the two horses. . . . Stories of horses are not many amidst us. . . . [Yet] the names Barasari and Nilaveni, the horses of Desingu Raja and his comrade Movuttukkaran [Mahaboob], are household words today in any part of Tamil Nadu." Arunacalam also remarks upon "the very peculiar galloping metre of the earlier ballad."[56]

In other versions of the story, there are also other horses, including mares. In a telling recorded in Rajasthan, a mare named Buli, an incarnation of the Goddess, is ridden by Bhoj (or Bhoju), the elder brother of Tejo (as he is called here):

How can I describe the mare Buli at that time?
It is very difficult; only one who sees her can describe her,
but there is no limit to the telling.
On the hooves of the mare Buli are horseshoes of gold.
The braces on her legs bounce up and down.
Her hair is the color of henna.
Her reddish-brown tail twitches.
She has a green-bordered saddle, made in Cittaur
With stirrups worth lakhs and lakhs; the goldsmith made them well.
On her head is a crest worth one and a quarter lakhs.
A pearl is strung on each and every hair.
And the reins of the mare Buli are studded with rubies.
Her head cover is studded with pearls. Her forehead shines like diamonds.
Bhoj Maraj mounted the Buli mare.
At that time, only Mother Earth supported the weight.
After performing salutations to Mother Earth,
did they tie the crowns upon the horses and mount the horses?
The groom is crazy, and the horses jumpy. . . .[57]

Stories about Teja are illustrated in popular pamphlets, one of which displays on the cover a picture of man on a horse, with a snake rising out of the ground to touch him. The pamphlet relegates the royal and martial concerns of other tellings to a previous life, concentrating now on more intimate family concerns and a more modest horse, a mare named Lila or Lilagar or Lila Gori, "Lila horse" (the same name as Dev Narayan's mare). Here is a summary of the story in the pamphlet, which introduces Shesha Naga, the great cobra on whom Vishnu rests as he sleeps in the cosmic ocean:

A woman worshipped Shesha Naga, her family god, who promised her a son and a daughter. The boy, Teja, grew up and went to visit the girl to whom he was betrothed, despite omens that he would be bitten by a snake. He put out the blaze in a burning forest, and with the head of his spear he rescued from the smoldering forest a black snake from the family of Kadru. The snake cried, "Why have you saved me? If I had burned, I would be free from all my troubles. I was a sardar who fought in the war between Prithvi Raja and Sahabuddin Muhammad Gauri, and I was killed without paying back the debt I owed for the purchase of my horse, as a result of which I was born in a snake's womb. Now I will bite you, and never let you escape." The snake also objected that, as his wife had been killed in the fire, Teja had now caused their separation by not killing the snake. But he agreed to let Teja go to see his wife, and then return to be bitten.

Teja went on and swam a river with his mare, Lila Gori. He let his mare graze in the garden without restraint and beat the gardener woman for having whipped the mare four times. His wife came to him, and with her and his mare he returned to the snake. Mare and wife offered themselves in his place, but the snake bit Teja on his tongue. The snake told them to prepare a pyre, and on it Teja, his wife, and the snake were cremated together.

Lila Gori was sent to bring the news to Teja's family, but she died. The family followed the bloody tracks of the mare and found the remains of the pyre. They performed the last rites. Henceforth, as the snake predicted, the statue of the god worshipped in the temple has been Tejaji, with the snake around his neck, and his wife Bodala standing nearby, with Lila Gori.[58]

We might see in the rescue of the snake from the forest fire an echo of the forest fire in the *Mahabharata,* a connection strengthened by the name of Kadru, mother of the snakes in that text. The close bond between the mare and the wife, and the interrupted wedding, are familiar features in Indian equestrian folklore.

GUGGA AND HIS MARE

Gugga (also called Goga, Gogo, and Gogaji), a folk god who seems to have originated in Rajasthan,[59] is often said to have been a Rajput warrior hero who lived, by various accounts, during the reign of Prithvi Raj (the last Hindu king of Delhi, c. 1168–92) or in the time of the last great Mughal ruler, Aurangzeb (r. 1658–1707)—that is, at either end of the Muslim reign. Some sources say that Gugga was a combination of a Muslim faqir and a Rajput warrior hero of the Chauhan caste in Rajasthan. He was a follower of Gorakhnath, a famous yogi who had special powers over snakes and who taught Gugga the art of charming snakes; Gugga eventually turned into a snake and disappeared into the earth. But he is said to have burned to death so many families of snakes that the remaining snakes all vowed to leave any place where his name is mentioned.[60] Gugga is worshipped both as a man and as a snake, and many legends seem to focus on him both as an enemy of the snakes and as a snake himself.

A nineteenth-century Punjabi version of the story of Gugga's birth involves the Epic serpents Basak (Vasuki) and Tatig Nag (Takshaka):

Before Gugga was born, his father saw a partridge on the right and a snake on the left. The pandit said, "On the left is a snake, Raja; I think the omen good." . . . One day, Gugga played his flute and pleased the birds of the forest, but Basak heard the sound and was displeased, because the sound had awakened all the sleeping snakes. Basak sent Tatig Nag to find out what had happened. When Tatig discovered that Gugga was a follower of Gorakhnath, he offered to help him.[61]

But Gugga is also closely associated with horses. As a man, he appears on horseback, carrying a long staff or spear on which a snake is coiled, or with the snake Basak Nag coming out of the ground in front of his horse.[62] Gugga rides a black mare. In yet another variant of the simultaneous birth of the foal and the child, we are told that Gugga had no children until his guardian deity gave him two barleycorns, one of which he gave to his wife and the other to his famous mare, who gave birth to his charger, hence called Javadiya or "Barley-Born."[63] When Gugga died, the earth opened and received him with his mare (also sometimes, confusingly, called Javadiya).[64]

In the Punjab and western Uttar Pradesh, Gugga is known as Zahar Pir, who controls snakes and whose worshippers carry his standard at a festival each year in July or August. On such occasions, disciples specially dedicated to the saint enjoy the privilege of acting as his horses. To carry the fiction of their equine nature still further, the "horses" are actually made to eat some gram and a few blades of green grass. Excited by the drumming and shouting, the "horses" imitate the pawing of spirited chargers.[65] During the ceremony, the participants sing songs about Raja Basak or Zahar Pir and Gorakhnath.[66] Susan Wadley has described the ritual in which the Naga king possesses the oracle; this possession is expressed through the metaphor that the snake "rides" the oracle:

MASTER: The snake is safe. Very happy is the snake. King Basak who is here, the king is happy?
ORACLE: Yes.
MASTER: His horse is happy?
ORACLE: Yes.

As Wadley remarks, "Now the master knows that the possessing deity is well and that the oracle, or horse, is also fit. Note that the image is that of riding, as shown by the use of 'horse' for the oracle himself."[67]

FIGURE 29. Gogaji on his horse. Rajasthan, nineteenth century. (© Victoria and Albert Museum, IS 156–1984)

A version of the story told in Chamba (in Himachal Pradesh) calls Gugga Mundalikh and adds equine details:

> Mundalikh's chief officer, Kailu, rode a horse who leapt over the river to Basak's camp. Kailu disguised himself as a Brahmin and suggested that Basak's chief officer conceal the army of snakes in the grasses and ambush Mundalikh's army as it came by. This they did, upon which Kailu, throwing off his disguise, summoned his horse, who came running; Kailu mounted the horse and struck him once, making him prance and rear. As he struck the horse a second time, sparks came from the hooves and set fire to the grass in which the army of snakes was concealed, completely destroying them all.[68]

As usual, the snakes are destroyed by fire, and as usual they perish under the hooves of a horse. According to another story, Gugga entered battle with his mare, who "literally flew about," and he beheaded his two brothers; when his mother disowned him, he turned from a Hindu to a Muslim and went to Mecca. Eventually, still mounted on his mare, he descended into the earth.[69]

Gugga also gets into one version of the story of Pabuji, who goes to Gugga's village and then sets out with him on a trip to the desert. They leave the horses to graze while they doze under a tree, but when Gugga sends Pabu to find the horses, Pabu finds that their legs have been shackled with serpents. He says nothing about this, simply saying that he could not find the horses. When the two of them return together, the horses are still grazing where they had left them.[70]

A version of the story of Gugga from Nabha State, in the Punjab, adds another figure, a sweeper woman (a Dalit, of extremely low caste), and explains how Gugga got his name, relating it to *gugal,* a resin used for incense and medicine:

> The legend tells us that the god Shiva and Gorakhnath went to the Naga Vasuki to ask for one of his hundred and one sons, but his queen refused to give one up. When Vasuki, in anger, foamed at the mouth, Gorakh quickly took some *gugal,* saturated it in the saliva, and gave it to the queen, who shared it with a Brahmin woman, a sweeper woman, and her mare, all of whom were impregnated.[71]

Again we see the simultaneous births of horse and hero, but now we encounter the subversive association of the horse, the Kshatriya animal par excellence, with both Brahmins and Dalit sweepers. Indeed, the equine imagery throughout this cycle of myths is, in a sense, subversive, since it argues for a positive valence for mares, whom the Sanskrit Vedas, Epics, and Puranas had demonized.

THE MARE WHO WAS A BUFFALO

In coastal Andhra, extending over a very wide area,[72] Madeleine Biardeau discovered what she regarded as a survival of the Vedic horse sacrifice in a complex ritual involving two South Indian goddesses (Mariyamman and Virakali) and a low-caste priest (*pandaram*):

> In the evening . . . a mare is brought by the headman who has hired it. It stops just in front of the goddess. The *pandaram* washes the mare's feet and puts a *pottu* [sacred mark] on her forehead. He offers a *puja* both to Virakali and to the mare and sprinkles the *puja* water on the mare. There is a very tense

silence among people waiting for the mare to shake her head, and the music stops playing. When she shakes her head, the headman takes the mare in procession. . . . The mare is sent back to her master, having completed her part. The buffalo is brought near a ditch that has been dug out just in front of the goddess. The headman must be present when the buffalo is sprinkled with *puja* water, shakes its head and is beheaded by the *pandaram*. Both head and body are pushed into the ditch and covered with earth. . . .[73]

Biardeau comments on this ritual, drawing upon the fact that the Sanskrit word for buffalo (*mahisha*) is (in its feminine form, *mahishi*) the word for the chief queen:

> The presence of a female animal is very rare in such rituals, and a mare was quite unexpected. . . . She is treated like the goddess and identified with her during the *puja*. But the foot wash and the sprinkling of the head can be seen as separate elements of the horse sacrifice. Before the [Vedic] sacrificial horse starts on its one year's wandering, he has his feet washed. . . . But the sacrifice is not performed. It looks as if, as a mare, the goddess were treated as a symbolic victim of a sacrifice that will take place later. . . . Just after the death of the [Vedic] sacrificial horse, a symbolic copulation must take place between him and the main queen—the *mahishi*. . . . Here the mare stands for the *mahishi*, but in the meantime the sacrificial horse has been turned into a *mahisha*, a buffalo.[74]

Thus the horse sacrifice is, as usual, interrupted, but this time the stallion and the queen are replaced by a buffalo and a mare. The buffalo is a demonic animal in Puranic Hindu mythology, whom the goddess Durga in her aspect of Mahishamardini ("Buffalo-killer") kills when she rejects his erotic overtures and embraces him in a fatal (for him) Liebestod.[75] Here he is killed, as in the myth, in the course of his "marriage" to the goddess, in a brilliant combination of ancient and medieval themes.

10 | ✿ | Horses of the British Raj

1700 to 1900 CE

FINDING AND BREEDING HORSES FOR THE BRITISH IN INDIA

The British rode over India on horseback, first under the aegis of the East India Company (or Honorable East India Company or John Company or just The Company) in the eighteenth century and then under the flag of the British Raj, after Queen Victoria made India an official part of the British Empire, in 1858. They stayed in India, with their horses, until India won its Independence in 1948. John Lockwood Kipling (Rudyard's father) described India as a place where "everybody rides—or ought to ride,"[1] a statement that reveals a stunning ignorance of the lives of Indians but was true enough of the British in India. As the British view of native horses in many ways paralleled the British colonial consensus about native people, the British mythology of Indian horses offers another variant on the link between horses and heroes that we have seen at play in the vernacular epics. Like the native epics, the British writings mixed in with the realistic data—about tack and heights at the withers—a great deal of material that speaks to other concerns: gods and rituals, for the equestrian epics, empire, race, and colonization, for the British.

As "it was not regarded as practicable, or economic, for a regiment's horses to make a voyage of 5,000 miles,"[2] at first the British left their horses at home. Though many argued that only "a well-bred hunter breed with Thoroughbred blood" could carry the nearly three hundred pound weight of a trooper with his full gear, and though they did import some Thoroughbreds during their first years in India, they were forced to seek most of their horses closer to India than to England. In this early period, cavalry purchased their horses in the open market or, "when opportunity offered," captured them from the enemy. (Corn-

FIGURE 30. *Scene in Camp,* from *The Campaign in India, 1857–1858.* By George Francklin Atkinson, 1781. Day & Son: London, 1859. (© The British Library Board, 1781.c.8, plate 4)

wallis "found himself richer by 3,000 troop horses" after the battle of Seringa-patam in 1799.) Many of them gradually came to appreciate some of the country-breds, such as "the excellent Kathiawari, a small 14 to 14.2 hh animal, fast and hardy."[3]

The British had, from 1810, a special "remount" department to supervise pur-chasing and supply.[4] In the first half of the nineteenth century they also imported vast numbers of South African Cape horses, which Dutch settlers had brought to South Africa in the seventeenth century and later crossed with Arabians and Thoroughbreds. The Cape horses (also called Boerpferde) had more stamina and height (ranging from fourteen to sixteen hands) than Arabian horses. Lord Auckland, governor-general of India, presented a pair of Cape stallions to Ranjit Singh, the great Sikh leader, "as a token of British friendship," though Ranjit pre-ferred his own grey 14.1 hands Punjabi stallion, "Pigeon."[5] After 1857, the Cape horses (as well as the country-breds) were superseded by Walers, which had been developed in New South Wales, in Australia, from Thoroughbred, Arabian, and Cape horses. They were fifteen to sixteen hands, more powerful than Arabian or Cape horses, and had more stamina. And although by the mid-nineteenth century stallions were seldom kept entire among troop horses in Europe, the British still used stallions in India. There were complaints: "The squeals, rearing and kicking that went on during assembly in the half-light of the early mornings were both vulgar and dangerous,"[6] and when the stallions broke loose, they "not only attacked any spare horse wandering around, but they would jump on the back of your own mount."[7]

The British also developed a taste for the horses that their predecessors, the Mughals, and the Mughals' predecessors, had imported into India. They came to prefer these imported horses to country-breds and even to the horses from their own stud farms. Arabian and Persian horses, imported from the Persian Gulf, as well as Kandaharis, were said to "stand their work and privations infinitely better than stud- and country-breds." In 1853, a British officer praised a Persian horse of 14 hands 3 inches who carried a man of the Fifteenth Hussars (who weighed, in full kit, twenty-two and a half stone [315 pounds]) for eight hundred miles, "with ease and keeping his condition well."[8] In 1876 one officer of the Fourteenth Hussars insisted that "the Arabian-bred came nearer to perfection in symmetry, beauty, temper and performance than any horses I have ever seen, and they were soon snapped up as chargers by our officers."[9]

But the British also attempted to breed horses in India. The general British consensus was that the best Indian breeding grounds for horses were on the broad northwestern fringe of the subcontinent.[10] They bred some horses in the Punjab, in Saharanpur, and encouraged breeding more generally in North India. They tried to establish a Bengal stud in 1794 and set up a small "committee for the improvement of the breed of horses in India" in 1801.[11] The Indian breeders that I spoke with in Pune in 1996 complained that the British didn't bother to find out where you could raise horses in India, didn't realize that some places are in fact suitable for breeding, while others are not. Moreover, they used the horses they bred only for cavalry; for racing, they needed to import stallions and mares.

The British, by their own accounts, encountered many problems in breeding and maintaining horses for their cavalry, and they wrote books about it. Let's consider two reports, one by William Moorcroft, Superintendent of the Honorable Company's Stud, in 1814, and one by the artist and art historian John Lockwood Kipling, in 1891.

WILLIAM MOORCROFT, *OBSERVATIONS ON THE BREEDING OF HORSES*

The preface to William Moorcroft's book *Observations on the Breeding of Horses within the Provinces under the Bengal Establishment,* 1814,[12] notes that it contains "measures in progress for procuring better Parent Stock, and for re-establishing the North-Western Horse Trade. It exhibits proofs of the general decline of good breeds of Horses in India, and endeavors to detect some of its causes." Moorcroft, an equine veterinarian, shares the negative view of Indian breeds that we have noted in earlier reports by foreigners in India as well as by some of the British. That view was still a concern of John Lockwood Kipling, who wrote, over seventy-five years after Moorcroft, "A controversy has been going on intermittently for years as to the merits of the country-bred horse and the question of Indian horse-breeding generally."[13] It has in fact been suggested that the strain of country-bred horses degenerated after the introduction of British rule in the Punjab around 1850.[14]

The stud was established twenty years before Moorcroft took it over in 1814. The site, at Poosah, in North Bihar, surrounded by indigo plantations, was chosen because it promised "security from an enemy, and a moderate price of grain and labor."[15] Its purpose was "[t]o raise within the British Provinces Horses for the use of Cavalry, instead of depending on exterior supply" and "to spread a better breed of Horses, through such parts of the British Provinces as are most fit for that purposes" (1, 7). Though the stud was supposed to import "good thoroughbred English stallions together with a supply of big, bony, half-bred English hunting mares to serve as a breeding-stock,"[16] Moorcroft paints a much darker picture, insisting that it began with a group of "Indian Mares, for the most part unfit for the purpose," and employed as stallions "[s]mall Arabian Horses . . . ill calculated to make amends for the deficiency of size and strength in the Mares. . . . Horses and Mares of other countries were received as gifts, and were also bought, with but little nicety of selection. English Horses, some excellent, some indifferent, were subsequently added" (1). Clearly, in Moorcroft's eyes, the project had been doomed from the start..

It gets worse:

> In an island [like, to take a case at random, the British Isles?], produce accumulates under circumstances favorable to breeding; but in a continent, with

a long and pervious frontier [like India, for instance], it is not easy to prevent clandestine exportation into neighboring countries, where it bears a higher price. . . . Original faulty composition, abuse or mistakes in purchases, local inaptitudes, from the site and from habits of the natives, exportation of improved Fillies, and losses by casualties, diseases, and accidents, have retarded the progress of the Stud generally. . . . Other difficulties derive from the annoyance of insects, from mismanagement, and from diseases brought on by peculiarities of soil, climate, and food. And experience drawn from History proves that there exist causes of rapid decline in the breeds of Horses, not yet sufficiently analysed. (6, 9)

Much of this is the traditional lament of foreign horsemen in India, but in Moorcroft it took on a particularly bitter edge.

Moorcroft grants that there were some remote parts of India where people did know how to breed horses: "In India Horse-breeding appears to be somewhat lasting on mountains, somewhat flourishing in grassy wilds and in the oasis of sandy deserts" (44). And he is particularly interested in the horses bred in the Northwest:

[In] the Countries beyond the Indus, which most abound with Horses, . . . are to be found Mares at a reasonable rate. Represented as strong, healthy, fruitful, well-tempered, and living to a great age, they are perhaps better adapted for breeding in Hindoostan than any other procurable. From Toorkooman Mares, crossed by Arab, Iran, and Irak Stallions, a race of Horses is raised near Khooloom, under the patronage of Meer Quleech Ulee Khan, said to be well suited for Military purposes. This Chief has a large Stud of his own, and his Cavalry amounts to 12,000. The Stallions now at the Stud have been drawn from England, Arabia, and Asia generally. (20)

But, "It is proved that Indian Mares are less prolific and have a shorter period of fertility than those of more Northern climates. . . . At one season their number and quality seem tolerably respectable, at another so wholly contemptible, as scarcely to warrant leaving a Stallion amongst them" (19, 32). And Moorcroft has a low opinion of most of the horses bred locally:

The Arabian Horses now on the Stud Register are nearly worn out, and some are only fit to be given away. Katheewar and Lukhee Jungal Horses will be most serviceable for the Mares of the farmers. They are preferred by breeders to English half-bred Stallion. This preference may have had its rise in these casts of Horses, originally employed as Stallions, possessing certain predominating forms, which by degrees have been acknowledged as essential to beauty. Long entertained, they are now adopted as standard characters of national choice and are capable of covering gross deformity in parts more important to action, or to strength of constitution. (20)

Moorcroft assumes that the native stock was generally inferior; the only hope of breeding "good" horses was to import the sorts of horses that the British bred in England:

The supply from England, considerable in itself, is small relative to its object. Thoroughbred Horses, which are strong, handsome, and have gained great celebrity on the turf in England, soon repay their original cost in this country. They seem also to last longer by coming with their constitution formed and inured to fatigue, than Colts which arrive before they have completed their growth. (20)

Compounding the problem, Moorcroft asserts, was the fact that the "natives of this country are not easily moulded into new habits" (10). He insists, over and over, that the "natives" must be taught British methods of breeding in order for horses to thrive in India. He has nothing but scorn for native Indian ideas about the qualities that distinguished good horses from bad horses: "Prepossessions of natives, resting upon a difference in the turn of the ear or in the shape and length of the neck, may be thought altogether unworthy of notice. Indeed, as far as the composition of the Home Stud is concerned, characters exciting predilections of favor or raising prejudices of antipathy amongst natives, from mere distinctions of caprice, may be safely disregarded" (21–22). And he shares the low opinion native breeds that we encountered among many of the earlier conquerors:

Seizing upon the race of the country, as the natural Stock on which improvement ought to be engrafted, [the Stud] did not sufficiently stop to enquire, whether this breed was really worth improving. Such an enquiry would have shewn, that the indigenous race, diffused over the whole of that immense tract of land, comprised betwixt the Sea and the North-western [mountains], betwixt the Indus and the North-eastern Alps, was only a race of Ponies, good indeed in quality, but smaller than the Welsh Pony, the Scotch Galloway, or the Irish Hobby. All other breeds were only acclimated productions of exotic sires imported expressly, or having conduced to establish breeds accidentally, by being dispersed after invasions, or battles. (9–10)

The recurrence of the word "race" in this indictment is no accident. Elsewhere, Moorcroft refers to "lame Horses of high caste" (47).

THE EQUINE CASTE SYSTEM

The main reason that Moorcroft offers for the failure of Indians to breed "castes" of good horses, as well as his proposal for the solution to that problem, is the Hindu caste system. Noting that "castes of people" have been set apart for the raising of cows, sheep, and goats, he remarks: "But there have been no castes appropriated exclusively for breeding Horses" (44). Indeed, he argues, "No Moosulman of reputation, no Hindoo of respectability will keep a Stallion for hire. Shame deters the former, caste prevents the latter taking money for such a purpose. Yet the Moosulman is a slave to licentiousness, the Hindoo to the desire of wealth" (46).

Maneuvering around the racist slanders, is there any possible truth in Moorcroft's assertion that no Indian castes were breeders of horses? That depends on what you mean by "breeder." Abu'l Fazl had remarked that "[s]killful, experienced men have paid much attention to the breeding of horses in India,"[17] but who were they? There certainly was a caste, an ancient caste, in charge of the care, and perhaps of the breeding, of horses; these were the Sutas, charioteers, grooms, and bards, whom we first encountered narrating the *Mahabharata*. But castes like the Charans, the Sutas who told the tale of Pabuji, were no longer involved in the care of actual horses, merely in the tales of mythical horses.

The Mughal army, in a list of menial occupations, distinguished horse keepers or equerries from horse breeders.[18] And under the British, there was a class of men who cared for horses in the stable and rode them; they were called Syces (a Hindi and Urdu word, from the Arabic *sā'is,* attributed in English since 1653). There were also Nalbunds, who worked as farriers and grooms. Lockwood Kipling speaks of "large castes of stable servants, contented with a low wage, [and] capable under careful superintendence of keeping their animals in a state of luxurious comfort."[19] But did such people breed the horses or merely care for them?

Moorcroft says that a "caste of Rajpoots, a dissipated class of Moosulmans, are now the keepers of Stallions for hire [as studs]. . . . But never having the means of buying good Horses, and being greatly deficient in judgment, such animals as they do procure accelerate the ruin of the breed" (46–47). Moreover, "The Hindoo Nalbund is an interloper. In the Western Province he is of the Bhat or Bard caste. In the lower [provinces], called Oobdesee or foreigner, he is a Rajpoot of inferior caste, of ruined fortune or blighted character" (47). Thus Moorcroft expresses his scorn for several groups of native breeders and stable workers that he regards as fallen Rajput castes. Such people, he believes, would not breed good horses.

The owners of horses, who might well have made the decisions about breeding, would not have constituted a separate caste. A ninth- or tenth-century Sanskrit inscription from Pehowa (in Kurukshetra, Hariyanna) mentions four Brahmin horse traders,[20] evidence that individual members even of high castes might be involved in trading, if not breeding, horses without necessarily forming a separate caste. (And, indeed, in the precolonial period castes were not as rigid as they became in the colonial period, nor as rigid as the British system of class and race.) Moorcroft argues that some native horse owners once may have done some breeding:

> Under the Moohummudan Government, Horses were given from the Emperor's Stables, as Stallions. Nobles, and wealthy land holders distributed also old, or lame Horses of high caste for the same purpose, and some even maintained one or two, at their own expense, for the Mares of their relations, retainers or tenantry. The same custom is continued by the Sikh Chiefs and by the Murhuttas. And a few respectable natives in the British Provinces occasionally allow the use of a Horse to the neighbouring farmers *gratis,* but the practice is almost worn out. (47)

He also mentions, as we have seen, several studs and breeders in India (as did Rudyard Kipling)[21] but (rightly) does not regard them as "castes." By this reckoning, there are only miscellaneous breeders, no Hindu castes of breeders.

Moorcroft goes on to argue why this is so: "The Horse was no favorite with the Hindoo law-givers, or they might not have known this animal in its most attractive form." And he notes: "They were probably aboriginal of the plains of India, for if they had come from any Horse country, they would have brought with them some proof of that fondness for the Horse which is found amongst its inhabitants" (45). This, at least, is complete balderdash. The "Hindoo law-givers"

were Brahmins, descended from the people who brought their horses to India
during the Vedic period. Yet Moorcroft goes on to assert: "The Hindoo hierarchs
considered the sacrifice of the Horse as the most noble, the most purifying, next
to that of man himself, and yet they did not make breeding Horses a business of
caste. Did this omission originate in advertency? Were all fine Horses bred in
other countries?" (45). We know that, *pace* the British, "all fine Horses" were not,
in fact, bred in other countries, though many of them were. But there does seem
to have been a sharp division between the groups of people who (1) maintained
the science of horses in the *ashvashastras* (people belonging primarily to the
Brahmin castes), (2) people who owned and bred horses (primarily but not only
Kshatriyas), and (3) people (of low caste) who took care of horses. This is actually
the situation in the horse world in Europe and America to this day, where the categories would be (1) bloodline experts and trainers (Brahmins), who are advisers
to (2) wealthy businessmen (Kshatriyas), who flaunt their wealth in Thoroughbreds and who employ (3) badly paid, often immigrant stable workers, exercise
riders, and jockeys (low castes).

Caste, the problem, is also the solution that Moorcroft proposes here:

> Were a Brahmun to discover a reading of the Shastras prescribing the pur-
> suit of Horse-breeding to some widely diffused caste of Hindoos, and this
> were credited, it would only be necessary for Government to find the first
> materials, and to collect the produce. By an impulse once given through re-
> ligious authority, the supply would keep pace with the demand, and stability
> would be ensured. . . . Facts seem to show, that amongst Hindoos no occupa-
> tion has yet reached a high degree of perfection, has even had a permanent
> character, which has not been carried on through the channel of caste. Though
> there be no caste of Horse-breeders, yet, under patronage of Government,
> a Colony of Horse-breeders may supply the deficiency. (46, 49)

Lest we miss the point, Moorcroft repeats this last statement a few pages later:
"And if a Cast of Horse-breeders cannot be created, a colony of Horse-breeders
may supply the deficiency" (54). So the potential native horse breeders of India
should be literally "colonized" by the colonial government in order to provide the
sorts of horses needed by the British Raj.

Moorcroft's most serious mistake was in focusing on castes of breeders rather
than castes of horses, which is to say, breeds. There were of course breeds of Indian horses, distinct types of horses, as we learn from the *ashvashastras*. And

there were criteria by which to distinguish a good horse from a bad horse; the *ashvashastras* had a great deal to say about that, too. But horses were generally identified not, like human castes, by their genealogy but by their geography; all the horses from one area might be regarded as one caste, and from another as another caste. The *ashvashastras* identify horses as "those bred in Kamboja, Sindh, Aratta, and Vanayu...those bred in Bahlika, Papeya, Sauvara, and Titala." The Sultans and Mughals labeled horses with geographical designations such as Turki, Yabu, and Tazi. In the Mughal army in the Deccan, "the muster master read a soldier's and his horse's features with common criteria—skin color, hair, scarring, and a range of other facial features—thereby creating a correspondence between portraits of man and animal."[22] But while the soldier's name, his father's and grandfathers' names, his region and place of residence, and his physiognomy would be recorded on one side of his identifying document, on the other side they recorded only the "breed" (i.e., geographical area) and condition of the horse, not the parentage.[23]

Even if there were not official "breeders" of horses, people who owned horses must have bred them—within their own stock or from neighbors' herds—choosing stallions and mares with the particular qualities they valued. How else would each of the geographical breeds have preserved its prized characteristics, the shape of an ear, the proportions of a hock, the color of a coat? What kept Moorcroft from recognizing that this was, in fact, breeding was the Indians' failure to record the names of the sires and dams and, perhaps even more important, their failure to *limit* the breed to the descendants of those sires and dams, practices that were then (and remained in our day, as we shall see) essential to the British concept of breeding. Moorcroft refers to an Arabian "Stud Register," but it is presumably a British rather than native document. Moreover, the passion to "improve" the local breeds with infusions of, first, Arabian and then, under the British themselves, Thoroughbred bloodlines tended to blur rather than refine the boundaries of the native Indian breeds.

JOHN LOCKWOOD KIPLING, *BEAST AND MAN IN INDIA,* 1891

John Lockwood Kipling (1837–1911) was a professor of architectural sculpture in Bombay and the principal of the Mayo School of Art, Lahore (the present National College of Arts, in Pakistan). He provided illustrations for his son Rudyard's *Jungle Books* (1894), but before that, in 1891, he wrote and illustrated *Beast and Man in India: A Popular Sketch of Indian Animals in their Relations with the People,* of which chapter 8 discusses horses and mules. It is a work of stunning bigotry and Orientalism; he remarks casually on "the unequestrian character of India," and states, "There are of course many fine horsemen in the country, but they have usually been taught by Englishmen.... [I]t is no libel to say that the average native horseman is timid."[24] He also states that, in India, "horses and horse-keep are cheap" (62), which was certainly not true. But his book provides a valuable window into British ideas about horses in India.

He begins with a European mythological allusion:

> India has been described by a European as the Paradise of horses, and from his point of view the phrase is not unfitting. The natural affinity between horses and Englishmen becomes a closer bond by residence in India, where everybody rides—or ought to. . . . The horses, however, which serve native masters are born to Purgatory rather than to Paradise. Those in the hands of the upper classes suffer from antiquated and barbarous systems of treatment, and are often killed by mistaken kindness or crippled by bad training, while those of low degree are liable to cruel ill-usage, over-work, neglect, and unrelieved bondage. (62)

We immediately recognize here the familiar colonial tropes of caste, misguided horse management, untrustworthy natives, backwardness, and barbarism—and a total silence about the notorious mistreatment of horses in England, though this was a hot topic at this time, and *Black Beauty* was translated into Hindustani in 1895.

Lockwood Kipling then provides a biting satire on the *ashvashastras* with their cowlicks or whorls (*avartas*) and "featherings" or "shadows" (*chayas*):

> The ideas current on the qualities, form, and vices of the animal are as antiquated as its treatment. Many are tied up in aphoristic bundles for better preservation. So many parts of the horse should be round, so many square, so many short, and so many long, and everybody speaks of the five vices and of the eight lucky white points of Mangal–Mars. There is an elaborate science of stray hairs with an obstinate twist, of the colour of the markings and the planting of the hair in the skin. . . . In Indian horse lore the set of these featherings (they are analogous to the radiating arrangements of birds' feathers), ending sometimes in circles or whorls, are all mapped out like currents on a mariner's chart, and each is named and interpreted for luck, temper, constitution, or quality; but mainly for luck. . . . From the Oriental point of view, . . . colour and colour

markings are the first things taken into account. . . . [T]here are many similar rules in the East, complicated by moral and fatalistic fancies. (68)

And he doesn't think much more of Indian folk knowledge of horses: "Among horse folk, unfamiliar with books, spoken lore takes such fantastic forms that you would think some fabulous creature was being talked of" (68).

But he does have some appreciation of some of the native "castes" of horses: "In the Himalaya there is a variety of ponies, sturdy *gunths,* and *yabus* that could carry a church and climb up its steeple, Bhutia ponies, and many other hill sorts" (69). And he grudgingly approves of some of the native breeds:

> The characteristic all-pervading horse of the hot plains is the *tattoo* or coun-
> try pony, a cat-hammed, shadowy animal seldom more than thirteen and a half
> hands high. . . . Among them you often come across distinctly Arab character-
> istics, and most are dashed with the noble Arab blood. Though seldom good
> to look at, lean and unkempt, vicious and ill to handle, he is a beast of immense
> pluck and endurance. (70)

Lockwood Kipling has, however, very little good to say about the ways in which Indians treat their horses, including the horses that pull the *ekka,* a small, two-wheeled horse-drawn carriage:

> In Bengal and Madras, non-equestrian provinces, the animal often shrinks
> to a framework caricature of a pony; a heavy head hung on a long weak neck,
> no chest to speak of, inconceivably slender in girth, with weak hind legs work-
> ing over each other like the blades of a pair of scissors. . . . In the North-West
> Provinces and the Punjab the creature improves, is useful as a pack pony. . . .
> Cruel over-driving and a heartless disregard of the creature's thirst are the
> worst features of the immense *ekka* traffic of Northern India. (70)

Lockwood Kipling confirms what we have learned about the grand scale of the importing of horses and adds some vivid details:

> You may see them in Bombay harbor, the horses standing a-row on the bags
> of dates that form part of the cargo, looking exactly like a Noah's Ark with
> the lid off. . . . From the countries north of Kabul a constant immigration of
> the animals we call Northern horses, or sometimes Kabulis, . . still continues

at the rate of about two thousand annually. . . . Many horses are annually imported from Australia, but they are mainly for the army and wealthy people on the Bengal side of India. (71, 72)

And he alludes to the British attempts to regulate the breeding of horses in India (about which William Moorcroft had so much to say): "The British Government has for some years been trying to improve the horses of the country by importing English thoroughbreds, Arabs, and Norfolk trotters who stand as sires at the service of farmers under certain conditions, which include the branding of approved mares" (72). At this point we may ask, "Approved by whom?" a question that will recur when we consider the choices made by a British breeder in establishing a Marwari stud.

Finally, it occurs to Lockwood Kipling to mention what people in India think about their horses:

> While speaking of the horse as he is, we are forgetting the popular estimate of him. In spite of ill usage, he stands for honour and state among both Hindus and Muhammadans. Centuries have passed since the Asvamedha or great Hindu horse-sacrifice was celebrated, but the tradition lingers even among unlettered folk. As associated with Surya, the Sun God, he is held in esteem. . . . The blandly receptive Oriental mind . . . does not take its stories to pieces as if they were clocks. There may be astronomical facts hidden in the horses harnessed to the chariot of the sun, but so far as the Hindu at large is concerned, they are inventions of European Scholars. Muhammadans unite to praise [horses], for the Prophet himself . . . has left a formal benediction: "Thou shalt be to man a source of happiness and wealth, thy back shall be a seat of honour and thy belly of riches, every grain of barley given to thee shall purchase indulgence for the sinner." . . . Written words are still said to "gallop on a paper horse," the order of Government goes forth "on a steed of air." (77)

So even "the blandly receptive Oriental mind"—particularly the "Muhammadan" mind—has some ideas about horses worth mentioning.

RUDYARD KIPLING'S *KIM,* 1900

In *Beast and Man in India,* Lockwood Kipling included a section that he introduced with this note: "From a series of letters written to the *Pioneer* by my son, describing a tour in Rajputana, I extract a description of a visit he paid to the establishment of a native prince well known on the Indian turf."[25] The notes by his son (Rudyard, whom Lockwood Kipling does not mention by name) on the horses of the unnamed "native prince" are more generous and favorable than those of his father: "This city of the Hoyhnhnmns was spectacularly clean, cleaner than any stable, racing or private, that I had been into . . . and quite as impressive was the condition of the horses, which was English, quite English. . . . A boisterous unschooled Arab, his flag spun silk in the sunlight, shot out across the road and cried ha! Ha! In the scriptural manner."[26]

Lockwood Kipling himself became the model for aspects of some of the British characters in Rudyard Kipling's novel *Kim.* The great old Lahore Museum, of which Lockwood Kipling was curator, figured as the Wonder House or Ajaib Ghar, with its cross-culturally appreciative Orientalist curator, at the beginning of *Kim.* And in 1870–72, Lockwood Kipling was commissioned by the government to tour the Punjab, North-West Frontier, and Kashmir, where he made a series of sketches of Indian craftsmen as well as of various sights and antiquities in these regions; those adventures are mirrored in the travels of the characters in *Kim,* to which we now turn.

The very first pages of *Kim* introduce a message about a war, coded in horses, which is also cited at crucial moments in subsequent chapters: "The pedigree of the white stallion has been fully established." It is a triple code, of which the first two levels are easy enough to crack: ostensibly, on the first level, it means that the Muslim horse trader Mahbub Ali, who has sent the message to the British master spy Colonel Creighton, is able to vouch for a valuable horse that the colonel may buy. The coded message on the second level is that rebellious natives in the Northwest are planning an attack on British forces there.

The third level of signification is more complex. The idea of a pedigree implies that you know all you need to know about a horse when you know its father and mother (or dam and sire); the *Ashvashastra* lists among the things one should know about a horse, "the family line" (*kula,* "bloodstock"). Kim, the hero of Kipling's novel, is a boy raised among Indians and generally thought to be an Indian. But the unspoken third code in the white stallion's pedigree means that we know who Kim really is because we know who his parents were. The white stallion implicitly represents Kim's British father, in the equine metaphor that Creighton and Mahbub Ali apply to Kim, behind his back: Kim is a colt who must be gentled into British harness to "play the game."[27] Kim is even said to have "white blood," an oxymoron. (In fact, as Kim's father was a feckless Irishman, Kim is actually subaltern in English eyes. Still, in comparison with an

Indian native, he is a white man.) This leads us back in Indian history to the idea of the classes (*varnas,* literally "colors") of horses and of humans, or the belief that the most important thing to know about another human being is who his or her parents were. And this belief, in British hands, supports more general concepts of racism. It is perhaps worth noting that, just as the British at first used native horses and then began to import them, so, too, at first, in the eighteenth century, British servants of the East India Company often married native women; in the nineteenth century, they imported their wives from England.[28]

I need not point out the significance of the color of the stallion in a book by Kipling (who coined the phrase, "the white man's burden").[29] (We might also note in passing that the horse in the code is a stallion, in the old Vedic/British tradition.) But we might recall that the Vedic stallion of the ancient Hindus, the symbol of expansionist political power, was already white, in contrast with the Dasyus or Dasas, the serpentine natives, who were said to come from "dark wombs,"[30] a reference not to skin color (that prejudice came to India much later) but to human value. British ideas about breeding in India, supported by a complex pseudoscientific ideology, rode piggyback (or horseback) on already existing Hindu ideas about class and caste. The Indian theory, which we would now say the British "appropriated," was conceived without the support of a proto-racist theory like that of the British; one might say that the Indians imagined caste for themselves before the British imagined race against them.

Here is perhaps the moment to comment on the role of the breeding of horses (and to a lesser extent dogs, and other domestic animals) in British ideas about inherited characteristics. The breeding of horses, of "bloodstock," of Thoroughbreds, a theory of race *avant la lettre,* laid the groundwork for a European theory of the breeding of humans. These ideas, which played a role in the development of the concept of race, culminated in some ways in Darwin, and in others in the ill-fated eugenics movements. It is no accident that the British upper classes, with their deep investment in the "breeding" of men and women, had an early and deep investment in the breeding of horses. In particular, the British invented the idea of the Thoroughbred (a term soon to be applied to humans) from three horses that they brought to England, ironically, from their colonies in what they called the Orient: the Byerly Turk (actually almost certainly an Arabian), the Godolphin Arabian, and the Darley Arabian. "Closing the stud book"—that is, decreeing that only the offspring of stallions you have already listed will be accepted legally as belonging to a particular breed—is a vivid metaphor for the barriers of classism, racism, and patriarchy.

COUNT ROUPEE. — Vide. Hyde Park.

FIGURE 31. *Count Roupee.* Caricature of Paul Benfield (1741–1810), hand-colored etching by James Gilray, published by Hannah Humphrey, June 5, 1797. 10¼ × 14¼ in. (260 × 361 mm) plate size; 10⅞ × 14⅝ in. (276 × 370 mm) paper size. (© The British Library Board, P1742)

Ideas of class and race are expressed through an equestrian image from British India in the etching *Count Roupee in Hyde Park* (the rupee being the unit of Indian currency), which depicts a dark-skinned man riding a good-looking horse in Hyde Park. This is James Gilray's 1797 caricature of Paul Benfield (1741–1810), a Madras merchant who bought himself a parliamentary seat and a fine country estate with his somewhat shady Indian profits. His dark complexion labeled him as "nouveau-riche and racially 'other.'"[31] The fact that he is, moreover, riding very badly indeed is clear evidence that he is an arriviste of low caste, not a gentleman.

On the other hand, Kipling's treatment of the various Indian characters in *Kim* as individuals, differing according to their geographical homes, religions, castes, professions, and personalities, belies any simplistic notion of class or race determinism. And when Kim has questions about his own identity (he felt he was "a Sahib among Sahibs," but "among the folk of Hind . . . What am I? Mussalman, Hindu, Jain, or Buddhist?"), Mahbub Ali responds by using horses as a paradigm for multiculturalism before its time: "This matter of creeds is like horseflesh . . .

the Faiths are like the horses. Each has merit in its own country."[32] Or, as the British saying goes, "Horses for courses."

Moreover, Kipling brilliantly undermined the idea of the Thoroughbred (both horse and human) in "The Maltese Cat," a story that he published a few years before *Kim*, in 1895. Now, the term "Maltese cat" ordinarily designates a grey cat of indiscriminate breed, a paradigmatic mongrel. But in Kipling's story, it is the name of a horse, a polo pony, presumably also of indiscriminate breed; we are never told its breed, though some of the other polo ponies are identified as Syrian or Arabian, while the Maltese Cat used to pull a vegetable cart. This is the story of a polo team of native troops, called the Skidars, whose horses are not fancy, not pedigreed. They are playing an important match against the team of the British army, the Archangels, who have better bred, bigger, and more expensive horses, and more of them, so that they can rest one set of horses while riding another set, which the Skidars cannot do.

So the Maltese Cat's team are the underdogs, more precisely the underhorses, but they are clever and brave—and in particular, the Maltese Cat is *very* clever and *very* brave (he plays to the end with a painful injury that makes this his last game, though he will continue to lead the squad in the parades)—and we are rooting for them, and they win! To name a native horse, a wise and courageous horse, the hero of the story, after a mongrel cat is to make a strong statement about the superiority of native breeds over Thoroughbreds—and of native Indians over English officers? The Maltese Cat snubs an Arabian horse from the Archangels' team.

The story is told from the standpoint of the Maltese Cat, who is the captain and tells the other horses what to do. Kipling throughout the tale shows a loving and sympathetic knowledge of the breeds, their anatomy, and the way they are treated by their human owners. And he rejoices in the way that native horses, presumably country-breds, triumph over the fancy imported horses. Indeed, even Lockwood had said (referring to ponies from Manipur, a state in northeastern India), "The Manipur ponies used for polo or chaugan [a game much like polo] are mostly dun, and are excellent beasts in their way, playing the game with very little help from either knee or bridle" (69). And Alistair Wilson, glossing "The Maltese Cat," refers to polo ponies from "India, where country-breds were largely relied on, very good animals not more than 13.2,"[33] that is, fifty-four inches high, i.e., not very big at all. And so in this story by Kipling the country-breds, human and equine, carry the day. So much for caste, pedigrees, and Thoroughbreds.

MOORCROFT AND OTHER HORSEY BRITISH SPIES

The white stallion in *Kim* is the key to a complex spy network involved in the "Great Game" of espionage that England was playing against Russia on the fields of Northwest India. It now transpires that Kipling's *Kim* was "practically a handbook for C.I.A. agents in Southeast Asia in the nineteen-fifties and sixties."[34] Allen Dulles, then the head of the agency, was said to have kept a copy at his bedside, and Edward Lansdale, a pioneer in psychological warfare in Vietnam, urged all his operatives to read it and to pay special attention to Kim's "counterintelligence training in the awareness of illusions,"[35] an allusion to Kim's intensive schooling in resisting what Lansdale would have called brainwashing.

But long before that, in recorded British history, horse-trading, horse breeding, spying, and Orientalism combined in the character of William Moorcroft, the author of the book on the Indian stud that we have considered above, but also an "explorer and horse-trader."[36] As Moorcroft himself wrote: noting that "the best foreign Horses for Military purposes I met with were clearly traced to the countries bordering the Oxus," north of the Indian Caucasus, he resolved to go there to find stallions and mares and even to revive "the ancient North-western Horse trade" (11, 12). Urged by the hope of gaining permission to visit these regions in quest of stallions and mares, he consulted "a Hindoo Priest of my acquaintance, who had traversed those countries," and found "an old Pundit, who had likewise been there" and who offered to conduct Moorcroft to them.

In 1812, Captain Hyder Young Hearsey accompanied William Moorcroft on an expedition to discover the source of the Ganges and to visit the sacred lake of Manasarowar, once considered the source of all the sacred rivers of India. They also wanted to seek out prospective trade routes. As Europeans were forbidden to travel to this area, the two travelers disguised themselves as Gosains or Hindu pilgrims. On the return journey, Moorcroft and Hearsey threw off their disguises and were arrested in October by the Gurkha rulers of Kumaon, who released them at the beginning of November. In that same year, 1812, Hearsey published a watercolor illustrating their trip. Moorcroft's account of the expedition was published in *Asiatick Researches,* 1818, volume 12.

In 1819, the British sent Moorcroft to Northwest India, Tibet, and Afghanistan on a Quixotic search for "suitable cavalry mounts."[37] Moorcroft had seen mares from Kutch that he thought might be suitable for the army, and he was granted official permission "to proceed towards the North Western parts of Asia,

FIGURE 32. William Moorcroft and his companion Hyder Young Hearsey. On the road to Lake Mansarowar (Tibet). The travelers are wearing Indian dress and riding on yaks; they are shown meeting two Tibetans on horseback with a loaded yak. Watercolor by Hyder Young Hearsey, 1812. (© The British Library Board, WD 350)

for the purpose of there procuring by commercial intercourse, horses to improve the breed within the British Province or for military use."[38] But he collected information not only on horses but also on political and economic conditions at the borders of the Empire,[39] and shortly before his mysterious final disappearance, he was briefly imprisoned in the Hindu Kush on suspicion of being a spy.[40] Moorcroft was lost, presumed dead, in August of 1825, and he was said to be "now chiefly remembered by the unfortunate termination of his second and last journey."[41] Clearly, horses were deeply implicated in the clandestine as well as the official British subjugation of India.

Moorcroft had delusions of Orientalism; he told a friend that he would have disguised himself "as a Fakeer" rather than give up his plan,[42] and after his death, legends circulated about "a certain Englishman named Moorcroft who introduced himself into Lha-Ssa, under the pretence of being a Cashmerian," or who spoke fluent Persian "and dressed and behaved as a Muslim."[43] According to one biographer, Moorcroft was thrilled by the stories he heard "from the northwestern horse-traders—swarthy, bearded men like Kipling's Mahbub Ali."[44] But

Kipling created Mahbub Ali fifty years after the publication of Moorcroft's papers, and aspects of the characters of Creighton, Mahbub Ali, and Kim himself may have been inspired by Moorcroft.

British soldiers stationed in India (and elsewhere in what they called the Orient) often went on what was euphemistically called "shooting leave," that is, official time off to go hunting (shooting things like tigers), but in reality to go spying (sometimes shooting things like human beings), often in fantastic disguise. Horse-trading was often a part of these enterprises, sometimes just a cover, sometimes a secondary objective.[45] In 1830, when the British decided to chart the Indus River, as a possible line of advance for the British to take over Sindh, Lahore, and the Punjab, Alexander Burnes led the expedition, "under the pretext of shipping four enormous dray horses [or, in another version of the story, "a coach and five enormous horses"][46] upriver to Lahore as a gift from King William IV of England to the Maharaja Ranjit Singh, ruler of the Punjab."[47] In another exploit of this sort, "When [Charles] Stewart called on the Persian governor at Mohammadabad, he told him he was Kwajah Ibrahim of Calcutta and that he had come to buy horses for the Bombay market. . . . He also had sources in the governor's circle and to exploit the use of these he had to lend credence to his role as a horse-dealer by actually buying occasional horses from the governor; he was somewhat over-charged, but reckoned it was worth the money to avert suspicion and keep his channels open."[48]

And so forth and so on.

Works of English fiction sometimes called upon the symbolism of horses to depict the relationship between the British and their Indian subjects. At the very end of E. M. Forster's *A Passage to India* (1924), an Indian (a Muslim, Dr. Aziz) and an Englishman (the schoolteacher, Mr. Fielding), riding their two horses side by side, find that apparently, as Kipling warned, "never the twain can meet."[49] Aziz had just said that someday his people would drive the English out of India. "'Then,' he concluded, half kissing him, 'you and I shall be friends.' 'Why can't we be friends now?' said the other, holding him affectionately. 'It's what I want. It's what you want.' But the horses didn't want it—they swerved apart. . . ." And the horses were right, of course.

11 | ✿ | Horse Myths and Rituals in the Absence of Horses

1800 to 2000 CE

We turn now from people (like the Rajputs and the British) who did have horses to those who did not, particularly people living, in recent centuries, in what Lockwood Kipling called the "non-equestrian provinces,"[1] but more broadly people who may once have had but now no longer had horses.

Since horses in India were so expensive to buy and maintain, no native, village tradition of farming with horses or riding horses developed there. The occasional landowner may ride a small, weedy cob, but even so he is on a high horse, as it were: he dominates the horizon, the terrain, and (like mounted police at parades or riots) he can see everyone, because no one else is on a horse. A few landowners-who-would-be-kings still keep a few horses as symbols of prestige, and in remote villages, some wealthy farmers keep mares and breed a few horses for such utilitarian purposes as riding to fetch doctors or paying visits to neighboring villages.[2]

Yet, despite the negative political symbolic associations of horses, and the widespread ignorance of actual horses, horses are worshiped in places where they have never been a part of the land, where most people did not have horses and seldom even saw a horse. The symbol of the horse became deeply embedded in the folk traditions of India and then stayed there even after its referent, the horse, had vanished from the scene. On my first trip to India, living in rural Bengal, I made this entry in my diary on September 15, 1963: "On the side of one of the clay, thatched huts I saw a bas relief of a horse, in stature and stance somewhat resembling the T'ang horses at gallop, and in style something like Picasso bulls, altogether one of the most beautiful things I have ever seen, and about eight feet long." Most of the stories and images of horses have no obvious link with classical Indian texts, or even with the history of horses in India, but they do share in the more general symbolic valences that arise out of the patterns of Indian history.

Many of these horsey stories are still told, indeed performed, in Rajasthan today, where the priests and the storytellers (Bhopas) are drawn from among villagers of the lowest castes.[3] Though, as we have seen, the ballad of Desingu has a
historical basis in a culture of Rajputs and Mughals who certainly had horses, it
is told by Tamil villagers who did not. Recently a patron of these performances
explained why they were beginning to die out: "When the stories used to be
told, everyone had a horse and some cattle. . . . Now, when a Bhopa tells stories
about the beauty of a horse, it doesn't make the same connection with the audience." The epics are surviving better in places where "the pastoral context of the
story"—of cows and horses and heroic cattle herders—is still intact.[4] But they
are also surviving, in one form or another, even in places that lack that context.

The Rathvas of Gujarat, a tribal people, have not traditionally kept horses,
though the Maharajas of Chhota Udaipur used to keep horses at the palace. A
recent observer remarked, "I've only ever seen one horse in the area—and that
a rather sickly looking one that I saw off in a distant field."[5] Elsewhere in the
Chhotaudepur district, in the last few years, a Rathva man has been keeping
horses and renting them out for marriage processions.[6] But still today the Rathvas
paint beautiful horses, generally illustrating the tale of Pithoro, all over the inside and the outside walls of their houses. In the story of Pithoro, the hero feeds
his horse silver hay before an important contest.[7] If Pithoro were a horseman, he
would know that you don't feed a horse anything (let alone silver hay) right before you gallop him. Similarly, during a wild party in a Rajasthani story, "even the
horses . . . were given a lot of wine to drink."[8] This, too, is a very bad idea.

The mythical horses in these villages are not drawn from life; they are drawn
from art, and from the imagination of horses. In the heartland of India, most of
the horses are clay (or stone, brick, or cement).[9] For these villagers, what value
horses have is purely emotional, through their association with royalty, nobility, and military might. The *idea* of the horse (what we might call the "equine
imaginaire") worked its way deep into the Indian soil where the practical role of
the horse failed to make any ultimate impact, surviving despite (or because of?)
the absence of the regular ownership or use of real horses. Working from art
rather than from life leads to inaccuracies, and many folktales and images from
non-horsey cultures betray the authors' or artists' innocence of things equine.

THE CRUELTY OF PEDDANNA

When the stories about magical mares that were told among the equestrians of
Rajasthan and other horsey parts of India were retold by people who did not have

FIGURE 33. Shankarbhai, one of the sons of Mansingbhai Dhanjibhai Rathwa, a famous Pithora painter, painting horses on the wall of their house. (Photo by Gregory Alles, taken April 7, 2009, in Malaja, Chhotaudepur Taluka, Gujarat)

a firsthand experience of real horses, the stories were distorted by that ignorance. Such is the case with the story of Peddanna, the hero of the Telugu *Palnadu Epic* (told in the region of Palnadu in Andhra Pradesh), in a version recorded in 1974 but drawing upon a tradition that may go back as far as eight hundred years.

When Dev Narayan in Rajasthan "rode in" the villain's horse, he eventually sent him down to the Underworld (where horses often live in Indian mythology), but he did not hurt him when he taught him to submit to his rider. In the Peddanna story in Andhra, however, the theme of taming the villain's wild horse becomes a metaphor for taming human violence, and the heroic rider who subdues the horse becomes cruel, as the *Palnadu Epic* projects onto the presumed natural orneriness of the untamed horse the known wicked machinations of evil people who would kill our hero.

The story begins when our hero gets a winged mare from a benevolent older woman, like the heroes of other equestrian epics that we have seen (Pabuji, Dev Narayan, Teja, Gugga):

> Peddanna Bada Raju was born of a Velama family in Palamacapuri, but he
> was lovingly brought up by Viravidyala Devi, the Raju's wife. One day she ac-

quired a winged mare and gave her to Peddanna Bada Raju, but she warned him not to go to the south. Peddanna flew down to the south, to Pedda Kancerla, and married the princess Mutyalakomma, the king's daughter. The other Rajus plotted to kill him.[10]

Peddanna's birth in Palamacapuri (in Madhya Pradesh) makes him an interloper and foreigner in the eyes of the men of Kancerla, in Andhra. It is also notable that he immediately disregards the advice of the older woman who gives him the winged mare.

The story then introduces another magic mare:

The farmers of Kancerla planted a crop of chick-peas. A pair of celestial horses, a mare named Storm Cloud and a stallion named Fair Cloud, came every day to graze on a field of chick-peas, and went away. The farmers, seeing that their crops were being destroyed, went to the local Raju and complained. He posted horsemen, elephants, and men with drums, war drums, and torches. Storm Cloud and Fair Cloud came whistling down from the sky and alighted on the chick-pea crop. As they began to graze, the mare, Storm Cloud, whinnied, and at that, all the men lit their torches and beat their drums. The stallion, Fair Cloud, rose into the sky. The mare, Storm Cloud, tried to follow her husband, but she was in her ninth month of pregnancy. When she tried to flee, the embryo in her womb miscarried and fell to the ground. The Rajus of Kancerla, thinking that she had a belly ache from eating too much, fell on the mare and killed her. Some of the other Rajus slew the stallion. The Rajus of Kancerla captured the foal, built a paddock, and raised him. But no one could ride him, as he was a celestial horse. (223–24)

Let us pause for a moment here and note a significant error committed by the author of this text. As the translator remarks, "The gestation period of a horse is, of course, eleven months, but horses are not common in the area and the singer would be more familiar with the gestation period of cattle and humans, both of which are nine months" (240n21). (That the equine gestation period is eleven months was already known and stated in a Vedic text, several centuries BCE.)[11] The poet who does not know how long mares carry their foals has no real sympathy for horses. Nor do the men who find the mare, mistake the signs of a recent foaling for a belly ache, and casually kill both the mare and the stallion.

The story now turns back to Peddanna:

Unable to think of any other way to kill Peddanna, the Rajus decided that he might be slain by means of the unridable colt born of Storm Cloud and Fair Cloud. The Raju called Peddanna to the court and said, "I have a colt in my stables, a most recalcitrant beast. One way or another, I must have him broken." "Bring him on! Bring him on, Father-in-law," said Peddanna. "As my name is Peddanna, I know horses." He preened his great sharp moustache; he combed his tiger moustache; his eyes reddened; he gnashed his teeth; his eyes glowed like the eyes of a spirit.

He bridled the colt with a bridle made of knives and saddled him with a cutting saddle. He took him to the court. Though his wife feared that the colt would kill him, he promised always to come and save her. The colt was bridled with a bridle made of knives and saddled with a cutting saddle. When the horse saw Peddanna, he reared and whinnied. Peddanna Bada Raju approached. The horse shied this way and that, not allowing him to mount. Then Peddanna called on his patron god, Cennakesvarasvami, and on Ishvara [Shiva]. He leaped a mile into the sky and landed on the horse's back. He spurred the horse, which leaped a mile into the sky and entered the clouds. No matter how hard Peddanna tried to rein him in, the horse did not slacken his pace. The knives on the bridle cut deep into the horse's neck, and streams of blood poured down. Then, riding the celestial horse, Peddanna disappeared into the sky. The Rajus took away his wife, Mutyalakomma, and prepared to burn her alive. . . . They tormented her most horribly . . . She swooned, and when she recovered, they tormented her unmercifully. (224–26)

Peddanna's enemies have already murdered two horses. The violent imagery used to describe the taming of the colt—cutting with knives and razors, told twice, for emphasis—was used earlier in this text to describe the birth of another prince (again with an unnatural period of gestation): "He remains in the womb for nine years and then senses that it is time to be born. He causes his mother great pain. He leaps up, striking her heart, and she swoons. Her body feels as if it is being cut by sharp knives and razors. Unable to bear the pain, she weeps" (154). Women and horses are in general the victims, though not the only victims, of violence in this poem.

While Peddanna's wife is suffering on earth, the story continues in heaven, where Peddanna, no longer riding the magic mare that he had been given as a young boy, now has the colt that he had so violently tamed. It is, I think, significant that he has lost his mare and now rides a stallion:

Peddanna was sitting with Brahma, Vishnu and Ishvara. The wandering divine sage Narada approached him and said, "What is this, Peddanna? They are tormenting your wife and causing her to suffer most horribly." When he heard these words, Peddanna remembered. He went to his horse, and the horse said, "O Sir, Peddanna Bada Raju, for some reason I went to the human world and fell into your hands. But I have now spent some time with my parents, and I will never return to earth." It was a celestial horse.

Then the gods called Narada and said, "Narada, you must go. Take charge of the horse, mount him, protect the three worlds, and give him to Peddanna." Narada took the horse. Because he ruled the three worlds, he made the horse take on a corporeal form. He brought him and gave him to Peddanna, who mounted the horse and descended through the sky to Kancerla. As he approached, Mutyalakomma was being tormented mercilessly. Peddanna took his silk turban from his head. Mutyalakomma grabbed the end of the turban, and Peddanna pulled her up onto the horse's back. When he had pulled her up, they rode into the sky.

From the back of his horse, Peddanna fought a terrible battle with the Rajus of Kancerla. He killed all the Rajus, and then plowed all of Kancerla and planted it with castor beans. After that, Peddanna and his wife mounted the horse and went to Palamacapuri. (226–27)

Peddanna tries in vain to force the celestial horse to return to earth; Narada's magic does the trick, without force. Peddanna then uses the horse to take murderous vengeance on his human enemies.

In another episode, which takes place after Peddanna's return to Palamacapuri, the enmity between Peddanna and his son-in-law, Ala Racamallu, is, again, expressed through violence against horses:

Peddanna still had his stallion that he had won from the Rajus of Kancerla. And Ala Racamallu had a mare that he had brought from a battle at sea. The grooms of the two horses led them to water and they met in front of the Cennakesvarasvami temple. When Peddanna's stallion saw Ala Racamallu's mare, he pawed the earth and whinnied. The two grooms argued about who should turn aside; they began to whip one another's horses. Peddanna's groom accidentally struck Ala Racamallu's mare in the eye. Unable to bear the pain, the mare bolted and fled to the stable. From that time on, the mare neither drank water nor ate food. '

Ala Racamallu saw the mare crying many grievous tears, trembling all over. He questioned the groom and found out what had happened. A terrible battle took place between Ala Racamallu and Peddanna, with both heroes on horseback. Brahma wanted to stop the fight. He came between the two mounted warriors and grasped Ala Racamallu's mare in his right hand, Peddanna's stallion in his left hand. He drove Peddanna's stallion back, but the horse charged forward toward Brahma. Realizing that this was Brahma, Peddanna reined in his horse with all his strength, checking him, and drove back Ala Racamallu's horse. But Ala Racamallu charged and made his mare trample on Brahma's feet, breaking Brahma's big toe. Brahma resolved to see Ala Racamallu dead. (267–73)

Here even a god is the victim of human cruelty (delivered, unwillingly, by a horse), as is the mare whose eye is painfully wounded (a mare, by the way, who seems to have been imported by sea, like so many of the best Indian horses). Ala Racamallu ultimately dies, in fulfillment of Brahma's declared resolution to see him dead.

But the only protest against all of this violence comes, finally, from a talking horse:

Before he died, Anapotu Raju's older brother had left a message in a *jammi* tree for him. Anapotu commanded his horse to take him to his elder brother. The horse went straight to the *jammi* tree where the brother had left the message. Anapotu Raju was delighted, thinking that his brother was still there. But after he tethered the horse, he could find no trace of his brother. He mounted his horse and began whipping him, cursing him for his failure to take him to his brother. The horse trembled and shook but did not move. Weeping, the horse told Anapotu Raju how foolish he was to abuse him so. Then, raising his head, the horse pointed to the message hanging in the tree. (333)

At last an earthly horse speaks, just as the celestial horse had done, but now to protest human cruelty to horses.

MALANCHA AND THE PAKSHIRAJ

A particular breed of magic horse, a Pakshiraj ("King of Those Who Have Wings"), plays a similar part in a violent human tragedy in the Bengali saga of Malancha:

Prince Chandramanik was born to a king whose favorite horse was a
Pakshiraj. At his birth, Chandramanik was doomed to die in twelve days; at
this news, the elephants broke their chains and fled from their stalls, the horses
died in the stable, and the Pakshiraj refused to touch any food. They married the new-born boy to Malancha, a twelve-year old girl, the daughter of
a low caste police chief (*kotwal*). When Chandramanik died, the king had
Malancha's hands and ears cut off. At that moment, the Pakshiraj went mad.
But, unknown to anyone but Malancha, Chandramanik was miraculously restored to life, and Malancha was restored to wholeness.

Malancha raised Chandramanik, who did not realize that she was his wife.
He grew up and found out that he could regain his kingdom by winning a
horse race. Malancha promised to get a horse for him and return in three days.
She came to the city, where she saw the palace gate closed and the doors of
houses all bolted from within. The good luck of the king had left him and the
city looked like a desert. The Pakshiraj had gone mad; he ran wild and killed
every man that walked in the city. When Malancha heard all this, she cried
out, "Where are you, Pakshiraj? Do you remember Chandramanik?'" Her
voice reached the horse, and he ran up to her with ears erect and said, "How
could you know the name of Chandramanik? Shall I ever get him back?"
Malancha said, "Pakshiraj, come with me." She set out for her home, followed
by the horse.

The citizens were astonished. "Chandramanik died years ago," they said.
But she had said his name, and she had caught the mad horse. Was she a magician? The queen said, "Who is she? Go and find out." Malancha had returned
with the horse. Fire came out of the horse's eyes; his ears were erect, and his
sharp hooves cut the earth and made it tremble. Malancha helped her husband
ride the horse and said to the horse, "You know what you should do; my husband is a boy; I place him in your charge." At this moment she held up the reins
so that her husband might catch them. Chandramanik said, "Who are you?
You are always near me, but you do not speak to me. Who are you to me?" And
she answered, "I am the daughter of the police chief." She hid her face with her
hair and then in haste drew out a thread from her cloth, put it round the neck
of the horse, and let it go. The thread had been made of all the virtues she had
acquired in her past lives, and her tears had cast a charm on it. The Pakshiraj
ran as if flying in the air. Malancha threw herself down on the bare ground in
grief, saying to herself, "Alas! Why did I not let him know who I am? Why did
I not tell him when he asked?'"

When the prince returned to the palace, pretending to be the gardener's son, everyone was surprised to see the horse. "It is of the Pakshiraj breed; we don't have such a horse in our stable; where could the gardener's son have gotten it?"

The race began. Like a newly-fledged bird feeling its wings just grown, the horse could not bear to be checked. Chandramanik held the reins tightly. The horse's body moved like a wave; his four feet struck the earth impatiently. Chandramanik won the race. But then he struck the Pakshiraj with his whip. The stroke tore off the thread Malancha had tied round the neck of the horse, and it fell into the dust of the earth, unnoticed. The Pakshiraj drew a heavy breath and set off.

The princess saw Chandramanik, fell in love with him, and insisted on marrying him. Now the Pakshiraj came back where Malancha lay on the dusty ground. When she saw the Pakshiraj before her, she asked, "What is it, Pakshiraj? Where is my husband?" Eventually Malancha found her husband, saved him, and lived with him happily ever after.[12]

In this story, which I have greatly abbreviated, the horse is capable of violence; he runs wild, killing innocent men in the city. But his madness is a reaction to human violence, beginning with the king's action in cutting off Malancha's hands and ears, and behind that the more subtle caste violence, and violence against women, in the act of forcing a woman of low caste to bear the brunt of a cruel prophecy of early widowhood. The prince is guilty of the pivotal vicious act, whipping the innocent Pakshiraj, an action typical of the worst sort of horsemanship at any time, but madness when applied to a magical, winged horse. The prince's viciousness counteracts all the virtue that Malancha has put into the control of the magic horse, and only by generating new virtues can she save the prince yet again. As usual, the mistreatment of horses is analogized to the mistreatment of innocent women, in this case a low-caste woman.

TWO SHORT TAMIL SATIRES

Two stories from South India satirize South Indians who are naive about horses. The first is a simple story in a book for people learning to read Tamil:

Once upon a time, a horse saw a cow and envied her. The horse generated ascetic heat in order to get two long horns. It was successful; horns sprouted and grew on the horse's head, and he had split hooves, and a cow's tail. Then something startled him and he started to run, but he stumbled like a cow. And then he had to chew his cud, which he didn't like. And he had no tail to brush away flies. Finally, the horse generated ascetic heat in order to get rid of his cow features. "I don't want horns and I don't want cow's hooves. Let what I eat be immediately digested; I don't want to have to lie down and chew cud. I want to run and jump and live!" said the horse, touching Paramasivan's feet. "So be it," said the Creator, and granted the boon.[13]

The perennial folk theme (the country mouse and city mouse who want to trade places; the husband and wife who want to switch their jobs), often regarded as particularly therapeutic for dissatisfied children ("Be happy with what you are; don't try to be someone else," or, "Be careful what you wish for"), is here given a cultural twist: the horse challenges the whole Hindu establishment of cows, and (like the horses in another Tamil satire)[14] manages to get rid of his horns.

Another Tamil anecdote about a horse satirizes other sorts of horse myths:

The wise minister of a lovelorn king, failing to advance the king's impossible passion for a girl whose painted image the king had seen in a temple, decided to commit suicide. He rode his faithful horse over wilderness, mountains, and forests until they came to the Western ocean. He looked at the horse and said, "O Horse!" [He used the Sanskrit word, *ashva*.] "You have been with me until now. We cannot remove the obstacle that has come to our king. There is no further use in our continuing to live. You go somewhere and live on." And so he entered the ocean. And the horse, thinking, "Our death would also be a good thing," followed him into the water. Unfortunately, the water came only to their necks. As they were about to plunge into deeper water, Parvati and Shiva intervened and saved them.[15]

This may be a satire on the widespread theme of the noble horse that will not live without its master; or a satire on the Indian myth of the mare underneath the sea; or just a story about a silly man and his silly horse, and the mercy of the gods.

THE HERMIT AND HIS THREE-LEGGED HORSE

A story about a three-legged horse was told by Poromananda Chattopadhyay, a Brahmin priest, in Tarakeshvar, in West Bengal, in 1977. It offers a down-to-earth village satire on the many high-toned stories of miraculous horses and miraculous riders in the vernacular Kshatriya epic traditions:

I cannot speak with certainty about the history of the Tarakeshvar temple, but what I do know has come from ancient stories [*purani kahini*]. In the beginning, this place was covered by a dense forest. In the forest lived an ascetic hermit who worshipped Shiva [Baba]. The people called him Dhumropan Giri, which means "He who is always smoking," because he was fond of marijuana [*ganja*]. The house of the king of the area was only three miles from where this hermit stayed, and the king often heard about the holy man.

The hermit had a horse with three legs. He looked after this horse like his own child. Now, the villagers started rumors that something was peculiar about a hermit taking such good care of a useless beast. This horse excited their suspicion. When the king asked the hermit about these reports of his behavior, a heated argument arose. The hermit maintained that though his horse was three-legged, he was not a useless animal. The hermit said he rode him frequently, far and wide.

The king then offered him a deal. If the hermit could ride this horse, the king would give him all the land that the animal could cover. The hermit then mounted his horse and began to ride. He rode from Burdwan to Midnapore and from there to Hooghly, to Amdanga Mattha, and to Gorbeta. From there he returned to Tarakeshvar again. The king verified the hermit's journey and found that he had visited the entire area. Then, as he had promised, he gave the hermit all the land that he had covered with his horse. And so the hermit became the first landlord of this place, the owner of the land.[16]

The horse's journey to claim all the land he can ride over may well be a satire on the ancient Vedic sacrifice in which the stallion did precisely that. That this role should now be played by a three-legged horse who is the prize possession of a pothead, and that the king should make him a landlord, is surely satirical.

AIYANAR: MASSIVE STATUES OF MYTHICAL BEASTS

Village potters all over India make equestrian images and votive horses in basic, primary shapes. Deposits of clay horses abound on the graves of Hindu Tantriks and Muslim saints near the village shrines of Bengal.[17] Throughout West Bengal, clay horses are offered to all the village gods, male or female, fierce or benign, though particularly to Dharma Thakur, the sun god. At Kenduli in Birbhum, West Bengal, clay horses are offered on the grave of a Tantric saint named Kangal Kshepa. Bengali parents offer horses when a child first crawls steadily on its hands and feet, like a horse.[18] At the Gambhira Festival on the Night of Shiva

FIGURE 34. Votive offerings at Aiyanar Temple. Aiyanar Temple, Tiruduraipundi, Tamil Nadu. (Photo by Anna Lise Seastrand, 2018)

(Shivaratri) in Bengal, the followers of Shiva ride a hobbyhorse, a wooden or bamboo stick decorated with colored paper and string; a dancing horse takes part in the dance in this festival.[19] Similar festivals take place at other seasons of the year, in other parts of the country.

In Orissa, terra-cotta votive horses known as *thakurani* are given to various gods and goddesses to protect the donor from inauspicious omens, to cure illness, or to guard the village.[20] In Balikondala, Orissa, *thakuranis* serve as vehicles for gods to ride at night as spirit riders to guard the villages, protect the fields, and visit the ill; and there are terra-cotta horses in the temple of Shiva on the edge of the village.[21] Rag horses are offered at the tombs of saints in Gujarat.[22] In Tanjore, horses are offered to male and female village gods.[23]

Perhaps the most dramatic expression of the worship of horses among the non-horsey village people of India is the construction in Tamil Nadu of massive figures of horses, alone or mounted, dedicated to Aiyanar, the son of Shiva, guardian of village boundaries.[24]

In the absence of real horses, the village potters of South India copy the images of horses that they have seen, images made by people who *did* have horses. The village potter-priest gives the horses basic shapes that reflect the naturalism of South Indian sculpture on such famous carvings as the rearing stone horses that support the roofs of the large halls of the stone temples in the Vijayanagar style of the sixteenth century.[25] As many as five hundred large clay horses may be prepared in one sanctuary, most of them standing between fifteen and twenty-five feet tall (including a large base) and involving the use of several tons of stone, brick, and either clay, plaster, or cement.[26] One group of three majestic forms stands over sixteen feet high and was built by village potters a century ago. Each one was made in a single piece, with three-inch-thick sides, and then fired on the spot.[27] They are a permanent part of the temple and may be renovated at ten- to twenty-year intervals; the construction of a massive figure usually takes from three to six months. Over the years, the horses accumulate in the sacred groves, and they are still built today. These massive figures are the most ambitious technical achievement in clay found anywhere in India.

The gigantic figures appear to be larger versions of the clay horse figures still commonly made by Tamil village potters for presentation to the night-riding gods in periodic festivals and worshipped in the sacred groves of South India.[28] Terra-cotta horses dedicated to the god Aiyanar and his troops by individuals or whole villages can be found in rural shrines in most districts of South India. Hollow clay horses such as these are believed to serve as mounts for the gods, who ride them at night around the borders of the village to protect each village.[29] When the horses have riders, the riders ride without stirrups, on saddled or un-saddled horses. The horse is usually built in a rearing posture and on a scale much bigger than that of the rider. Chickens, billy goats, and cocks are sacrificed to Aiyanar at the Aiyanar temples.[30] Aiyanar is often accompanied by the demon Karuppan, the Dark God,[31] a sinister aspect of the Aiyanar horse that may stem from the Epic and Puranic tradition of demonic horses.

A TAMIL HORSE TEMPLE

The following notes were written by Father Selva Raj, on September 17, 1990, based on an interview with Mangalanatha Pillai, chief trustee of a horse temple in Tamil Nadu:

There is no written document or evidence for the origin or history of this temple. Oral tradition and architectural evidence are the only available documents. According to oral tradition, the temple is a century old. It includes a gigantic, impressive horse statue located at the entrance of the temple. A seven-foot wall surrounds the temple and the inner sanctum. The horse was built in memory of and dedicated to Gauripulla Thevar, a prince of Sivanga. And so the temple is known today as the Gauripulla Thevar Kovil temple.

The origins of this temple are traced to an amorous adventure of prince Gauripulla Thevar, who fell in love with a woman from the village of Padamathur, about two miles away from his palace, and used to visit her every day. When the villagers of Padamathur heard about this, they became upset and decided to do away with the prince at the village council meeting. When the prince learned of this plot, he resolved to abduct his beloved. So, accompanied by a few soldiers of the palace, the raja went to the village and rode off with the woman on his horse. But while he was returning to the palace with her, groups of villagers intercepted him along the two-mile road and beat and stabbed the prince and his entourage so severely that they all died of their injuries at Padamathur village.

There are two horses in this temple. The larger one (approximately thirty feet long and thirty-five feet tall), made of bricks, is located at the entrance of the temple, and the other, smaller statue (six feet long and five feet tall), carved out of a single black granite stone (a stone called "Karungal" in Tamil Nadu), is inside the temple. This statue depicts the horse with the king and his lover mounted on its back. Both horses are adorned with garlands. The temple and the outer horse were built in the same year (1879), and both were renovated in 1980.

In addition to the garlands, the outer horse is adorned with all the decorations usually found on royal horses in their artistic depictions as well as with various demonic figures (*asuras*). The horse's raised front legs are resting on the heads of two gigantic demons (*bhutas*), subordinate to the horse. Its significance, according to Mangalanatha Pillai, is "so that the weight of the horse may not fall upon the earth." The horse also stands as a symbol of royal power.

Inside the temple, beside the statue of the king and the horse, there is also a statue of the goddess Kali. Separate *pujas* are performed for these three principal deities of the temple. Each of these statues represents a different world order: the horse the animal world, the Raja the human world, and Kali the divine world. Assembling these three distinct categories of figures within the confines of a single temple brings together and forms a harmonious relationship between the three worlds that enclose the worshipper. Separate *pujas* of appeasement are offered to these three principal figures of the temple.

Despite the inclusion and presence in this temple of Kali, who is almost invariably associated with blood offerings, no animal sacrifices or blood offerings are ever made here. Only *pujas* of coconuts, flowers, incense, and sweetened rice (*pongal*) are offered to the horse in this temple.

There are, by contrast, many temples in the vicinity of Padamathur where animal sacrifices and blood offerings are made, even though the horse is either the principal figure or very prominent. In Aiyanar Temples, for example, where the horse is given a place of prominence, animal sacrifices are offered, even today, to Aiyanar and his horse. But at the Aiyanar Temples, Aiyanar is the primary, direct recipient of this sacrifice and the horse is only a secondary, indirect recipient, venerated only as the vehicle of Aiyanar. In the Gauripulla Thevar temple, by contrast, where the horse is the primary object of worship, there are no animal sacrifices.[32]

Evidently, despite their traditional association with death and battle, horses in some South India temples shun violence.

DALIT HORSES

The equine folklore of India expresses the connection not only between horses and foreigners but also between horses and resident aliens, as it were, such as the Dalits, formerly known as Untouchables, Scheduled Castes, or Other Backward Castes. Dalits, in 1980, made up 52 percent of the country's population. The paradigmatic Dalits, the sweeper castes,[33] also called "scavengers,"[34] are condemned to perform tasks such as carrying away human waste and human and animal corpses. Yet Dalits are a vital part of the equestrian storytelling tradition.

A story about the Lalbagi sweeper caste, recorded in North India during the nineteenth century, may be a satire on the Vedic horse sacrifice:

> There is a horse miracle story told in connection with Lal Beg, the patron saint of the sweepers. A valuable horse belonging to the King of Delhi died, and the sweepers were ordered to bury it, but as the animal was very fat, they proceeded to cut it up for food for themselves, giving one leg to the king's priest. The king, suspecting what had happened, ordered the sweepers to produce the horse. They were dismayed by the order, but they laid what was left of the animal on a mount sacred to Lal Beg and prayed to him to save them, whereupon the horse stood up, but only on three legs. So they went to the king and confessed how they had disposed of the fourth leg. The unlucky priest was executed, and the horse soon after died also.[35]

This is a horse sacrifice in the shadow world of the Dalits, where Vedic traditions turn inside out. True, the horse comes back to life (like the horses in the tales of Dhyanu and Harishchand), but not for long, nor does the priest fare well. The point comes through loud and clear: a horse is not a Dalit animal. The three-legged horse in this story may be satirical, like the three-legged horse in the story about the hermit who wins land from the king.

It may seem strange at first that Dalits should be associated with this elite animal, but a traditional reason is provided to explain it: It is said that many low castes, including Dalits, traded leather to the Portuguese in the seventeenth century in exchange for horses. This caused tremendous anger in high castes, since low castes were not supposed to ride on horses (or elephants or palanquins). Some of these horse-owning Dalits were killed and are now worshipped with offerings of images of horses.[36] This argument views the fact that there are now *myths* about horse-owning Dalits as a direct result (or rationalization) of the fact that there once *were* but no longer *are* horse-owning Dalits.

In the late nineteenth century, Hindu traders did not allow the Muslim Boharas to ride on horseback.[37] Rajputs in the 1930s wouldn't let Jats, whom they regarded as a Dalit caste, own horses.[38] In our day, the Indian bias against Dalit horse owners has often been cruelly enforced. On March 31, 2018, BBC News ran a headline: "Indian lowest-caste Dalit man killed 'for owning horse.'" The article went on to state:

A young farmer from the lowest rung of India's caste hierarchy—the Dalit community—has been beaten to death, apparently for owning and riding a horse. Police in Gujarat state said three upper-caste men had been detained for questioning. The victim's father said his son had been warned not to ride the horse as this was an upper-caste privilege. Owning a horse is seen as a symbol of power and wealth in parts of India. . . . Pradeep Rathod, 21, was found dead in a pool of blood near Timbi village in Gujarat State late on Thursday. The horse was also found dead nearby, his father said. In a complaint filed to police, his father said his son had loved horses so he had bought him one. "My son's love for horses led to his murder," the father said according to AFP news agency, which has seen the statement. "About a week ago, when I was riding the horse with my son, one of the persons from the upper caste Kshatriya [warrior] community warned us not to ride the horse in the village. He said that people of Dalit community cannot ride horses, only Kshatriyas can ride horses. He also threatened to kill us if we did not sell the horse," the complaint read.

The *Hindustan Times,* March 30, 2018, ran this headline, "Dalit man killed by upper caste duo in Gujarat for owning, riding a horse," and added some details to the story:

> The Gujarat police has launched a manhunt for two upper caste men who allegedly killed a Dalit man in Bhavnagar district on Thursday night for owning and riding a horse. "The body of Pradeep Rathod (21) was found late on Thursday night from a farm house in Timbi village. The horse that he had bought two months ago was also lying dead nearby," said an official of the Umrana police station in Bhavnagar district. . . . Police said the man's father had told them that Pradeep intended to sell the horse following threats from upper caste villagers but that he had convinced him against doing so. The police said the father had presented his son with a horse as the young man was very fond of riding and raising horses.

Though the murdered boy is a Dalit, his surname, Rathod, is a variant of Rathore, which is generally a Rajput name that is a surname of Pabuji and of Rajput families associated with the breeding of Marwari horses. This may explain Pradeep Rathod's fatal attraction to horses.

TRIBAL HORSES

Closely associated with Dalits as people living in India on the blurred fringes of the pale of Hinduism are the tribal people or Adivasis ("First Inhabitants"), formerly called Scheduled Tribes. Adivasis are seldom owners of horses, but the horses in the tribal art and legends of India rode deep into the interior of the country.

The creation myths of the Birhors and Munda, tribal people of Chota Nagpur, and the Santal tribals of Bengal share a story in which the creator makes the first man and woman out of clay, but then a winged or fiery horse (sometimes named Pankraj [Pakshiraj]) comes and tramples these first creatures, until the gods invent a dog that keeps the horse away. According to a variant told by the Kho in Chitral (the Hindu Kush), before humans were created, the world was populated by horses, who trampled the clay figure of the first man under their feet until a watchful dog protected him from the horse.[39]

Tribal people may not have horses, but they do have many horse images and rituals, which often persist among dynasties that have emerged from a tribal background.[40] The tribal gods ride horses.[41] Across the tribal belt of India, from the

FIGURE 35. Gond horse. Kondh (Khond), Orissa, twentieth century. Metal alloy, beeswax-thread technique, a regional variation of lost-wax casting (dhokra). 4¾ × 1¹¹⁄₁₆ × 5⅝ in. (12.1 × 4.3 × 14.3 cm.) (Philadelphia Museum of Art, Purchased with the Stella Kramrisch Fund, 2002-93-13)

Bhils, Bhilalas, and Kolis in the west to the Santals and Gonds in the east, clay representations of horses are used as votive objects.[42] Some Rajput Bhils worship a deity called Ghoradeva ("Horse God") or a stone horse; the Bhatiyas worship a clay horse at the festival of Dussehra; and the Ojha Kumhars erect a clay horse on the sixth day after the birth of a child.[43] The Korkus, a smaller tribe living in southern Madhya Pradesh, carve tablets naming their dead and depicting them in positions of honor, usually on horseback, and all of the tablets for each village are placed together under a sacred tree.[44] The Gonds often make brass statues of horses.

These tribal horses are often associated with sacrifice—not the sacrifice *of* a horse (to a god) but the sacrifice of a sheep or a goat *to* a horse. The Kunbis (who do actually have real horses) wash their (real) horses at Dussehra, decorate them with flowers, sacrifice a sheep to them, and sprinkle the blood on them. The Gonds (who do *not* have horses) have a horse god, Kodapen, whom they worship at the opening of the rainy season with a stone dedicated to him outside the village. A Gond priest offers a real, live heifer and a pottery image of a horse, saying, "Thou art our guardian! Protect our oxen and cows! Let us live in safety!" The heifer is then sacrificed and the meat eaten by the worshippers.[45] In sacrificing a goat or a heifer to a horse, these tribal people are doing what the Vedic priests did when they killed a goat as part of the horse sacrifice: the (scape) goat carries away the evil from the horse. But unlike the tribals, the Vedic priests killed the horse, too.

BHILS AND RAJPUTS: HORSES TAKEN FROM TRIBALS

The Bhils ruled over their own country, in what was later to become Rajasthan, until the Rajputs arrived and took it from them.[46] Nowadays, there is such a blurred border between Bhils and Rajputs that they intermarry frequently.[47] The Bhils, who have horse rituals but no horses, have taken their equine cult from their neighbors on the north, the Rajputs, who do have horses, while the Rajputs have taken from the Bhils their right to have real horses. Though the Bhils do not raise or own horses themselves, at least their gods are made to ride horses; the Bhils have assimilated from their conquerors, the Rajputs, the values of horse-manship, without the actual use of the horse. These may be attempts by tribal peoples to bring (back) into their own traditions an aspect of Rajput behavior,[48] a step at what one might see as Kshatriyazation:[49] through the (virtual) horse, the Bhils seek and find a higher status, linking the tribal world and that of the feudal aristocracy.

The Bhils, Kolis, and Korkus commemorate fallen heroes with stone slabs engraved with a horse and rider, in an imitation of prestigious Rajput styles. Brass figurines of a rider on a horse play a great role in the Bhil funeral ritual called *nukto,* in which the purified spirit of the dead man is said to ascend to the clan of ancestors and to dwell with God (Bhagavan) in the beyond.[50] In some ways, the Bhils are *plus royaliste que le roi:* they use the Rajput horses in ways that the Rajputs did not. In fact, Rajput memorials generally do not depict horses, or stress the equestrian form of their dead,[51] while the Bhils, through their equine and equestrian rituals, confer on their ancestors the nobility of the horseman, the cavalier. The Rajputs emphasize the qualities of the horse that symbolize power and fertility, playing down the closely related death symbolism of the Vedic sacrificial stallion and the Puranic doomsday mare. But the Bhils bring out the horse's ancient power to symbolize death.

The Bhils appear in Hindu folklore not as people to whom the ownership of the land and the custom of riding horses were denied but, on the contrary, as people who steal other peoples' horses: "Devnarayan had written a letter to Bhuna asking him to free his father's mare Tejan from the Bhils . . . Bhuna fought with the Bhils and freed the mare Tejan."[52] The projection of blame from the usurpers to the usurped in this way is a common feature of mythology everywhere: the people from whom one steals are depicted as thieves from whom one is merely *retrieving* one's own treasure. Thus the *Rig Veda* tells us that Indra took *back* the cows of the Dasas[53]—the demonized natives of the land to which his people had migrated and whose cows Indra himself had stolen. The story of the Bhils' rustling was supported by the always available mythology of the thieving outsiders (or Dalits or tribals), and the myth took root.

Lal Beg, patron saint of the Lalbagi Dalits, is often identified with Zahar Pir, whom we have met as Gugga. So, too, Bhils and Dalits are connected with the story of Pabuji, which is *about* horsey Rajputs but is told *by* Dalit Nayaks (and now sung to nomadic, camel-owning Rebaris).[54] In that story, fighting on Pabuji's side are Bhils (who in this context are regarded as Nayaks), Rajputs, and Rebaris. In one episode, Deval Charan decides to drink up all the blood shed in the battle, which has been flowing together in a single stream; she builds a bank to keep separate the blood that flows from the three different caste groups. But Pabuji objects: "O goddess, let this blood mingle! These have died in my service, they are my own warriors: let their blood mingle. If their blood remains separate, then (in future) Bhils will not protect Rajputs and Rajputs will not protect Bhils, and nobody in the world will recognize Pabuji. Honor my oath, and let the blood of my warriors mingle!" The goddess breaks down the bank, the blood flows together, and she drinks it all.[55] This episode is a vivid and moving parable of the way in which some lower castes have become a part of the cult of horses.

HORSES MYTHS AND RITUALS WITHOUT HORSES

People who do not know horses often fear them. To some extent, the natural reaction to any large animal coming fast right at you is, "It's going to eat me!" This misconception was the source of many myths in which horses devour people, or doomsday flames come out of the horse's mouth. In the story of the jackals that became horses, the fear of the horse's mouth was a clue that the authors of that story were not familiar with horses. But even a Persian translation of a Sanskrit textbook on horse management, presumably from and for people who do have horses, ends with a vivid painting of a mare, her ribs exposed from starvation, who has torn off her ropes, kicked off her back fetters, and is biting the neck of her groom (who is also thin, as well as dark-skinned and almost naked—low caste).[56]

The back hooves of a horse are also feared, and with better reason; in tribal myths, as we have seen, horses trample the original human beings to death. A Sanskrit text from about 900 BCE connects those back hooves with the power of the gods: "When the gods went to heaven, the anti-gods went after them and joined up with them. The gods became horses and knocked the anti-gods away with their hooves. That power of the hooves is the essence of the horse; he who knows this attains whatever he wants. Therefore a horse is the swiftest of animals; therefore a horse strikes backwards with his foot; he who knows this strikes evil away."[57] Even the anti-gods cannot withstand those back hooves.

The myths of horse-owning cultures may sentimentalize the mind of horses, attributing to them human emotions and loyalties. But the myths of non-horse-owning cultures often lack the intimacy and affection toward horses that marks the myths of horse-keeping people, and this lack leads to fantasies of fear and violence. In this context, our original broad working distinction between people in India who have horses and people who do not have horses must now be more carefully qualified. Among people who *have* horses—who know horses and ride them and drive them and feed them and, perhaps, sacrifice them—we must distinguish between ancient kings, who drive white stallions in chariots and are known to us from Sanskrit texts, and more recent aristocrats, like Rajputs, who ride astride black mares and are known to us from contemporary vernacular as well as historical sources. These two subgroups have different, albeit related, horse myths.

Within the non-horse-owning group, we must also distinguish further subgroups. First would be the horse myths of people who have never had any contact with horses at all. Technically, unless one believes (as I do not) that people are born with an archetypal horse in their heads, there can be no such group; people who have literally *no* contact with horses (even by hearing about them or seeing pictures of them) cannot invent them. But there certainly are people who have never actually seen a real live horse. Their myths of horses may be inspired by other peoples' myths of horses, or by pictures or sculptures of horses.

The second non-horsey subgroup would contain people who have no horses now but may once have had horses. Some tribes in the northwest of India who do not have horses are connected with horses through their name, such as the Assakenoi, mentioned by historians who came to India with Alexander the Great, and the Asmakas or Ashvakas;[58] there are even people called "horse-faced" (Ashvamukha, Turaganana).[59] Such names might be derived from the practice of wearing the skin and head of the sacrificed equine victims during feasts.[60] And then there are people like the Bhils, who have been deprived of their horses.

Cultural memory can be long. For people who do not have horses but may have once had them, the horse still holds the memory of meaning. The symbol got into the folk consciousness and then stayed there even after its referent, the horse, had vanished from the scene. As Claude Lévi-Strauss wisely remarks, "[A]n animal that is absent in a new environment can nevertheless retain a metaphysical existence in mythical imagination. . . . [I]f a species is absent in a given environment but remains present in myths, it is then projected into 'another world,' where the semantic functions the myth assigned to it elsewhere—when it was an animal in the real world—are systematically reversed."[61]

Moreover, people who have never had horses may have had or still have direct contact with other people who do have horses (people like Arabs, or in the case of the Bhils, Rajputs). And even though the people of the tribes and villages did not usually *own* horses, they may well have been the people who were employed to *care* for the horses of the richer classes.[62] Such knowledge would, however, still have been limited to a small part of these village or tribal cultures. And the people who told the local stories, and made the local horse images, would not, perhaps, have been the ones who had ridden or even driven horses, let alone sacrificed them. But they may have fed them and groomed them and, indeed, spent more time with them than their owners did. Each of these groups has its own, different sort of horse myths.

In attempting to hear the voices of the often mute village images, we might draw upon what we know people have said about horses in cultures (particularly but not only in India) where horse myths gloss the actual uses of horses. For horses in India may also express more general human responses to horses, concepts that are held in common with and may be illuminated by other cultures.[63] The Greek tragedian Aeschylus contrasted, on the one hand, "beasts yoked in the yokes, made the slaves of trace chain and pack saddle, that they might be man's substitute in the hardest tasks" with, on the other hand, horses "harnessed to the carriage, so that they loved the rein, horses, the crowning pride of the rich man's luxury."[64] The first sort of horses may well have been exploited by the poor, sacrificed to "the hardest tasks," "man's substitute" in slavery, suffering in his place. But the second sort of horses were not always exploited by the rich, whose horses may indeed have "loved the rein," loved the taming. That, at least, is the myth told by people who love horses. Extremes of such love often find their way into the equine epics; one of Pabuji's companions "travelled fast, carrying his horse under his arm when it grew weary."[65]

In Europe and America, when horses vanished from general use after the advent of the steam engine and the automobile, they remained vivid only in certain pockets of the modern world: in the working world of the cattle-herding West of the United States, on dude ranches, pulling carriages for tourists in big cities, and so forth. Among the moneyed and privileged, people still ride to hounds, and in the *imaginaire*, horses thrive in Western movies and in artistic representations in the American West. But horses are no longer widely diffused in art forms in Europe and America, as they were in the nineteenth century[66] — and still are in parts of India. For the myth survives in India even when the mythmakers have no horses; the symbolism has power even where there can be no actual material basis for its importance to the people. What is, finally, one of the most striking things about the mythology of horses in India is that it exists, in such quantity and diversity, in places where horses themselves have never been truly a part of the land.

12 | ✣ | Horses in Modern India

1900 to 2020 CE

THREE TWENTIETH-CENTURY HORSE HEADS

Modern Indian writers found ways to use the ancient theme of horse heads on human bodies to score contemporary points.[1] The Telugu writer Viswanadha Satyanarayana (1895–1976) wrote a short story, entitled "Ha Ha Hu Hu: A Horse-Headed God in Trafalgar Square," about a Gandharva who has the body of a *very* large man, the head of a horse, and, eventually, golden wings. The Gandharva arrives, by some unexplained accident, in Trafalgar Square, is treated very shabbily and stupidly by the English, and eventually leaves.[2]

In the play *Hayavadana* (The horse head), written in Kannada in 1972 by Girish Karnad (1938–2019), a creature with the head of a horse and the body of a human man acts as a foil for two men who accidentally switch heads and spend the rest of the play reconciling their heads to their bodies. As the head is more important than the body, the head of each man eventually changes his transformed body back into the same body he had originally had. Meanwhile, the horse-headed creature in the frame keeps trying to get rid of his horse's head and become all human, but in the end, by the same rule that applied to the men, his body changes to that of a horse, to match his head. And that turns out to be the perfect solution.

A horse head played a central role in a street performance of a play in the Gingee area of South India, in April of 1982. The play is based on the story of the birth of the hero Ashvatthaman in the *Mahabharata,* who got his name ("Voice of a Horse," or "Whinny") because, as soon as he was born, he whinnied like the stallion Ucchaihshravas.[3] The Tamil comedy suggests that Ashvatthaman, generally regarded as an incarnation of a portion of Shiva, is a reverse centaur, with horse head and human body (the more usual Indian form), fathered by Shiva under slapstick rather than Epic circumstances:

FIGURE 36. *Lightning,* M. F. Husain, 1975. (Courtesy of the owners, Kent and Marguerite Charugundla)

Shiva in disguise visits Kripi, Drona's childless wife, and insists that she serve him food, wearing no clothes at all. She weeps and resists, but finally gives in and serves him naked, with only her long hair covering her vagina. At the sight of her, Shiva is overcome with desire and ejaculates into his rice; he then leaves without eating it. Kripi orders her servant to feed the rice to a horse. Offstage, the horse (presumably a mare) gets pregnant, delivers, and dies; onstage, Kripi turns around with a little boy on her arm, plucked from the audience. Drona appears. He finds Kripi's story hard to believe, and at first doubts her chastity, as well as expressing concern that the baby's face looks like that of a horse, while his body is human. But they name the child Ashvatthaman.[4]

This horseplay satirizes the theme, well known from the vernacular equestrian epics, of the foal and prince born from shared food. More broadly, it makes fun of the Epic heroes, the Epic gods, and the whole mythology of mixed marriages and mixed births of humans and horses.

M. F. HUSAIN AND *LIGHTNING*

The artist Maqbool Fida Husain (known as M. F. Husain), who was born in Bombay in 1919 and died in London in 2011, was widely regarded as India's greatest contemporary artist (or, according to Wikipedia, India's "most prolific, saleable, and world-renowned artist"). But he was harassed by lawsuits and warrants for his arrest and threats against his life because of his portraits of nude Hindu goddesses as well as for paintings with political messages critical of the Indian government, and because he was a Muslim. He was accused of "advocating the coupling of Hindu goddesses with beasts of the field," an image familiar from the

ancient Vedic horse sacrifice. After his paintings were ripped apart and his apartment in Bombay bombed, he died in self-imposed exile.[5]

Husain included horses in his paintings for many years, but perhaps his greatest horse painting was *Lightning,* a mural depicting ten horses that he painted in 1975, inspired by Prime Minister Indira Gandhi's Congress Party rally that year in Bombay, and more generally by the "Emergency" in which she trampled into the dust human rights in India. *Lightning* consists of twelve panels, each ten feet high and five feet wide, the largest work Husain ever made. The panels don't connect with one another; they were meant to be moved about and displayed in different sequences from time to time. The ten horses, naked of any saddlery, are bucking and kicking and rearing and plunging, their mouths open.

One horse clearly references the horse in Pablo Picasso's painting *Guernica,* which protested the Nazis' devastating casual bombing practice on the Basque town of Guernica during the Spanish Civil War in 1937. Juxtaposed with *Lightning*'s contemporary references are images of horses that Husain modeled after historical prototypes, such as the horse from T'ang Dynasty tomb pottery and the ink paintings of the twentieth-century Chinese master Xu Beihong.[6] There do not seem to be any Indian referents. Husain has said of *Lightning,* "This is one of my most significant paintings. The horses in 'Lightning' have sheer energy in a minimum of lines. They say that when there is lightning in the sky white horses are cutting across the spaces."[7] It is perhaps significant that the name of the winged horse that carried Muhammad from Mecca to Jerusalem, and up to heaven and back, was Buraq, derived from the Arabic word for lightning.

Daniel Herwitz brilliantly conjures the connection between horses and Mrs. Gandhi's Emergency:

The Emergency came like thunder and lightning: guns, the imposition of state authority, Prime Minister Indira Gandhi riding the whirlwind of power against the forces of corruption, galloping down the streets of the Indian Wild West, fighting the black market, imposing order against Marxist revolt, putting blinders on the unruly horse of history which, reeling from the formation of the Indian nation out of the British Jewel in the Crown, not yet over the tumult of Partition, uneasy with the strong-arm tactics of the Congress Party, could not help but balk. No one expected it any more than anyone can predict the moment lightning will strike. . . . [The horse of history] balked with the fury of horses unleashed into their own unruliness, rose up and kicked at the air, screamed into the blue of space, thrust its body towards the ground, elongating its neck and twisting its haunches, refusing the beauty of its own shape . . . the war of rider against horse, horse against horse. This picture of a moment of lightning when the Indian state is on the verge of collapse is the incarnation of an endless battle between warring families, a remaking of the Mahabharata in contemporary times. . . . And so the Emergency becomes referred to as myth.[8]

The horse is the perfect image to forge this link to the ancient myth, for in horses "freedom, contortion, control, and the fact of headlong immersion into a shifting landscape towards the unknown, become human."[9] And it took a Muslim painter, the inheritor of the great tradition of Muslim paintings of horses, to create this realization of the *Mahabharata* within the complexities of twentieth-century Indian politics.

MARES AT WEDDINGS

Despite such literary and artistic survivals, the only real live horse a visitor to India today is likely to encounter is the horse ridden by the groom in many Indian weddings.

Back in 1891, John Lockwood Kipling had remarked, "Horses take a great part in most Indian weddings. Both Hindu and Muhammadan bridegrooms ride in procession, while the bride is borne in a canopied litter. . . . The equestrian marriage parade is probably an ancient custom based, it may be, on the marriage by capture of which we hear so much."[10] Bridegrooms still ride to weddings on horses, preferably on Marwari horses.[11] But nowadays there is much debate about both the history of this custom and the nature, more precisely the gender, of the horse: is it a mare, a stallion, or a gelding? A fine example of this debate was captured on the pages of an Indian website, on February 25, 2019, under the intrigu-

FIGURE 37. Amit, a bridegroom on a Marwari (or part Marwari) horse at the triple wedding of Bhoju Gujar's daughters, Ghatiyal, Rajasthan, 2011. (Photo by Iqlak Mohammed)

ing heading, "Why do Indian grooms always come sitting on a mare instead of a horse?"[12] Several ingenious, and quite different, answers were offered by eight Indian readers, indicating an impressive knowledge of the history of horses in India, the symbolic value of stallions for the control of the senses (and, sometimes, of wives), the limiting of horses (or just stallions) to the use of the ruling classes, and the decline in the use of horses in the modern period, as well as expressing a rather cynical concern for the groom's possible escape route. The list of eight views reads much like the list of competing opinions in traditional Sanskrit logical debates.[13] I have omitted the names of the contributors and standardized the punctuation, but made no other changes:

1: This is an old tradition of Rajputs, where they used to win brides and take them, riding on horses. Hope you remember Prithvi Raj and Samyukta Love Story.[14] They always rode horses, not mare. That too without castration. [Photograph of a Mughal painting of a man with a woman on a strutting horse; there is a circle in blue drawn around the horse's obvious testicles.] Nowadays, riding horses are kept castrated, to reduce their virity [sic] & power (just reduce ... they are still very powerful) without which it's close to impossible for Todays' Generation (Eating GM Food) to ride or even control a Horse! Now, the reason why groom sits on mare is based on above point only. Mare is docile and easy to handle. No one wants to get embarrassed on Wedding Night!

2: From what I've learnt, the horse and the groom come together to take the bride away and surely two males can't take one female (Pandavas' case not to be considered here);[15] hence the animal has to be a mare. My grandma told me about this, but one thing I've noticed is that there's always a more practical reason for Hindu customs that are very scientific ...

3: I think the most logical reason behind this ritual is as follows (this is my assumption): during that era horses are considered as a main source of transport and expensive (may cost more than a BMW). As the best of the best or most of the horses are saved for army, king and royalty, what is left is used by commoners or civilians, hence mares.

4: Not all Indian grooms do. It is a ritual in some parts of the country.

5: The influential, kings and others of nobility, even rode an elephant or a chariot, and some of the tales in Hindu mythology point to that. But, for others, horse (or a mare) was the practice. I have seen both, bride and the groom, sitting on separate horses, during the marriage procession, in Pandharpur, of Maharashtra. Not only sitting on a mare, the groom is even holding a sword, in parts of north India. The sisters of the groom feed pulses to the mare. Priests have developed some verses for the occasion of the riding of the horse, even though none of this is mentioned in the ancient books of rituals, and the meaning of the verses recited on the occasion have nothing to do with riding the mare. In the medieval age, the marriage was often associated with war, and many a time, the groom had to wage a war to win the bride. That is why the practice of riding a horse (or a mare) [is] associated with marriage. Nowadays, the riding of the mare is just a part of the ritual, and while most of the procession is made to ride the cars, a mare is engaged a few metres away from the house of the bride, for the sake of the rituals. ...

6: Horses have significant importance in Hindu tradition. Some traditions include Ashwamedha Yagna in ancient times, Krishna as a charioteer of Arjuna in Mahabharata, the Sun God driven by 7 horses. It signifies controlling the senses, letting go of childish behavior and entering a new phase of life. Hence a groom riding a "ghoodi" [mare] as it is called in Hindi signifies sacrifice, faithfulness and devotion as the man enters a new phase in his life of being a married person.

7: At that time there was no automobile. Kindly note horse was reserve for kings and forces or Rajpoot. Ghodi (Female horse) is used in marriage not horse.

8: A fun-filled event in entire wedding rituals, where the groom wears a traditional Sherwani and pagdi [long coat and turban] and will be seated on a decorated horse or elephant. According to traditions this ritual shows that an eligible bachelor in their family is going to start a new life. Coming to the question, why he is seated on horse: because one needs to have great control and power to handle a horse, so here it resembles that the groom has the same quality to lead his relationship. In other words, we can say a groom is very anxious to see his bride, so he rides on a horse to reach her. Or we can say that this is his last chance to escape from the wedding.

And that, perhaps, should be the last word on the subject of horses (more particularly mares) at weddings.

BREEDING MARWARIS IN INDIA

Let me conclude these scattered glimpses of horses in contemporary India with a longer tale of a group of horses, Marwaris, that an Englishwoman brought from India to America at the turn of the twenty-first century. The importing of horses has been, as we have seen, a central motif in Indian history, but in this instance that current was reversed, and these horses were *exported from* India. The story of the Marwaris touches on themes that have been woven throughout this book, questions of rational and irrational attitudes to certain breeds of horses.

Marwaris comes from Marwar ("Desert Area"), a district in Rajasthan whose capital is Jodhpur ("City of War"), the same place that gave us those flared riding trousers and short riding boots that the British adopted in the nineteenth century. A Marwari horse is a desert horse with a thick, arched neck, long-lashed eyes, flaring nostrils, and highly distinctive ears that curve inward to a sharp point, meeting to form an almost perfect arch at the tips. Aficionados compare the shape of the Marwari's ears to the lyre, to the scorpion's arched stinger, and to "the Rajputs' trademark handlebar mustaches, turned upright and set on their thick, bushy ends."[16] (The telltale equine ears are the best clue for guessing whether a twentieth-century Hollywood film about India was shot in India or in the deserts of Lone Pine, in Southern California: if the horses in the film have those curved ears, it was shot in India, as both Bollywood and Hollywood usually used Marwaris on location in India, but not in California). They average between 14.2 and 15.2 hands (fifty-eight and sixty-two inches)[17] and often exhibit a natural ambling gait, close to a pace. Nowadays they are used for light draught and agricultural work, riding, and carrying bridegrooms at Hindu weddings. They are said to be passionate, showy, quick-tempered, and brave.

Close to the Marwari horse in many ways, including the special ears, but not quite so tall or long,[18] is the Kathiawar horse, from the Kathiawar peninsula off nearby Gujarat. Another breed, the Balochi, now found in Pakistan, has "pointed ear tips almost touching each other,"[19] a description strongly reminiscent of Marwari horses (which are, after all, bred in that same general area of the subcontinent, Sindh and the Punjab); the Balochi, medium-sized, with a fine head and neck, is noted for its endurance under all conditions. Another breed, the Waziri (which John Lockwood Kipling described in terms also very strongly reminiscent of the Marwari), is also bred in Pakistan, where it is often used for polo.[20]

There are many different stories about the origin of the Marwari horse. According to one widespread narrative, Marwaris were bred from Arabian and Turkmen stock by the Rathores, a clan of Rajputs who were forced from their kingdom of Kanauj in 1193, withdrew into the Great Indian and Thar Deserts, and founded the ruling dynasty of Marwar in around 1212. They bred the Marwari horse for battle, starting with an army of only two hundred animals. Kesar Kalmi, the magical black mare of the Rathore Pabuji, comes from Marwar. Others say that the Marwari is descended from native Indian ponies crossed with Arabian horses (and perhaps some Mongolian influence from the north). Still others argue that the Mughals in the early sixteenth century brought Turkoman horses to supplement the breeding of the Marwari.[21] Another theory is that the Marwari breed originated in northwest India on the Afghanistan border, and in Uzbekistan, Kazakhstan, and Turkmenistan,[22] or that Arabian horses from a shipwreck swam ashore and covered Marwari mares.[23]

The original Marwari horses were said to be small and hardy, more like ponies, but with "poor conformation," until the influence of the infused Arabian blood improved their appearance without compromising their hardiness.[24] We will return to this idea of "conformation," which often means only that the horse's appearance conforms to whatever standard of beauty the writer happens to hold, usually coupled with the assumption (originally among Arab riders and writers but then more widely embraced) that Arabian horses set the standard for equine beauty. A study conducted in 2007 to assess genetic variation among five major Indian horse breeds found that Marwaris were closely associated with Arabian horses, while the four other breeds were supposedly descended from Tibetan ponies.[25]

Penelope Chetwode, in 1980, met with Randhir Singh, formerly chief instructor at the Remount Training School of the Jodhpur Lancers, who was "absolutely crazy about Kathi [Kathiawari] horses," and she recorded this anecdote:

> Many years ago Pandit Nehru asked him [Randhir Singh] what percentage of Arab blood [Kathiawari horses] had and was told about 90%. Randhir Singh told us that were he asked that question today he would reply 10% only! He is convinced from reading old texts in Sanskrit (of which he is a scholar) that the finest horses in the world have come from India. I would not mind betting that he could find a text proving that the Arabian himself originated in the sub-continent![26]

A very similar argument has been made, by Indian nationalists, about all things Indo-European, including horses.

When, in October 2002, the Marwar Horse Society tried to draft a studbook, the first sentence read: "It is difficult to exactly trace the origin of the true Marwari horse with precision, but undoubtedly it has connections with the Arab and may have mixed with the Turkmenian breed and the horses of invading armies." After agreeing to delete the word "undoubtedly," the members of the Society began to argue about the link to the Arabian and Turkmenian horses, as Hindi-speaking breeders insisted that the Marwari could not be a Muslim horse. Eventually, after much haggling, the group settled on a statement that was by then indisputable: "It is difficult to trace the origin of the true Marwari horse."[27]

The Rathores bred into the Marwari horses their most distinctive physical characteristic (the curved ears) and used them for cavalry. At that time, only members of Rajput families and Kshatriya warrior castes were allowed to ride these horses.[28] During the late sixteenth century, the Rajputs of Marwar, under the leadership of the Mughal emperor Akbar, formed a cavalry force over fifty thousand strong.[29] In 1813, a Colonel Stanhope wrote that his regiment, the Seventeenth Dragoons, horsed chiefly in Kathiawar, was better mounted than any other regiment in the service of the East India Company.[30] A century later, during the First World War, the Marwar Lancers (also known as the Jodhpur Lancers) under Sir Pratap Singh fought for the British and defeated a large host of Turks and Germans in the Battle of Haifa (1918).[31]

Englishmen in India during the time of the Raj were in general more appreciative of Marwari and Kathiawar horses than of other native breeds. William Moorcroft had referred to Kathiawar horses as belonging to "those casts [*sic*] of Horses, originally employed as Stallions, possessing certain predominating forms, which by degree have been acknowledged as essential to beauty." He admits that these beautiful Kathiawars were bred by native Indians: "The Khumbaet Rajahs formed a breed, the Katheewar, at an expense almost exceeding belief. This has lasted longer than many others, from local circumstances, and from its former extension, but now touches upon its ruin."[32] But then he qualifies this credit to the native breed, arguing that the Kathiawars had originally been imported:

> The breed called Katheewar, raised by native Princes at great expense, through Parent Stock imported from the countries bordering on the Red Sea and the Persian Gulph, produced the best and finest Horses in India for Military purposes. And at periods, when breeding was much encouraged, these Horses were procurable in great plenty. For a Governor of Guzzerat sent three thousand, as a present to a Moghul Emperor. But within the last twenty years, the breed has much declined both in number and quality, and is now in danger of being lost.[33]

It's worth noting that this idea of the degeneration of this breed was already in the air as early as 1814.

John Lockwood Kipling mentioned what he called "the Waziri horse" which is "remarkable for a lyre-like incurving of the ears, which is a beauty or a defect as the amateur may choose,"[34] and he went on to write, with thinly veiled sarcasm:

> There are several varieties of indigenous horses recognizable at once ... Marwari horses are prized especially by native chiefs for their size and form. . . . The animals most liked are the stallions of Marvvar or Kathiawar. White horses with pink points, piebalds, and leopard spotted beasts are much admired, especially when they have pink Roman noses and light-coloured eyes with an uncanny expression. Their rippled, highly arched necks, curby hocks, rocking gait, and paralytic prancing often proclaim them as triumphs of training. (69, 65)

And he quoted a British expert who referred to "Arabs, Barbs, Marwars, and Kathiawars" as "the finest horses that India could produce" (62).

He also quotes his son Rudyard, who was highly appreciative of the breed: "High above everything else, like a collier among barges, screaming shrilly, a black, flamboyant Marwari stallion, with a crest like the crest of a barb, barrel-bellied, goose-rumped, and river-maned, pranced through the press" (65). Rudyard Kipling also quotes the positive assessment by the English Master of the Horse in his principality in India: "'We've got one stud at Bellara. . . . They raise Marwaris there too, but that's entirely under native management. We've got nothing to do with that. The natives reckon a Marwari the best country-bred you can lay your hands on, and some of them are beauties! Crest on 'em like the top of a wave!" (76, 77).

But Marwaris did not thrive under the British Raj. Since most (though, as we have seen, not all) of the British preferred other breeds,[35] particularly Thoroughbreds and Arabian polo ponies, they neglected the Marwari, along with the Kathiawari,[36] reducing the reputation of the Marwari to the point where even the inward-turning ears, the pride of the breed, were mocked as the "mark of a native horse."[37] The breed further deteriorated in the 1930s, when poor management practices resulted in a reduction of the breeding stock;[38] and Indian Independence, in 1948, led to the obsolescence of warriors on horseback and a decreased need for the Marwari. After Independence, too, the Nawab of Junagadh, one of the chief breeders of Kathiawars, moved to Pakistan.[39]

But it was, ironically, the Rajputs' own glorification of their mounts that nearly proved the Marwaris' undoing at this time. Because the Rajputs had long ago created a "parallel caste system for horses" and barred anyone but Kshatriyas from owning or riding their best horses, the Marwaris had become "a hated symbol of feudalism and oppressive social divisions."[40] Many of the horses were subsequently killed.[41] Then, in 1956, when the Indian government deprived the Rajput noblemen of their estates, including most of their horses, thousands of Marwari horses were shot, castrated, or consigned to hard labor as draft animals or pack horses. Indigenous horse husbandry fell, for the most part, to rural farmers, who preferred small, hardy ponies to larger, more delicate horses.

Marwaris were on the verge of extinction as a distinct breed until the intervention of Maharaja Umaid Singhji in the first half of the twentieth century; the continuation of his work by his grandson, Maharaja Gaj Singh, saved still more Marwari horses. Yet, as a direct result of "indiscriminate breeding practices," in 1995 an estimated only five hundred or six hundred Marwaris remained "untainted by crossbreeding," and as of 2001, by other accounts, only a few thousand "purebred" Marwaris existed.[42]

CONSERVING MARWARIS

Enter Francesca Kelly, born in 1955, the half-English, half-French stepdaughter of Sir Harold Beeley, the United Kingdom's ambassador in Cairo from 1961 to 1964 and again from 1967 to 1969, which meant that Kelly was able to spend much of her childhood in Cairo, galloping about on Arabian horses on the sands surrounding the family's desert retreat. In 1995, Kelly made her first trip to India, soon discovered Marwari horses, and fell for what she described as their "incredible, otherworldly presence" and their "combination of beauty and wildness of spirit."[43] In 1999 she joined an Indian horseman, Raghuvendra Singh Dundlod, to rehabilitate the now "endangered" Marwari horse by breeding "top-quality horses" in Rajasthan.[44] They founded the Indigenous Horse Society of India to encourage breeders to adopt more modern methods.

The danger, they felt, was that "ignorance and indiscriminate breeding"—that is, breeding to mares and stallions of mixed breed and to Marwari horses that lacked the good qualities for which the breed was prized—would lead to the demise of the Marwari as a distinct breed. Most recognized horse breeds are protected by pedigrees that trace the lineages of the "pure" animals back for generations. All registered Thoroughbreds, for instance, are ultimately linked by pedigree to one of the three Arabian stallions brought to England in 1704. Breeds such as Thoroughbreds and Arabians were standardized in Europe and England and the United States by a method that required records, studbooks, and codified breed standards, which define animals that are suited to produce pedigreed offspring. We have noted the rather unsuccessful effort that the British made to establish "scientific" breeding methods to produce better horses in India. We might view the Marwari affair as a direct descendant of that earlier effort.

But in the case of the Marwari, there were no records, no studbooks, and no codified breed standards by which to preserve the integrity of the breed. Considerable interbreeding had already taken place. Without a useful, agreed-upon description of the Marwari and the introduction of a registration system, the breed would remain highly vulnerable, in a sense porous. If we consider the language used in the texts reporting on the Marwari breeding projects,[45] we find patterns suggestive of European ideas about breeding derived from concepts of purity and pollution of race, class, and caste. We recognize these terms from the idea of the Thoroughbred and the concept of racial purity that we encountered in the dis-

FIGURE 38. Francesca Kelly riding her Marwari mare Shanti. Shanti, ridden here as always in a bitless bridle, was the first filly of the stallion GajRaj and one of the six horses that Kelly imported into the United States in 2000. (Photo taken in Chappaquiddick in 2015; courtesy of Francesca Kelly)

cussion of Kipling's *Kim*. That is what it means to standardize a breed—of horses or humans.

And so the Marwar Horse Society (a branch of Francesca Kelly's Indigenous Horse Society of India) organized, in Jodhpur, the first national breed standards conference, where, as we have seen, they encountered difficulties even in agreeing on the history of the breed. At first, the breeders of indigenous horses had no collective strategy for preserving the breed. They despaired of tracing the Marwari foundation sire, but they tried to draft a breed standard, beginning by registering those "prime Marwari specimens" whose immediate sires and dams could be identified.

Kelly's goal was to conserve, not merely to breed, Marwari horses. "The fact that the breed wasn't really being taken care of, either through ignorance or lack of money or appropriate breeding practices, pushed me into finding out as much about them as possible," she said. "I saw these horses, all pegged out like slaves, tied at the head and at the back, nose in the manger, no room to breathe. Nobody was going to ride them. They were the saddest specimens of crossbreeds that you will ever see." She was determined "to continue with creating our own breed standard."[46] And so she and Dundlod and experts from the Indigenous Horse Society defined their own breed standards and subsequently translated them into Hindi. Registration with the society became compulsory for anyone who wanted to export Marwari horses or compete with them in the national indigenous horse show, and the National Research Centre on Equines, located in Hisar (in Haryana), as well as most other veterinary departments, accepted and agreed to disseminate Kelly and Dundlod's breed standards.

EXPORTING MARWARIS

While all of this was happening, Kelly was also fighting a war on another front: she was determined to export some Marwaris to America and Europe. At first, the only step the Indian government had taken to conserve the Marwaris was to block their exportation. In 1992, they banned the export of indigenous horse breeds (though they allowed the export of [presumably Arabian?] polo ponies and Thoroughbreds), and they signed a global biodiversity pact declaring India's indigenous livestock part of the country's "national wealth." "The view was that there were too few [Marwaris] to export them," said Dundlod.[47] The ban drew on sound logic. With the Marwari gene pool already depleted, sending stock overseas seemed foolish, even potentially disastrous. And if, as seemed possible then, the best ones were to be exported, for extravagant prices, to America, the breed in India would be diminished. Moreover, despite a few exceptions, most rare breeds have failed to prosper outside their original homes.[48]

But Kelly decided, "The future of this horse is outside as well as inside India."[49] In 1995, shortly after her arrival in India, Kelly had bought her first Marwari, already with the intention of bringing the horse to the United States. Then, between 2000 and 2006, the Indian government allowed a small number of exports. In 2000, Kelly brought six Marwari horses home with her to her stables on Chappaquiddick, at the end of Martha's Vineyard, an island off the coast of

Massachusetts; after a few years, she moved the horses to Vineyard Haven, at the other end of the island. Since then she has sent a number of mares and stallions to the Kentucky Horse Park, the Musée Vivant du Cheval in Chantilly, Paris,[50] and other sites throughout the world.

Satyendra Singh Chawra, a Rajput breeder, expressed skepticism about the Marwari export project: "One of the strongest arguments in favor of exports is that they have revived a lot of our dying handicrafts, but there's a big difference between handicrafts and horses. There may be a demand [overseas]. But we at the moment do not have adequate stocks to meet that demand."[51] The point about handicrafts is well taken, for even in that area the admitted "revivals" have not been without their costs. Under the Raj, the British encouraged the production of Persian carpets, but particularly carpets with the sorts of patterns and colors that would please the British and European market, thus influencing the very nature of the native industry.

Then, in the mid-twentieth century, the art historian and British administrator William George Archer (1907–79) first made known in England the stunning paintings made by the desperately poor women painters of Mithila, in Bihar. Near the end of the twentieth century several foundations in the United States began to support these women and their art. As a result, Mithila women have preserved rather than discarded their paintings (as they used to do)[52] and have found an international market for their work that has significantly relieved their poverty and given their children a healthier life and a more promising future.[53] The themes of the paintings, however, are no longer purely traditional, but include scenes of social criticism, such as rich women bringing their babies to be vaccinated while poor women are sent away, and political commentary, such as scenes of the attack on the World Trade Center and the burning of the Taj Mahal hotel in Mumbai. They are very different from the paintings that William Archer saw and loved, and much of that difference can be attributed to foreign influences,[54] though some of it is simply an inevitable artistic response to a changing world. The British used to justify their plunder of various Indian artifacts by arguing that they were saving them from extinction. That memory threatens to cast its shadow over the Marwari breed standardization project.

GOOD BREEDING, AND OTHER SUBJECTIVE CULTURAL ASSUMPTIONS

European and American ideas of breeding influenced the choice of horses that were registered as pure Marwaris in India. The danger that Francesca Kelly's project would change the Marwaris into horses that suited European rather than Indian tastes at first seemed very real. Insisting on certain criteria for breeders raised the danger of exerting on the Marwaris in India the same external influence that had changed the carpets and the Mithila paintings.

But Kelly was determined "to continue creating our own breed standard."[55] In 2018, she said:

> I select by eye alone, maintaining a vigilant eye on lineage but not always. Conformation of the Marwari has greatly evolved in the last decade with a fair amount of out-crossing to the Thoroughbred and other non-Orientals even to maximize height, which I don't support as it dilutes the desert characteristics and strengths of the Oriental influences of the past. In essence, balanced conformation, beauty and soundness are my guidelines. Much as judging any other breed. The Marwaris' distinctive temperament, ears and eyes, all make for exceptional character, and one wants to see this in hand and under saddle.[56]

These are historically and scientifically informed criteria. In particular, Kelly was determined to breed not only for soundness, intelligence, and health but also for those qualities that have historically made the Marwari unique, qualities that we know from centuries of verbal and artistic representations of Marwaris—the curved ears, of course, but also many other particular characteristics of the breed. In this, Kelly is part of a broader British movement to preserve indigenous species and indigenous qualities in many areas, including breeds that have been manipulated, often with a loss of soundness and/or intelligence, further and further from the early unique types. This is surely a good idea.[57]

At the same time, there are highly subjective criteria involved in the judgment of such qualities as beauty, always in the eye of the beholder. ("The owner's eye maketh the horse fat,"[58] is a wise old saying in horsey circles.) More particularly, equine beauty is in the eye of the beholder's culture, in this case, British culture. Kelly chooses horses that are sound, but also that are beautiful—in English eyes. Indian standards of equine beauty, which often echo *ashvashastra* ideals, are very different from British or American standards. For example, although Marwaris can be bay, gray, chestnut, palomino, piebald, skewbald,[59] or white, the official breed colors are bay, black, chestnut, roan, piebald, skewbald, dark brown, dun, and gray. The white horses that are bred specifically for religious use in India (including weddings) are generally not accepted into Marwari stud books, as white has not been a traditional color among Marwaris. But Indian breeders consider black horses unlucky, as the color is a symbol of death and darkness, while they consider horses lucky if they have the white markings of a blaze and four white socks.[60]

The shadow of the *ashvashastras* falls even more heavily on other equine qualities, such as hair whorls and their placement, which are important to Indian horse breeders but not to British and European breeders. Horses with long whorls down the neck are called *devman* and considered lucky, while horses with whorls below their eyes are called *anusudhal* and are unpopular with buyers.[61] Whorls on the fetlocks are thought to bring victory.[62] Indian breeders also expect Marwari horses to have correct proportions, based on the width of a finger, said to be the equal of five grains of barley. For example, the length of the face should be between twenty-nine and forty fingers, and the length from the poll to the dock should be four times the length of the face.[63]

Indian breeders continue to breed Marwaris by their own standards. The annual horse and camel fair held in Pushkar, Rajasthan, is the country's largest gathering of horse breeders. There, men who had been excluded from the decision-making process at the conference that decided the "breed standards" continue to breed by far the largest number of Marwari horses in the world. And so the Marwari horse is not, in fact, constrained by the breed standards of the Indigenous Horse Society. The Persian carpet/Mithila painting/European taste danger is a danger only if it is the only, or primary, available option, and in fact there are many Marwari options. America and Europe are now enriched by a critical mass of magnificent Marwari horses, but not at the expense of India. Some follow the new breed standards and some the traditional *ashvashastra* standards; there are more Marwari horses, and more varieties of them, and more people get to enjoy their beauty. This, too, is surely a good thing.

POSTSCRIPT: TWO ENGLISH HORSEWOMEN

When I first heard Francesca Kelly's voice on the phone in 2008, for a split second I thought it was the voice of Penelope Chetwode coming to me from 1986: the strong, confident voice of a well-bred Englishwoman who had been put up on a pony before she could walk, had lived her whole life among horses and was used to telling large unruly animals what to do and having them do it, a voice that often seemed to be set in upper-class upper-case letters. As I began to get to know her, Francesca's all-consuming love of horses and her deep knowledge of them also conjured up Penelope for me.

Moreover, Penelope had actually anticipated, by two decades, Francesca's ambitions to "save" an Indian breed, in Penelope's case the Kathiawari, the closest thing to a Marwari. In December 1979 (when she was sixty-nine years old), Penelope had paid her first visit to the Paddocks, the Government Stud Farm near Junagadh, in Saurashtra, that had been established before Independence by the Nawab of Junagadh. Penelope's concerns ring a familiar bell:

> A real effort is being made to save and improve the breed. . . . The young stock were often backed as yearlings which did NOT improve their hocks, and this is one important point which the new studs . . . have got to concentrate on. Others are to get them deeper through the heart, as most Kathi horses are very rangy at present, and to improve their necks, which are on the weak side so that they easily become stargazers. That this is going to be possible I can vouch for as I rode three stallions and one mare, all of which had good conformation—minus the faults listed above—and gave me a series of delightful rides.[64]

She commented on the fact that (for reasons we have often noted) the local farmers particularly liked a white-grey stallion, "as colour and lucky marks still play a considerable part in horse-breeding in the Indian peninsula!"[65] She traveled on to a number of other studs, rode many other stallions and mares, and was in general full of praise for the horses ("sweet-tempered and free from vice") and helpful suggestions for the trainers, such as handle the mares regularly, lead the foals out after their dams,[66] use a Cavesson noseband, use a snaffle, lunge the young horses in head-collars, and, above all, don't use heel-ropes: "If I were a horse this would TURN ME INTO A BADMASH"[67] (Urdu for a hooligan or rogue). (Lockwood Kipling had also complained about those heel-ropes, and Francesca Kelly had bemoaned the horses "tied at the head and at the back.")

Penelope's great love was Arabians (and, in India, Kathiawaris); Francesca's, Marwaris. But the three breeds are similar in many ways and in their contrast with Thoroughbreds—smaller, more lithe, more curved, more self-willed, more playful, more graceful. Discovering the bonds between Penelope and Francesca, I felt a sense of closure, the two ends of my life with horses, and of my book about horses, rising to touch one another gently, like the ears of a Marwari horse.

13 | ✿ | The Gift Horse

Throughout Indian history, horses have belonged only to people who were not merely economically "other" than the Indian villagers but politically and often religiously other. Any Indian equine tradition is likely to reflect the influence of the many foreigners who brought horses into India. The first waves of these foreigners established the first patterns of Indian horse myths and horse rituals, patterns that we may still detect in contemporary folklore. But the themes are not merely repeated, parroted; they are changed, challenged. The fact that they often appear in inversion, or even, perhaps, in subversion, may suggest a submerged, perhaps even repressed, resistance against the imported equestrian forms.

Though these foreign equestrians were often of low (or no) social status in the caste system, they had to have had superior political or economic or military powers to be able to afford the cost of maintaining horses in India. The horse represented this power, the power of the sorts of people that make other people want to tell them to "get down off your high horse." The punitive military expedition rode into the village on horseback, trampling the crops; the tax collector rode into the village and took away nine-tenths of the year's harvest, leaving the villagers to near starvation; policemen and petty officials were mounted and everyone else was not. Materially, the horses and their owners were the enemies of most Indian villagers. There is still a Hindi saying that advises you, "Stay away from the fore of an officer and the aft of a horse." It was as wise to avoid those people as to keep out of the range of those back hooves. Tribal mythologies in India speak of horses trampling to death the first humans created by the gods, and, over the centuries, Indian artists depicted horses trampling on people. No wonder that horses were demonized and treated cruelly in some of the texts created by Indians who did not have horses.

FIGURE 39. Rider on a stallion riding over a man. War scene, Narumpunathaswamy Temple, Tiruppudaimarudur, Tamil Nadu, seventeenth century. (Photo by Anna Lise Seastrand, 2007)

Horses remained Kshatriya animals, with all the negative connotations of that class—power, domination, extortion, death—to which was sometimes added another factor: some of these equestrian Kshatriyas were not Hindus but Muslims. The Indo-Persian poet Amir Khusrau (1253–1325), spoke of the forces of Ala-ud-din Khalji (r. 1296–1316) destroying the Shiva linga in the Nataraja temple in Citamparam as "the kick of the horse of Islam."[1] The poet Vidyapati, in the early fifteenth century, included horses in a damning condemnation of "Turks":

The Turks coerce passersby into doing forced labor.
Grabbing hold of a Brahmin boy, they put a cow's vagina on his head.
They rub out his *tilak* and break his sacred thread.

FIGURE 40. A horseman tramples a foot soldier. *Nata Ragini,* made in Malwa Region, Madhya Pradesh, ca. 1650–60. Opaque watercolor with gold on paper. Image 7 7/16 × 5¾ in. (18.9 × 14.6 cm.). (Philadelphia Museum of Art, Gift of Stella Kramrisch, 1987-52-3)

They want to ride on horses. They use rice to make liquor.
They destroy temples and construct mosques.[2]

"They want to ride on horses"—apparently that is a sin tantamount to destroying temples.

In the seventeenth century, a Hindu from Afghanistan insisted that, when he died, he wanted to be buried where he couldn't hear the hoof steps of Mughal horses.[3] And in the nineteenth century, the British preference for Muslims (in part because the Muslims were better horsemen than the Hindus) generated great resentment. One nineteenth-century story depicts the wicked cobra king, Tatig the Nag (the Naga Takshaka), "reading the books of the wisdom of the Quran."[4] But, as we have seen, Muslim ideas and Muslims often played a positive role in the lore of horses in India. The equine mythology of India reveals a surprisingly affirmative attitude to the many foreign equestrian rulers of India.

THE MYTH OF HORSES FROM THE WATER

In many myths, magical horses come down to earth from heaven. This is an old theme in world mythology, reflected in the pervasive Indian notion of the horse as a semidivine creature, and it was enriched in India by the historical memory of horses coming down from the northern mountain passes, as close to heaven as anyone could imagine. In the story of Desingu, the horse comes from the sky but also from the Muslims. These Muslims are the enemies of the ruler—they kill Desingu—but they are also the source of the magic horses.

There are even more stories about magical horses that come from the waters, the old myth compounded by the historical experience of the importation of horses from the sea. (The idea that horses come out of the water may also have been fortified by the easily observed fact that they so often try to get [back] into it. As Francesca Kelly remarked of her prize Marwari brood mare, Shanti, on the shores of the North Atlantic, "She loves the water. It is hard to keep her out of it if we are near the ocean."⁵) Before drawing together the threads of this theme, let us consider just one more story (well, two more) about horses coming into India from the water.

A group of Chinese pilgrims came to India in the seventh century CE to bring Buddhist texts back to China. They told a mythologized version of their own story, the story of foreigners who came to India from another world:

> To the north of a city on the eastern borders of India, in front of a Deva temple, there is a great dragon lake. The dragons, changing their forms, couple with mares. The offspring is a wild species of horse ("dragon-horse"), difficult to tame and of a fierce nature. The breed of these dragon-horses became docile. This country consequently became famous for its many excellent horses.⁶

Since Chinese dragons are part horse, part snake (sometimes part bird), it was a simple matter for the Chinese pilgrim to assimilate his native dragon myth to the Indian myths of horses and Nagas from a watery underworld. The exotic magical horses fertilize the native mares, as the wild become tame.

Another version of this story was recorded among the Pamirs of the Himalayas:

> The lakes are believed to be full of sea-horses, especially lake Shiva in Badakhshan and lake Yashilkul in High Pamir. During the night these sea-horses

come out of the water to graze and pair with the horses in the fields; this cross-breeding is said to be very good for the breed. To venture out onto these lakes is fatal, as the sea-monsters would immediately pull one down into the deep.[7]

The cross-breeding is good for the horses but not for the humans who own the horses—a fine example of the ambivalence with which Indian folklore regards horses, particularly horses who come from foreigners. As long as the cross-breeding takes place only among animals, it is entirely welcome; this is a theme repeated in a number of texts. But it is worth wondering whether this welcome fertilization is not a remarkably positive displacement onto the animal world of the widespread human experience of rape at the hands of invading foreign armies.[8]

These stories know that, whether from the sky or the sea, the best horses came to India from somewhere else. One simple reason for the positive attitude to the visitors from heaven/mountains and the sea is the belief that there would not be horses in India—or, at least, not such good horses—but for these foreigners.

THE SEVENTY-TWO RIDERS OF KUTCH

A story about horses from the sea was told from time to time about Kutch (also spelled Katch, Cutch, or Kachchh), on the Arabian Sea, in Gujarat. Kutch is where Abu'l Fazl, the Mughal historian, said the best horses in India were bred,[9] and where Moorcroft had seen mares that he thought might be suitable for the British army.[10] Volume 5 of the 1880 *Gazetteer of the Bombay Presidency* cites sources from 1610 that speak of a Cutch Raja "who had a greed of horses 'not to be matched in the east.' They were valued at £1500 (Rs. 15,000) and were said to be far above the Arabians not only for swift running, but for staying power, 'so that a man might ride one of them almost at full speed a whole day and never draw bit.'"[11] The *Gazetteer* goes on to speak highly of these horses: "Cutch horses have long been held in much esteem. Generally a little over fourteen hands, they are well made, spirited and showy in action, with clean bony limbs, thin long neck, large head and cheeks, outstanding ram-like brow, full sparkling eyes, and small soft ears. His chief defects are his ill temper, the length of his cannon bone, and his ugly heavy brow. . . . The trade in horses is small. A very few are imported from Sindh."[12] But it precisely on this matter of the importing of horses into Kutch that the mythology takes over, in the *Gazetteer* narrative about the Sanghars, mixed Hindu and Muslim cattlemen who lived on the north shore of the Gulf of Cutch:

[One] story is that in the eighth century of the Christian era, King Punvar oppressing the Sanghars, they sought the aid of some foreigners from western Asia. Seventy-two horsemen came, and, establishing themselves on a hill three miles from Punvaranogad, took the fort and killed the chief. . . . In their honour the Sanghars made images of the seventy-two horsemen, set them on a railed platform in Punvaranogad, with their faces toward the south, and instituted a fair on the second Monday of *Bhadrapad* (September– October). This fair lasting two days is attended by about 16,000 pilgrims, mostly Cutch Hindus.[13]

Throughout the twentieth century, villagers in Kutch continued to make statues of the seventy-two men and one woman, mounted on horses, and to offer sweet rice to the horsemen and ask them for boons.[14]

The incident at the heart of this story allegedly took place in 985 CE, when a ruler named Punvro (also known as Punvar or Punvaro) had built the stronghold of Padhargadh (also known as Punvaranogad) and then is said to have "cut off the hands of his chief architect to prevent that great artist from doing similar work for another prince." Soon after that, the legend continues, seven Sanghars who worshipped the god Jakh came to Kutch from Byzantium. They offended Punvro (there are several versions of what precisely it was that they did), who imprisoned and tortured them; they prayed to their god Jakh, who came from Byzantium with seventy-one brothers and a sister; they killed Punvro and destroyed Padhargadh. The story, still retold in Kutch in the twentieth century, sometimes adds that "white-skinned, horse-riding foreigners from Central Asia" were the ones who came and freed the Sanghars from Punvro.[15]

Other versions of the story say that the seventy-two riders, including one woman, came from the sea, and that after the riders saved the local villagers from the depredations of a demon, their horses were sent to Delhi and, on the way, fertilized the local mares;[16] or, according to another variant, the riders blessed childless women, including the Queen, with children.[17] Seeing a connection between Jakhs and Yakshas, the *Gazetteer* tells us that "the Sanghars, out of respect for the saviours, called them Yakshas after the fair-skinned horse-riding demi-gods of that name."[18] Most versions of this myth emphasize the skin color of the foreigners; they were "white-skinned foreigners said to have come in the thirteenth century from Anatolia and Syria,"[19] or "white-skinned, horse-riding foreigners from Central Asia," or Greeks, Romans, Scythians, or White Huns, "tall and of fair complexion, blue- or grey-eyed."[20] According to the *Gazetteer,* most of the

Sanghars of Cutch "worship *jakhs* or white horsemen."[21] And the *Gazetteer* speculates on the whiteness of these riders:

> According to both Brahman and Buddhist writings the Yakshas are a class of superhuman beings, white, handsome, and mounted on horseback. Mentioned in the Veda, they are generally supposed to have been a Himalayan tribe with whom the Aryans had dealings, during, or soon after, their entry in India. Who the Cutch Yakshas were is doubtful. Fair horsemen from the west, the fact that their traces remain only on the coast would seem to show that they came by sea. This excludes from the number of possible Yakshas, the Greeks (324 B.C.), the Yuetchi or Indo-Skythians (100 B.C.–100 A.D.), and the White Huns (500 A.D.). There remain the Romans of the first, the Persians of the sixth, and the Arabs of the eighth centuries. The Romans may be rejected. Their invasion is doubtful, and they could hardly have brought horses. Arabs too seem unlikely. They would strike the Cutch people as ruddy not as white, and by their conquest of Sind and their attacks on western India, the Arabs were too well known to become centres of legend. It therefore seems probably that these Yakshas were the Persians who, at that time the chief seafaring nation in the Indian seas, in the sixth century conquered the lower Indus, but did not settle, withdrawing as soon as the local ruler agreed to pay tribute.[22]

L. F. Rushbrook Williams remarks that "a number of British, and even of Indian, writers have set themselves to extract whatever solid basis of historical fact may underlie this mixture of credulity and folk-lore, and could thus serve to account for the unique Jakh temples with their curious equestrian images, which Kutch alone possesses."[23] He scorns what he refers to as "the 'standard' account of Kutch (otherwise a generally reliable source) in Volume V of the *Gazetteer*" (83). And he offers, instead, from "'memorialized history,' passed down through many generations of the Royal Bards of the Jadeja dynasty, a perfectly consistent and intelligible version of the Jakh affair, which, so far as the present writer knows, is here written down for the first time" (86). This is his version:

> Early in the reign of Punvro, there arrived on the shores of Kutch seventy-two men and one woman. They had been shipwrecked and they landed on rafts at the anchorage of Jakhao, the name of which still preserves their style or title of Jakhs. They were tall and of fair complexion, blue- or grey-eyed. . . . It was thought they came from somewhere near Byzantium. . . . They were well-

liked and were presented with horses so that they could travel about more easily. (86)

This telling emphasizes the arrival by sea and makes the horses native rather than imported, the gift *from* rather than *to* the people of Kutch. As Williams's story continues, eventually the Jakhs' popularity made Punvro nervous; he persecuted them and one of them killed him; his widow, in revenge, had them all murdered. The people revered them as saints and set up temples to them (87). Williams speculates that they may have been "adventurous members of the Varangian Guard of the Byzantine army," or, more likely, "Zoroastrians from the northern parts of Iran, who, during the whole of this period, were emigrating to India in search of the religious toleration which Islamic persecutors denied them in their own country" (88). And he remarks that the Parsis of Bombay have a tradition that some of the ships bringing their ancestors from the coast of Iran to the coast of India went astray . . . perhaps north to Kutch?

Stella Kramrisch argues, however, that these riders are not people fleeing from Muslims, but Muslims themselves: "Harking back to other, untold memories from Inner Asian horse-herding cultures, these apocalyptic horsemen transmute the fear generated by Muslim invasions into India into a liberating legend in which the evil power does not come from outside but is local, embodied in the tyrant Punvaro."[24] The myth of Punvro, in Kramrisch's gloss, turns the usual story on its head, telling us that the Muslims saved the good citizens of Kutch from their tyrant, an inversion of the self-serving British story, still repeated widely in Chennai today, that the British, especially the early East India Company, liberated Hindus in South India from Muslim control and played not merely a neutral but a positive role in establishing an evenhanded attitude to all religions in its new territory.[25]

Thus, different variants of the equestrian myth cast different actors as the native villain and the foreign heroes. As the nature of the foreigners changes, so does the nature of the tyrant. The story of Punvro may have grafted upon the widespread myth of the tyrant who cuts off the artist's hands not "untold memories" of Inner Asia but, perhaps, a memory of such an act of cruelty perpetrated by an ancient ruler, or another, much more historically specific, myth about the British. For the British treated the weavers in Bengal so cruelly (there is abundant testimony about this)[26] that agents of the Raj were widely believed (apparently on no evidence) to have cut off the weavers' thumbs, or (on the basis of one piece of dubious evidence) to have so persecuted the winders of silk that they cut off their own thumbs in protest.[27] The legend lived on into the end of the twentieth century in a myth about an artisan from Kutch who made a diabolically clever box with a gun inside it, which fired when anyone opened the box. He gave it to the Marquess of Dalhousie, the governor general of India, who gave it in turn to his adjutant to open; the adjutant was killed, and Dalhousie had the crafts-man's hands cut off.[28] The myth of the weavers' thumbs may also have been en-hanced by a memory of the famous *Mahabharata* story of Ekalavya, a low-caste boy whose skill at archery rivaled that of Arjuna, the greatest of the noble Pan-davas; to maintain the Pandavas' supremacy as archers, their teacher demanded that Ekalavya cut off his right thumb, which the obedient boy did.[29]

The myth that depicts benevolent foreigners bringing horses into India also underlies an older myth about Kutch. Abu'l Fazl wrote, "It is said that a long time ago an Arab cargo ship was wrecked and driven to the shore of Kutch; and that it had seven choice horses, from which, according to the general belief, the breed of that country originated."[30] This myth (which also bears a suspicious resemblance to the versions of the Punvro story in which the foreign saviors, sometimes said to number seven, with or without horses, are wrecked on the shore of Kutch) was then adapted into a tradition that the Arab horses swam ashore and fertil-ized Marwari mares or were taken to the Marwar district and used as foundation bloodstock for the Marwari.[31] Penelope Chetwode knew this as a story about Kathiawaris and Mughals, and about a deliberate, historical landing rather than a mythologized shipwreck:

> It is an established fact that the Moghul Emperors, during the sixteenth, seventeenth and eighteen centuries, imported a large number of Arabian horses in India, and that these were landed at Saurashtrian ports on the west coast. They were then led or ridden to Delhi or Agra or Lahore, and on the way may well have been allowed to cover some of the country-bred mares. In the late nineteenth century the Nawab of Junagadh, and possibly some other lo-cal rulers, imported Arabian stallions and used them in their studs. However, none of these facts can explain the enchanting little ears of the Kathi breed.[32]

We have seen another version of this myth in one of the tales of Pabuji, when a glorious horse comes out of the sea and fertilizes Pabuji's mare, who gives birth to a magical foal.[33] The mythology of shipwrecked Arabian sires surfaces in Ireland: it is said that Irish horses owe much of their beauty to the infusion of Arab blood resulting from the wreckage of the Spanish Armada off the Galway coast in 1588:

the men swam ashore and fertilized the women (hence the "Black Irish" of Galway), while the stallions swam ashore and fertilized the mares (hence the Arab heads of Connemara ponies).[34] Here, unlike the Indian tales, the story draws a direct, though still positive, link between the desirable fertilization of the mares and what might well have been the rape of the women.

The Kutch traditions may or may not know the ancient Vedic myth of the hegemonic horse trampling the native/demonic serpent; we have here the anthropomorphic, and quasi-historical, form of the myth, foreign horsemen trampling natives. The corpus of myths that depict foreigners bringing horses into India seems to have assimilated the historical experience of the importation of horses not only to the lingering vestiges—the cultural hoofprints, as it were—of Vedic horse myths but also to the more widespread theme of magical horses brought from heaven or the watery underworld. The Vedic horsemen are replaced by Arabs or Anatolians or, by implication, the British, while the Dasyus, or Vedic Others, are replaced by a demon or a tyrant. This plasticity kept the myth alive in widely varying contexts,[35] which express, in very different ways, the ambivalent connection between horses and foreigners. The Vedic bias is maintained: the foreign horsemen, whoever they are, are the heroes. In all instances, the foreigners ride to the rescue of the natives, like the American cavalry arriving, in old Hollywood movies, to save the women and children from people ironically called "Indians." But with such different actors playing the roles (the Vedic horsemen replaced by Arab horsemen, their enemies the Dasyus by a Patan tyrant), is it really the same myth at all? I think it is, though another historian of religions might not.

The confusion of the villains and the heroes in the story of Punvro is no accident; the myth is rife with obfuscation. Certainly it is a myth about, and probably by, foreigners to India, a myth that manipulates the native symbolism of horses and snakes in such a way as to make the foreigners the heroes, the natives the villains, in a myth that then took root within the folklore of the natives. It's all done with mirrors, which is to say, with myths. We must take account of the people who constructed this myth, who perpetuated it, recorded it, translated it, selected it. The popular legends concerning the horses of Kutch were first collected on the spot and written down by Major (later Sir) Alexander Burnes in 1826;[36] they were embodied in volume 5 of the *Gazetteer of the Bombay Presidency* in 1880 and copied, with minor variations, by several people. It is not hard to guess why the British might have wanted to preserve this myth. But we are still hard pressed to explain the acceptance and perdurance in India of other forms of this mythology of liberating foreign horsemen, such as the myth of the jackal horses, which is unlikely to have been subjected to British mediation.

LEVELS OF POWER

The relationship at the heart of all mythologies joins the supernatural powers—gods and demons—with humankind, heaven and hell with earth. In India, the gods have power over humans, sometimes cruelly used, sometimes the source of all that is desired. And what humans are to the gods, horses are to humans. Like the villagers who worship them, horses have been robbed of their freedom by human beings who made up stories about horses. For people who do not have horses, taming—particularly brutal taming—may appear as exploitation. And, on another level, the relationship between horse-having people and horse have-nots certainly involves exploitation. The myths of those who do and those who do not own horses differ not merely because one group knows horses better (and hence creates a mythology more accurate in horse lore and, perhaps, more sympathetic to the horse) but because many equine myths are inspired not merely by the horse itself but by the *relationship* between the horse and humans, a relationship that may come to symbolize other human relationships: sexual, political, parental, or all of the above. And this interactive factor will clearly play different roles in the myths of people who have different sorts of contact with real horses.

A power relationship is expressed through the symbolism of horses in contrast with serpents, on the one hand, and riders, on the other. God is to rider as rider is to horse as horse is to snake. First comes the power structure between gods and humans, then between humans and horses, and then between horses and snakes. Onto this basic pattern the people of India superimposed, like so many plastic overlays on an anatomical model of the human body, several parallel relationships expressed through horses, between people of power (physical, political, economic, or religious) and people without such power—between men and women, foreigners and natives, British and Indians, and Hindus and Dalits or tribals. These relationships supply not only the background but much of the foreground of the complex equine myths, the message as well as the medium. Power and domination travel down the line from gods to rulers to villagers as from riders to horses to snakes. But who is represented by the horse in each story, who by the serpent, and who is the rider?

Horses are, after all, contradictory symbols of human political power. Horses are animals that invade other horses' territory, but their first instinct is always not to attack but to run away. Some humans think of horses as lions (or jackals), but horses often behave as if they think of themselves as deer. The fragility of horses is well represented by the fragile, ephemeral medium in which villagers usually represent them: clay. And think of the tormented horses in Picasso's *Guernica* and Husain's *Lightning.* Horses are prey rather than predators, as is evidenced by the fact that they have their eyes toward the back of their heads, the better to bolt, rather than in the front, like the cats and other hunters, the better to attack. Horses flee, fast, from predators, protecting themselves with their best weapon, their hind legs. When the gods become horses, they kick backward rather than attack from the front. But the myths also suggest a contrast between wild horses as predators and tame horses as prey. Horses are thus seen as simultaneously vulnerable and dangerous, fragile and powerful, frightened and angry, victims and victimizers, a ready-made natural/cultural metaphor apt for the uses and misuses of political power.

The history of the mythology of horses in India demonstrates the ways in which the people of India first identified horses with the people who ruled them on horseback and then identified themselves with the horses, in effect positioning themselves as their own exploiters. A Marxist might view the survival of the mythology of elite horses among the proletariat as an imposition of the lies of the rulers upon the people, an exploitation of the people by saddling them with a mythology that never was theirs nor will ever be for their benefit, a foreign mythology that distorts the native conceptual system, compounding the felony of the exploitation itself. A Freudian, on the other hand, might see in the native acceptance of this foreign mythology the process of projection or identification by which one overcomes a feeling of anger or resentment or impotence toward a more powerful person by assimilating that person into oneself, *becoming* the other,[37] a kind of equine Stockholm syndrome.

Like all great symbols, horses are often susceptible not only of inversion—the horse of the conqueror becomes the horse of the conquered—but also of subversion, in which the values of the conquerors are first assimilated and then reversed by those who are conquered, expressing, as it were, the snake-eye view of horses, but in a positive light. At what point do structuralist inversions turn into Marxist subversions? But this is subversion turned on its head, as it were, subversion inverted, subversion from the bottom up.

And this is not all that is happening.

THE STRANGER'S GIFT

Though there is much to be said for this set of interpretations, in this final lap of the track I would want to augment them by pointing out that horses are potent natural symbols of things other than political and economic power. The village terra-cotta horses may express an implicit wish for the power of the horse itself—horsepower in the true sense of the word: strength and fertility and beauty and freedom. For the taming of horses often functions as a metaphor for the taming of human sexuality as well as human violence.

The myth of horses was, like the horses, a gift from the sea, or from the sky—from another world that was generous, even if only accidentally and ambivalently generous, divine as well as demonic. We know we should not look a gift horse in the mouth (to guess its age from the erosion of its teeth, a fairly reliable criterion), because we don't want to appear ungrateful (and perhaps because people who don't understand horses fear their mouths). But we learn from Indian history that it is often necessary to look a gift horse in the myth. Where horses gave the nobles power, horse myths gave the villagers another kind of nobility, if only through glimpses of the glamor of the dominant classes (such as the Rajputs) or the political power of the conquerors (such as the Mughals or the British). The association of horses with Indian kings contributed to the continuing popular identification of horses with power and the gods,[38] as symbols of royalty and grandeur. The villagers may be worshipping horses in order to gain some of that power for themselves. This is an otherness not loathed but admired, not despised but coveted; it is an otherness that has been assimilated into the native system of values. This yoke, at least, the villagers, like good horses, willingly accepted.

Horses are also worshipped for their beauty, which people continue to care about even when it is clearly not in their best interests to do so. From early times, horses were not just something to be eaten, hunted, or worked; they were valued for the direct impact of their beauty, and were decorated to emphasize that beauty. Horses are numinous; they captivate the eye, they inspire desire, they have magic. Their allure infects even people who know, on a rational level, that horses aren't good for them. And this allure is what Indian artisans try to capture in their religious images; it is what makes them treat horses like gods. The foreigners' horses became a positive factor in the lives of those whom they conquered or dominated, the myths and images of horses a source of beauty that was a surrogate for the real horses that the conquered people could not own, just as horses were a surrogate for humans in the sacrifice and in the heaviest work in the fields.

Horses have played an essential role in the life and religion of all the people who have had direct contact with them, and India was no exception; horses have been charismatic symbols throughout Indian history. In the end, then, horses are the sign of desire; they symbolize whatever one longs to have. (Perhaps this aspect of horses underlies the old English saying: If wishes were horses, all beggars would ride.) In this, horses are like dreams, in Freud's view: for the poor and the oppressed, they are wish fulfillments. The Hindus speak of a "wishing-cow," a *kama-dhenu,* that one can milk of whatever one wants. If cows grant all desires through the metaphor of milk, horses grant all desires through the metaphors of taming and heavenly flight, becoming "wishing-horses" or *kama-ashvas.*

Horses can easily become symbols of sex, politics/economics, and religion (what Hindus call *kama, artha,* and *dharma*), holding out great hope for anyone who has been unable to win a share in that triad of human goods. Horses, who are sexually vibrant, politically luxurious, and supernaturally beautiful, have a strikingly ambivalent hold on the unconscious of people who want sacred/royal power, martial power, economic and political power, as well as fertility, or sexuality, or eroticism. The images of horses also give shape and intensity to those dark forces that are the shadows of the happier human qualities that make people who have horses love them. Hippophilia and hippophobia are two sides of the same coin; we are crazy about horses, one way or another.

In India, where most people don't have horses, horses may well take on their shadow persona, as an *un*fulfilled wish, as the symbol of what one *doesn't* have, of what is possessed by someone else. This lends horses, over and above their natural allure, all the glamor and pathos of the interior room watched by the child outside, pressing her nose against the windowpane. This is an exoticism that has been assimilated into the native system of values as a complex source of ambivalent meaning. The Indian mythology of horses is a testament to the vitality of the imagination and to the human drive to go on and on responding merely to the memory, or to the view from afar, of a charismatic animal.

Notes

PREFACE

1. For a badly fictionalized description of this event, see Mary Alexander, *Mrs. Betjeman,* 137–41. For a much better novelized portrait of Penelope as a cavalry general's daughter, see Evelyn Waugh's *Helena* (1950), dedicated to Penelope.

2. See Penelope Chetwode, *Kulu: The End of the Habitable World.*

1. HORSES IN INDIAN NATURE AND CULTURE

1. These carvings occur, most notably, on Stupa 1, the Eastern Gateway and the Western Gate; Stupa No. 2, the Northern Gateway; and Stupa 3, the Southern Gateway.

2. It may be thought that even though invading armies had the advantage of horses, the native Indian rulers had the advantage of elephants. But Simon Digby, in his definitive book on warhorses and elephants in India, remarks: "[T]he elephant is a picturesque animal, and medieval authors are all convinced that it was a great asset in battle. Examples of its performance on the battlefield during the Sultanate period do not decisively support this view" (*War-Horse,* 52). For one thing, elephants, despite their value as the ancient equivalent of tanks, are so much slower than cavalry: "The Indian elephant is capable of what has been called 'a fast shuffle of about fifteen miles an hour'" (53). Moreover, "When wounded, elephants were liable to get out of control and escape at the top of their speed" (50). Indian texts offer support for these views; the *Ashvashastra* (3.4) remarks: "Horses will always draw the chariot at the time of battle, which the lordly elephants, proud of their strength, cannot do." There is much more that one might say about elephants, but aside from a few references to clashes between horses and elephants in the Rajput epics, this is a subject that I will leave to others. (See, for instance, Trautmann, *Elephants and Kings.*)

3. Doniger O'Flaherty, *The Origins of Evil,* 321–48.

4. Leshnik, "The Horse in India," 56.

5. *Ashvashastra* 26.4–5.

6. *Agni Purana* 288.1–10.

7. Notes from a meeting with David Robertshaw at Cornell University, 1989.

8. Digby, *War-Horse,* 26.

9. Leshnik, "The Horse in India," 57.

10. Leshnik, "The Horse in India," 57. See also Thomas Trautmann, cited in Bryant, *The Quest,* 261.

11. From a conversation with Dr. Faroukh Wadia at the Wadi Stud, in Pune, January, 1996.

12. From a conversation with Dr. Faroukh Wadia at the Wadi Stud, in Pune, January, 1996.

13. Iskandar, *Mirror for Princes,* chapter 26.

14. Herodotus, *History,* 3.106.

15. Huntington and Huntington, *The Art of Ancient India,* 187–88. The statue is in the Lucknow Museum.

16. Horses are traditionally measured by height, and in "hands," units of four inches, from the ground to the withers. The "hand" unit was originally defined as the breadth of the palm, including the thumb.

17. Digby, *War-Horse,* 20.

18. Kossack, *Indian Court Painting,* 53.

19. John Lockwood Kipling, *Beast and Man,* 62.

20. Marco Polo, *The Travels,* 356–57; *Marco Polo,* 174.

21. Moorcroft, *Observations,* 48.

22. Scharfe, *The State in Indian Tradition,* 194n217.

23. Keay, *India,* 277.

24. Marco Polo, *The Travels,* 357.

25. Abu'l Fazl, *A'in-i Akbari,* 1:142.

26. Gommans, *The Rise of the Indo-Afghan Empire,* 72.

27. Notes from meeting with David Robertshaw at Cornell University, 1989.

28. Hayes, *A Guide to Training,* chapter 3: "Varieties of Food," 20.

29. Hayes, *A Guide to Training,* 22, 29.

30. Lockwood Kipling, *Beast and Man,* 62.

31. Lockwood Kipling, *Beast and Man,* 62–63.

32. Gupta, "Horse Trade in North India."

33. Tavernier, *Travels,* 84, 226.

34. Digby, *War-Horse,* 31.

35. *Taittiriya Samhita* 5.5.10.6.

36. *Arthashastra* 2.30.8, -11, -18.

37. Brereton, *The Horse in War,* 91.

38. *Gazetteer of the Bombay Presidency,* 1880, 5:38.

39. Marco Polo, *Marco Polo,* 357, 174.

40. John Lockwood Kipling, *Beast and Man,* 62.

41. John Lockwood Kipling, *Beast and Man,* 62–63.

42. Marco Polo, *Marco Polo,* 174.

43. Digby, *War-Horse,* 31.

44. Personal communication from Stephen Inglis, March 26, 1985.

45. Digby, *War-Horse,* 14.

46. Keay, *India,* 276–77.

47. Scharfe, *The State in Indian Tradition,* 194–95; Keay, *India,* 189.

48. Law, "Animals in Early Jain and Buddhist Literature," 103–4.

49. Keay, *India,* 276–77.

50. Gommans, *The Rise of the Indo-Afghan Empire,* 71.

51. Gommans, *The Rise of the Indo-Afghan Empire,* 78.

52. Digby, *War-Horse,* 31.

53. Keay, *India,* 211.

54. Personal communication from Romila Thapar, Oxford, England, May 25, 1986.

55. Leshnik, "The Horse in India," 56–57. Cf. also Leshnik, "Some Early Indian Horse-Bits."

56. Notes from meeting with David Robertshaw at Cornell University, 1989. See also Epstein, *Domestic Animals of China;* and Zeuner, *A History of Domesticated Animals.*

57. Bühler, "The Peheva Inscription." Also known as the Prthudah or Pehoa inscription.

58. Digby, *War-Horse,* 29.

59. Digby, *War-Horse,* 30.

60. *Akananuru,* trans. George Hart, *Pattina-palai,* lines 185–93. Thanks to Elayaperumal Annamalai for this citation.

61. Inglis, "Night Riders."

62. Personal communication from Stephen Inglis, March 26, 1985.

63. Nagaswamy, "Gateway to the Gods."

64. Mookerji, *The History of Indian Shipping,* 195.

65. Nagaswamy, "Gateway to the Gods."

66. Digby, *War-Horse,* 31.

67. Majumdar and Pusalker, *The Struggle for Empire,* 523.

68. Marco Polo, *The Travels,* 356–57; *Marco Polo,* 174. See also Keay, *India,* 277.

69. Moorcroft, *Observations,* 53.

70. Leshnik, "The Horse in India," 56.

71. Digby, *War-Horse,* 30.

72. Keay, *India,* 306.

73. *Encyclopaedia Britannica,* s.v. "Horse latitudes."

74. Leshnik, "The Horse in India," 56.

75. Moorcroft, *Observations,* 48.

76. Hayes, *A Guide,* chapter 11, "Management of Horses on Board Ship," 138.

77. Alder, *Beyond Bokhara,* 50–51.

78. Notes from meeting with David Robertshaw at Cornell University, 1989.

79. Notes from meeting with David Robertshaw at Cornell University, 1989.

80. West, *Indo-European Poetry,* 417. The French continue to eat horses, but the French care more about food than about sentimentality (or just about anything else). And almost all horsey cultures have been known to eat horses in times of starvation.

81. Platte, *Equine Poetics,* 5.

82. An anti-god masquerading as a deer lures Prince Rama into the forest and away from his wife, thus initiating the central action of the *Ramayana.*

83. *Yogavasishtha* 3.104–9, 120–21; Doniger O'Flaherty, *Dreams,* 132–71.

84. I am assuming that the reader of this book—the sort of person that I have in mind when I say "we," from time to time—will be someone who belongs, as I do, to the English-speaking world, particularly but not only in America, Great Britain, and the lands of the former British Empire (including South Africa, Australia, and India), where horses are known.

85. The ancient Sanskrit texts were aware of another sort of functional gender ambi-

guity in mares, but only when they were harnessed as draught horses: the draught mare is neither male nor female, "for in that it pulls the cart it is not a female; and being female, it is not a male." *Shatapatha Brahmana* 5.5.4.35.

86. Doniger O'Flaherty, *Women*, 239–59.

87. Though the *Kamasutra* (2.8.1–17), the locus classicus for such things, does not use pejorative terms like "perverse" or "upside down," it does refer to this position as "the woman playing the man's part," assuming the missionary position as the norm. See also Doniger, *The Mare's Trap*.

88. Young, *Women Who Fly*.

89. *Ashvashastra* 3.1–17.

90. *Rig Veda* 2.11.8, 4.19.4 and 6.30.3; *Ramayana* 1.13.27; Sontheimer, "The Mallari/ Khandoba Myth," 162n17; Jettmar, *Die Religionen des Hindukusch*, 292 and 295.

91. Kapp, "Ein Menschenschopfungsmythos."

92. Crooke, *Popular Religion*, 2:207.

93. In the Wellcome Institute for the History of Medicine; personal communication from Dominik Wujastyk and Nigel Allan, March 1968.

94. Translated by Paula Richman, in Richman, "Subramaniya Bharati's Ramayana," 15–18.

2. HORSES IN THE INDO-EUROPEAN WORLD

1. West, *Indo-European Poetry*, 12.

2. Platt, *Equine Poetics*, 2.

3. For more of this discussion, see Doniger, "Ekwos."

4. Sherratt, "Plough and Pastoralism."

5. Dent, *The Horse*. Cf. also Dent, "The Earliest Wave."

6. Sherratt, "Plough and Pastoralism."

7. Pausanias, *Description of Greece* 3.4.20; Xenophon, *Cyropaedia* 8.3.ll.

8. Doniger O'Flaherty, "The Tail."

9. Xenophon, *Anabasis* 4.5; Herodotus, *History* 1.216.

10. Herodotus, *History* 4.71–72.

11. Polybius, *Histories* 12.4b; Plutarch, *Quaestiones Romanae* 97, 287A; Festus, *Breviarium*, s.v. "October equus," 178.5ff.

12. Giraldus Cambrensis, *Topographia Hibernica*, 169.

13. Doniger O'Flaherty, *Women*, 161. Citing *Vajasaneyi Samhita* 23.22; *Shatapatha Brahmana* 13.5.2.4.

14. Ovid, *Fasti* 4.731–34; Propertius, *First Roman Elegy* 4.1.19–20.

15. Johannson, "Ueber die altindische Gottin," 97; Doniger O'Flaherty, *Women*, 165.

16. Platte, *Equine Poetics*, 52–53: "If Doniger O'Flaherty should prove correct in her suggestion that the original sacrificial horse was a mare and that the killing of the horse before the ceremony is an Indian innovation to circumvent the difficulty, and danger, of compelling a stallion to mate with a human woman, then the smothering must be an attendant innovation" (n. 38; Doniger O'Flaherty, *Women*, 149–212). He continues: "Doniger O'Flaherty argues that the *ashvamedha* itself contains vestiges of a previous version of the ritual in which a man did indeed copulate with a mare. She points to a ready iden-

tification of the horse with the king, mediated by frequent solar symbolism which is pertinent to both figures, and focuses especially on the sexual abstinence, of both the king and the stallion, practiced during the preparation for the ceremony. . . . The switch from mare to stallion would make the horse the active, or penetrative, partner, and a live horse could not be counted on to perform this ritual function. The killing of the stallion and the subsequent fiction that the stallion is merely sleeping is a practical solution. Although this reasoning is tempting, I prefer to plot a more conservative course."

17. Thapar, *Early India,* 115.

18. Platte, *Equine Poetics,* 5.

19. Witzel, "Harappan Horse Myths."

20. Most recently, Devdutt Pattanaik, in "What Puranic Historians Won't Accept," uses the evidence of horses to establish persuasively that the civilization of the Vedas cannot be older than the civilization of the IVC.

21. The long-held assumption that the Aryans invaded India has been qualified and reevaluated in different ways by Trautmann, *Aryans and British India,* and Klostermaier, *A Survey of Hinduism,* taking into account contemporary Indian scholarship. See also Doniger, *The Hindus,* 89–95.

22. Though many have tried, from early attempts by Soviet scholars to the more recent work of Asko Parpola and several Indian scholars.

23. Dales, "The Mythical Massacre."

24. This was also a proverb ("For want of a nail [shoe; foot; horse; rider] a kingdom was lost"), on which Shakespeare riffed ("A horse! A horse! My kingdom for a horse!" [*Richard III,* 5.4.7–10]).

25. Thapar, *Early India,* 109 and 85.

26. Witzel, "Harappan Horse Myths."

27. Doniger, "Another Great Story."

28. Personal communication from Andrew G. Sherratt, Oxford, May 28, 1986.

29. Horses are not indigenous to Africa, for instance, but were apparently first introduced into Africa with the Hyskos' conquest of Egypt about the middle of the second millenniums BCE. Fairservis, *The Ancient Kingdoms of the Nile,* 162.

30. Stacul, *Prehistoric and Protohistoric Swat.*

31. Sontheimer, "The Mallari/Khandob Myth," 162.

32. Romila Thapar, personal communication, Oxford, England, May 18, 1986. Drawings of men on horses are said to have been found at the Bimbetka caves in prehistoric times, but it is now believed that these images date only from the historic period. See Dubey-Pathak, "The Rock Art," 6.

33. Personal communication from David Robertshaw, at Cornell University, March, 1989.

34. Leshnik, "The Horse in India," 57.

35. Thapar, *Early India,* 85, 88, 92, 95–96, 107.

3. HORSES IN THE VEDAS

1. *Rig Veda* 1.117.9; 1.118.9; 1.119.10. See also Macdonell, *Vedic Mythology,* 148–149; Vogel, *Indian Serpent Lore,* 11.

2. Shulman, "The Green Goddess," 129; cf. 130–31.

3. *Rig Veda* 1.163.1, 5, 6, 8–13; Doniger O'Flaherty, *The Rig Veda,* 87–88.

4. The French Indologist Louis Renou, in a *méchant* moment, translated "perfectly cooked" as "*au point.*"

5. *Rig Veda* 1.162.3, 6, 8–12, 17, 20–22; Doniger O'Flaherty, *The Rig Veda,* 89–93.

6. *Rig Veda* 10.17.1–2. "Tvastri is giving a wedding for his daughter: people come together at this news. The mother of Yama, the wedded wife of the great Vivasvant, disappeared. They concealed the immortal woman from mortals. Making a female of-the-same-kind, they gave her to Vivasvant. What she became bore the twin equine gods, the Ashvins, and then she abandoned the two sets of twins — Saranyu."

7. He is also the divine artisan, called Tvashtri, "the Fashioner," or Vishvakarman, "the All-Maker." Hephaestus is his Greek counterpart.

8. The sun is called Vivasvant, "the Shining One."

9. *Rig Veda* 10.72.8–9; *Shatapatha Brahmana* 3.1.33.

10. *Rig Veda* 10.14.2; *Atharva Veda* 18.3.13.

11. *Rig Veda* 1.50.8–9.

12. Doniger, *Splitting the Difference,* 43–55.

13. *Brihaddevata* 6.162–63, 7.1–6. The core of this text may date back to 400 BCE, but material was added as late as the 10th century CE.

14. *Panchavimsha Brahmana* 20.4.5.

15. Lommel, *Kleine Schriften,* 272–74.

16. *Ashvashastra* 3.2.

17. Doniger, "Saranyu/Samja." For contemporary versions of the story, see Narayan, "Who Is Vishwakarma's Daughter?"

18. *Panchavimsha Brahmana* 6.1.1–4.

19. *Shatapatha Brahmana* 12.7.2.21.

20. Patanjali's *Mahabhashya* on Panini 5.3.57.1. Thanks to Gary Tubb.

21. *Kashika* on Panini 5.3.9. Thanks to Gary Tubb.

22. *Jaiminiya Brahmana* 1.67. Cf. also *Taittiriya Samhita* 7.1.1–3.

23. Desai, *Erotic Sculpture of India,* 158. There is one example of such a stone in the Baroda museum, and one in the Prince of Wales Museum. Personal communication from Devangana Desai, 1995.

24. *Kamasutra* 2.6.21, with the commentary of Yashodhara.

25. *Mahabharata* 13.38.25–29; *Shiva Purana* 5.24.29.

26. *Mrichchakatika* 10.19. A connection with donkeys is implied just a few verses later in this play (10.53), when the villain of the play uses the same metaphor to complain that he had escaped "like a donkey that has broken loose from his reins," but was then brought back like a bad dog.

27. *ashvAya, ashvAyati;* also *ashvayu,* desiring horses: *Rig Veda* 51.14, 4.30.14, 8.45.10, 8.66.9, 9.35.6, 9.63.4. Cf. Panini 7.4.30.

28. *Ashvasya, ashvasyati.* Panini 7.1.51.

29. Harsha, *Naishadhiyacharita* 19.17. I am grateful to David Shulman for bringing this verse to my attention. The solar chariot horses here are presumably male, going against the Vedic tradition (as in *Rig Veda* 1.50.8–9) that regards them as the daughters of the Sun.

30. Grottanelli, "Yoked Horses."

31. Thapar, *Early India*, 122.

32. These ideas owe much to a conversation with Jan Heesterman, back in the 1980s. See also Heesterman, *The Broken World of Sacrifice.*

33. Doniger O'Flaherty, "The Tail."

34. Platte, *Equine Poetics*, 35. He continues: "a ritualistic shift in identity between horse and human was central to the event [of the horse sacrifice]."

35. *Shatapatha Brahmana* 13.2.2.7.

36. *Shatapatha Brahmana* 13.3.8.1–6; Doniger O'Flaherty, *Textual Sources*, 18–19.

37. *Shatapatha Brahmana* 13.1.2.5.

38. Hooykaas, *Agama-Tirtha*, 23; cf. *Shankhayana Shrautasutra* 16.1.15; *Baudhayana Shrautasutra* 15.8.

39. *Kaushitaki Brahmana* 15.4.

40. *Aitareya Brahmana* 4.9.

41. *Shatapatha Brahmana* 2.1.4.23–24.

42. *Taittiriya Brahmana* 2.6.13.3.

43. *Shatapatha Brahmana* 14.1.2.20; *Vajasaneyi Samhita* 37.9.

44. *Shatapatha Brahmana* 1.9.9.

45. Doniger O'Flaherty, *Women*, 157–58.

46. *Rig Veda* 10.86. See Doniger O'Flaherty, *The Rig Veda*, 257–63, and Doniger, "Indra as the Stallion's Wife." Stephanie Jamison, in *Sacrificed Wife*, 77–88, further developed this connection between the horse sacrifice and RV 10.86, and showed that the monkey is a mock horse, and the poem a mock horse sacrifice. She also argues that the queens did not merely mime the copulation with the horse, but here I disagree.

47. *Shatapatha Brahmana* 13.2.8.1–4.

48. *Vajasaneyi Samhita* 23; *Taittiriya Samhita* 7.4; *Shatapatha Brahmana* 13.2.8–9; etc. See Doniger O'Flaherty, *Textual Sources*, 16–17, and *Women*, 154–62. See also Jamison, *Sacrificed Wife*, 65–88.

49. Kirfel, "Siva und Dionysos"; Platte, *Equine Poetics*, 51, citing Puhvel, *Comparative Mythology*, 272, suggests that they "strangle the stallion because that produces postmortem tumescence."

50. *"na ma nayati kash cana sasasty ashvakah." Vajasaneyi Samhita* 23.18.

51. Doniger O'Flaherty, *Women*, 161, citing *Vajasaneyi Samhita* 23.22; *Shatapatha Brahmana* 13.5.2.4.

52. Dumézil, "Bellator Equus."

53. *Ramayana* 1.13.27–28.

54. *Ramayana* 1.17.6–9.

55. *Ramayana* 1.8.7–23, 1.9.1–32, 1.10.1–29, 1.11.1–11. The obscene version is in the *Alambusa Jataka* (# 523), bowdlerized with asterisks in the standard Cowell translation but fully translated in Doniger O'Flaherty, *Asceticism*, 42–50.

56. *Harivamsha* 3.5.11–17.

57. *Arthashastra* 1.6.6. Commentary cited by Kangle, *Arthasastra* 1.6.6.

58. Doniger, *Splitting the Difference*, 88–111.

59. I owe this inspired idea to Katherine Ulrich, personal communication, April 7, 2020.

60. *Naishadiyacharita* canto 17, verse 201.

61. Doniger, *Against Dharma*, 123–50.

62. Madhava, *Sarvadarshanasamgraha*, 6–7.

63. Alberuni, *India*, 548.

64. Griffith, *The Texts of the White Yajur Veda*, 230–31, 213.

65. "Subject: In Reality Urva Means Powerful And Rukam Means Addiction," September 23, 2019 at 11:57:26 p.m., EDT.

66. Indeed, severed horse heads remain powerful outside of India in our day: recall the scene in Francis Ford Coppola's *The Godfather* (1972), in which a man who has incurred the wrath of the Godfather wakes up to find the severed head of his prize racehorse in bed with him.

67. *Rig Veda* 1.116.12, 1.117.22. "Through a horse's head, Dadhyanch told the Ashvins where the mead was hidden. The Ashvins gave Dadhyanch a horse's head and Dadhyanch told them the place of the hidden mead."

68. *Shatapatha Brahmana* 14.1.1.18–25.

69. *Ramayana* 2.40.13–16. The line about creatures with ears appears only in the Vulgate edition (Guajarati Printing Press ed.), where it is 2.45.14. Thanks to Gary Tubb for this verse.

70. *Brihadaranyaka Upanishad* 1.1.1–2. My translation, drawing upon Patrick Olivelle's.

71. *Brihadaranyaka* 1.2.6–7.

72. *Taittiriya Samhita* 5.5.10.6.

73. *Brihadaranyaka* 1.4.3–4.

74. But see Doniger, "Sacred Cows."

75. *Rig Veda* 10.61.7, 1.71.5, 8; 1.164.33; 3.31.1.

76. See Doniger O'Flaherty, *Other Peoples' Myths*, chapter 4.

77. *Aitareya Brahmana* 3.33–34; Doniger O'Flaherty, *Hindu Myths*, 29–31.

78. Though there is little evidence that human men were actually sacrificed, there are intriguing stories about the moment when people *stopped* sacrificing humans, rather like the tale of Abraham and Isaac. See Shulman, *The Hungry God;* and the tales of "Why Coconuts Are Offered to the Goddess" and Harishchandra in chapter 10 of this book.

79. *Katha Upanishad* 3.3–6.

80. Manu 2.88.

81. *Kamasutra* 2.7.33.

82. "The truth" is the Upanishadic mantra "You are that." From Vidyaranya's *Shankaradigvijaya,* canto 10, verse 50, p. 391. Cited and translated by Maitra, "The Rebirth of Homo Vedicus."

4. HORSES AND SNAKES IN THE UNDERWORLD

1. Manu 10.11.

2. Manu 10.47

3. *Mahabharata* 4.3.1–4.

4. *Rig Veda* 1.58.2, 1.149.3, 1.60.5, 2.4.4, etc. *Aitareya Brahmana* 15.5.1–7.

5. *Rig Veda* 1.35.3, 1.164.47, 2.11.6, 5.6.6, 8.72.16.

6. Doniger, "Horses and Snakes."

7. *Mahabharata* (southern recension) 8.26.16.

8. *Mahabharata* 3.63.

9. *Mahabharata* 13.102.

10. Vogel, *Indian Serpent Lore,* 84–87; cf. *Vishnu Purana* 2.10.

11. *Mahabharata* 1.218–19, 1.3.145.

12. *Panchavimsha Brahmana* 25.15.1–4.

13. Personal communication from Peter Kepfoerle, 1987.

14. *Mahabharata* 1.18–19.

15. *Mahabharata* 1.60.65–68.

16. *Kathasaritsagara* 4.22.

17. Blackburn, "Domesticating the Cosmos."

18. *Mahabharata* 5.104–17.

19. *Mahabharata* 1.3.85–195. Cf. the story of Bhrigu, who sees strange sights in the underworld in the *Jaiminiya Brahmana* (1.42–44), and Nachiketa's similar experience in the *Mahabharata* (13.70–71); see Doniger, *Tales of Sex and Violence,* 32–40.

20. *Mahabharata* 1.33.24.

21. *Mahabharata* 14.55–57.

22. See Ahalya in Doniger, *Splitting the Difference,* 88–109.

23. *Rig Veda* 1.163.1; *Brihadaranyaka Upanishad* 1.1.2; *Mahabharata* 1.15.

24. *Ramayana* 1.37.1–24, 1.38.1–26, 1.39.1–28, 1.40.1–26, 1.42.1–24, 1.43.1–3.

25. *Rig Veda* 4.18.18, 5.34.9, 10.127.9.

26. I owe these ideas to Katherine Ulrich, personal communication, May 31, 2020.

27. *Shiva Purana* 5.38.48–57; *Linga Purana* 1.66.15–20; *Vayu Purana* 2.26.143–78; *Brahmanda Purana* 3.46–53; *Vishnu Purana* 4.4.1–33; *Bhagavata Purana* 9.8.1–31, 9.9.1–15; *Ramayana* 1.38–44; *Mahabharata* 3.104–8.

5. HORSES IN THE OCEAN IN THE SANSKRIT PURANAS

1. *Shatapatha Brahmana* 7.3.2.14.

2. *Brihadaranyaka Upanishad* 1.1.2.

3. *Mahabharata* 1.169.16–26, 170.1–21, 171.1–23.

4. *Mahabharata* 1.172.1–17.

5. *Taittiriya Samhita* 5.5.10.6.

6. Sayana on *Rig Veda* 2.35.3.

7. *Rig Veda* 1.116.12, 1.117.22, 1.84.13–14.

8. Sayana on *Rig Veda* 1.84.13–14.

9. *Skanda Purana,* 7.1.32.1–128, 7.1.33.1–103; cf. *Padma Purana,* 6.148.27ff.

10. He is mentioned in the *Atharva Veda* and is said to be the author of the *Prashna Upanishad* of the *Atharva Veda.*

11. Monier-Williams, *Sanskrit-English Dictionary,* s.v. "Pippalada." An Arabic expression for a bisexual person is one who eats both pomegranates and figs.

12. *Matsya Purana,* 175.23–63; cf. *Harivamsha* 1.45.20–64.

13. *Mahabharata* 13.56.4–6.

14. *Mahabharata* 1.19.14. The mythology of horses' heads and mouths is complicated by the fact that the Sanskrit word *mukha* can mean "head" or "mouth" or "face."

15. *Gopatha Brahmana* 1.2.18.

16. *Rig Veda* 3.30.19; Sayana: *urva iva anavaptakamo vadavanala iva.*

17. *Brahma Purana* 110.85–210.

18. *Shiva Purana* 3.24–25.

19. Doniger O'Flaherty, *Asceticism and Eroticism,* 40–82.

20. *Mahabharata* 13.83.53; *Shiva Purana* 2.3.19–20; *Kalika Purana,* 44.124–36; *Matsya Purana* 154.251–52; *Bhavishya Purana* 3.4.14.53; *Kumarasambhava* 10.1–25. See also Doniger O'Flaherty, *Asceticism and Eroticism,* 286–92.

21. *Brahma Purana* 116.22–25.

22. Personal communication from Sandra King Mulholland, in the 1980s.

23. *Abhijnana-Shakuntala* of Kalidasa 3.2 (alternative verse).

24. *Mahabharata* 12.137.41.

25. *Shiva Purana* 5.24.29; *Mahabharata* 13.38.25–29.

26. *Prabodhacandrodaya* 6.8.

27. Hooykaas, *Agama-Tirtha,* 109; citing *Kauravashrama* 78.

28. *Markandeya Purana* 105.1–13.

29. *Devibhagavata Purana* 6.17–19.

30. Mahalingam, "Hayagriva," 196–97.

31. *Panchavimsha Brahmana* 7.5.6; *Taittirya Aranyaka* 5.1; *Taittiriya Samhita* 4–9.

32. *Mahabharata* 12.335.44–54.

33. Doniger O'Flaherty, *Hindu Myths,* 179–97.

34. *Mahabharata* 12.335.1–64, 3.193.16.

35. *Vishnu Purana* 5.17.11; *Bhagavata Purana* 5.18.1–6.

36. *Tiruccenturt Talapuranam* of Venrialaik Kavirayar (Tirucentur: Tevastanam Publications, 1963), canto 9.422–81. I am indebted to David Shulman for this text and the translation.

37. *Mahabharata* 5.128.49.

38. *Devibhagavata Purana* 1.5.1–112; Doniger O'Flaherty, *Women,* 224.

39. *Skanda Purana* 6.81.1–10, 6.84.7.

40. Hopkins, *Epic Mythology,* 203–4.

41. *Mahabharata* 1.63, 3.213.2–20, 3.223.

42. *Mahabharata* 5.130.64.

43. *Harivamsha* 44.66–68.

44. *Bhagavata Purana* 10.2.1; 38.20; 37.1–8, 25; 43.25. See also *Vayu Purana* 98.100; Gopinath Rao, *Elements of Hindu Iconography,* 1:221.

45. *Vishnu Purana* 5.1.24, 5.4.1–2, 5.12.21.

46. *Rig Veda* 10.136.5; *Mahabharata* 3.30.12, 3.36.2; *Bhagavata Purana* 10.37–38.

47. *Mahabharata* 3.188.14–93, 3.189.1–13. See also *Vishnu Purana* 4.24.25–29.

48. *Bhagavata Purana* 2.7.36–39.

49. *Harivamsha* 31.148; *Agni Purana* 16; *Bhagavata Purana* 12.2.16–25; *Brahmanda Purana* 2.3.73.104–24; *Kalki Purana* 1.1–4; 2.6–7; 3.1–2, 14–16; *Linga Purana* 1.49; *Matsya Purana* 47; 248–63; *Saura Purana* 4; *Skanda Purana* 7.5.1; *Vayu Purana* 2.37.390ff; *Vishnu Purana* 4.24.25–29, 5.7, 6.1–2.

50. Gopinatha Rao, *Elements of Hindu Iconography,* 1:221.

51. Ivanow, "The Sect of Imam Shah," 62–64.

52. Doniger O'Flaherty, *The Origins of Evil,* 38–39 and 200–202.

6. *ASHVASHASTRA,* THE SCIENCE OF HORSES

1. *Arthashastra* 2.30.1–3. I have relied heavily on Patrick Olivelle's translation, simplifying it and clarifying (or eliminating) some of the non-equine technical points.

2. *Arthashastra* 2.30.4–7.

3. *Arthashastra* 2.30.8–13.

4. The best horse would be about five feet high and ten feet long.

5. *Arthashastra* 2.30.14–26.

6. *Arthashastra* 2.30.27–30.

7. *Ramayana* 1.7.20.

8. *Arthashastra* 2.30.32–38.

9. The text actually speaks of six, nine, or twelve yokings, and then five, seven and a half, or ten yokings. A *yojana* or "yoking," i.e., a "stage," the distance a horse can travel before being replaced by another horse, is variously estimated as between five and ten miles. I have used the lower calculation, which seems, in this particular passage, already beyond the capacity of most horses. The three different distances are for the best, middling, and worst horses of each of the two categories, chariot horse and riding horse.

10. *Arthashastra* 2.30.39–48.

11. See McClish, *The History of the Arthashastra.*

12. *Arthashastra* 2.30.50–51.

13. For the general secularity of the *Arthashastra,* see Doniger, *Against Dharma.*

14. The edition I am using here is the *Ashvashastra* of Nakula, ed. S. Gopalan.

15. Law, "Animals in Early Jain and Buddhist Literature," 104.

16. Pinault, *Horse of Karbala,* 126.

17. *Ashvashastra* 1.1–38; 3.2.

18. Anjum, "Horses in Mughal India," 281.

19. *Mahabharata* 1.16.

20. The identification of parts of the horse with elements of the cosmos owes much to the beginning of the *Brihadaranyaka Upanishad,* the meditation on the identity of the cosmos with the sacrificial horse.

21. *Arthashastra* 1.13.25, 1.14.12.

22. This seems to be what we would call a martingale.

23. From the *Agni Purana* 288.1–52

24. Digby, *War-Horse,* 13. See Huda, "Faras-namah-i-Hashimi and Shalihotra"; and Earles, *A Treatise on Horses.*

25. Dayal, "Making the 'Mughal' Soldier," 883, citing Anand Ram Mukhlis, *Siyaqnama* (Lucknow: Kishore, 1879), 149.

26. Iskandar, *Mirror for Princes,* 112–16, trans. Reuben Levy.

27. Doniger O'Flaherty, "Contributions to an Equine Lexicology."

28. From 2012 to 2020 he was the president and CEO of the Field Museum in Chicago.

29. *Kamasutra* 1.3.3–10.

30. Personal communication from Suzanne Rudolph, May 10, 2008.

7. BUDDHIST HORSES

1. The animals on the Indus Valley seals also have this quality of breath from within, and may have been a distant influence on the Ashokan animals—though not, of course, on the horse in particular, for as we have seen, there are no horses in the IVC.

2. Law, *Tribes*, 17 and 112.

3. Law, "Animals," 6–7.

4. *Jataka* #254; Law, "Animals," 6–7.

5. The name means "Necklace," the significance of which escapes me.

6. Ashvaghosha, *Buddhacharita* 5.3, 7, 22, 68, 73–81; 6.3, 4, 11, 53–55; 8.3–4, 14–23, 38–49, 73–76. I have made my own translation, leaning heavily on Olivelle.

7. Ashvaghosha, *Buddhacharita,* 15.1–7, 13, from Tibetan translations; cited by Conze, *Buddhist Scriptures,* 53.

8. *Ashvashastra* 23.6. Some Greek horses also weep, famously in Homer (*Iliad* 17.426).

9. Ohnuma, *Unfortunate Destiny,* 101.

10. *Nidanakatha,* cited by Ohnuma, *Unfortunate Destiny,* 105.

11. Ohnuma, *Unfortunate Destiny,* 119–20.

12. Ohnuma, *Unfortunate Destiny,* 123, citing Doniger, "A Symbol in Search of an Object."

13. There is a story about this. Apparently a British scholar once expressed to an Indian colleague his surprise that horse-faced women should be regarded as beautiful. The Indian scholar replied, "O yes! Horse-faced, like English women." Personal anecdote from Gary Tubb (in Chicago, November 13, 2019), citing the scholar Kalipada Tarkacharya. Lady Ottoline Morrell, in particular, was often said to be horse-faced, but there were so many others.

14. Kalidasa, *Kumarasambhava* 1.11.

15. The Ashvamukha is sometimes called Hayavaktra or Hayagriva or other synonyms for "horse head."

16. The animal part of the Kimpurusha, particularly in Southeast Asia, was sometimes a bird rather than a horse. Parpola, "The Pre-Vedic Indian Background," 62; Hopkins *Epic Mythology,* 142–59. For the connection between horses and birds, see chapter 4 of this book.

17. Magha, *Shishupalavadha* 4.38.

18. See, for example, paintings in the Government Museum at the Gadh Mahal in Jhalawar.

19. *Venkatacalaviharasatakamu* 7, by an anonymous author, in *Sri Venkatesvara Laghukrtulu.* I am indebted to David Shulman for this reference and translation. I have omitted the last two lines, which would require a lot of non-horsey commentary: ". . . . all the way to Golconda, O Satrusamhara Venkatacalavihara!"

20. Rawson, *Erotic Art,* 42. I am indebted to Dr. James C. Harle of the Ashmolean Museum, Oxford, for calling my attention (back in 1969) to similar reliefs on temples 7 and 9 at Aihole.

21. *Mahavamsa* 10.53–62 (Geiger ed.).

22. Though some texts distinguish the male and feminine forms, this text uses the

masculine form (Yakkha) for both male and female. To avoid confusion, I will call her a Yakkhi.

23. *Padakusalamanava-Jataka, Jataka* #432.

24. Meech-Pekarik, "The Flying White Horse."

25. *Valahassa Jataka,* #196; Cowell ed., 2:89–91.

26. Holt, *The Buddha,* 49–51.

8. ARABIAN HORSES AND MUSLIM HORSEMEN

1. West, *Indo-European Poetry,* 467.

2. Keay, *India,* 211.

3. Keay, *India,* 275.

4. *Encyclopedia Britannica,* s.v. "Polo."

5. *Manasollasa* of Someshvara, 211–24.

6. Keay, *India,* 240.

7. Babur, *Baburnama,* 446 and 463.

8. *A Drunken Babur Returns to Camp at Night.* From a *Baburnama,* attributed to Far-rukh Beg (act. early 1580s to 1619). Now in the Arthur M. Sackler Gallery, S1986.231. I am grateful to Audrey Truschke for telling me about this image.

9. Abu'l Fazl, *A'in-i Akbari,* 1:132.

10. Abu'l Fazl, *The History of Akbar,* 4:211; Schimmel, *The Empire,* 203.

11. Digby, *War-Horse,* 26.

12. Abu'l Fazl, *A'in-i Akbari,* 1:140.

13. Keay, *India,* 325.

14. Abu'l Fazl, *A'in-i Akbari,* 1:132.

15. Digby, *War-Horse,* 25.

16. Jahangir, *Tuzuk-i-Janhangīrī,* 42.

17. Jahangir, *Tuzuk-i-Janhangīrī,* 151; Anjum, "Horses in Mughal India," 278.

18. Temple, *Legends,* 2:507.

19. Digby, *War-Horse,* 27.

20. Digby, *War-Horse,* 28.

21. Digby, *War-Horse,* 28, quoting Barani.

22. Digby, *War-Horse,* 27.

23. Anjum, "Horses," 282; Abu'l Fazl, *A'in-i Akbari,* 1:143.

24. Abu'l Fazl, *A'in-i Akbari,* 1:133.

25. Anjum, "Horses," 278.

26. Bana, *Harshacarita,* 201.

27. Abu'l Fazl, *A'in-i Akbari,* 1:94; 2:51, 78–79; Jahangir, *Tuzuk-i-Janhangīrī,* 106, 131.

28. Digby, *War-Horse,* 48, citing a translation of Amir Khusrau Dehlavi by M. Habib, Madras, 1931.

29. Tavernier, *Travels,* 2:205.

30. Digby, *War-Horse,* 28, quoting Barani, 21–22, 34–35, 53.

31. Abu'l Fazl, *A'in-i Akbari,* 1:133; Keay, *India,* 327.

32. *Arthashastra* 2.30.27–30.

33. *Manasollasa* of Someshvara, cited by Gode, "Studies," 98.

34. Anjum, "Horses," 280–81, citing *A'in-i Akbari*, 234.

35. Barani, cited by Eaton, *India*, 53.

36. Hiltebeitel, *Rethinking*, 314.

37. Hiltebeitel, "Muttal Ravuttan," 1.

38. Hiltebeitel, "Muttal Ravuttan," 18, 22, 19.

39. Hiltebeitel, *Rethinking*, 314.

40. The story is told principally in the *Tiruvacagam* of Manikkavacakar; the *Tiruvilaiyatal Puranam* of Paranjoti Muniva, the *Tiruvatavurar Purana* of Katavul Mamuniyar; and the *Pandyakulodaya* of Mandalakavi. It is retold in Mahadevan, *Ten Saints of India*, 61–73; in Pope, *Tiruvacagam*, xx–xxvii.; and in Butler, *The Life of the Tamil Poet-Saint Manikkavacakar*.

41. "The Story of the Foxes That Became Horses," from Narayana Rao, *Shiva's Warriors*, 77.

42. *Tiruvatavurar Purana* 2–3. Summarized by Yocum, in *Hymns*, 51–53, and in "Brahmin, King, Sannyasi," 5–6. Vatavurar is here usually called Tiru Vatavurar, with the honorific prefix "Tiru," equivalent to the Sanskrit "Shri."

43. Mandalakavi, *Pandyakulodaya*, chapter 7, lines 1–48, from David Shulman.

44. Yocum, "Brahmin, King, Sannyasi," 25–26.

45. Yocum, "Brahmin, King, Sannyasi," 26. He notes, "This information is derived from an interview with a priest at the Tirumarainatacuvami Temple in Tiruvatavur, a village about fifteen miles northeast of Madurai" (26n35).

46. *Tiruvacagam* 2:27, trans. Yocum, *Hymns*, 61.

47. Yocum, "Brahmin, King, Sannyasi," 38n8. A minor problem is posed by the fact that Perundurai/Perunturai is not, in fact, a seaport, as the myth suggests, nor is it east of Madurai; it is north of Madurai and inland, though on a river which does connect with the Bay of Bengal.

48. Yocum, "Brahmin, King, Sannyasi," 42n35.

49. Yocum, *Hymns*, 62n26.

50. From a conversation with Mr. Chenoy, in Pune, January, 1996.

51. Khan, "Horses in Pakistan."

52. Pinault, *Horse of Karbala*, 127.

53. Gottschalk, *Beyond Hindu and Muslim*, 50.

54. Pinault, *Horse of Karbala*, 114. In the following discussion of the celebration, citations to Pinault are in the text.

55. Crook, *The Popular Religion*, 2:206; quotation citing Rousselet, *India and Its Native Princes*, 116.

56. Bhattacarya, *Folklore of Bengal*, 49.

57. Sontheimer, "The Mallari/Khandoba Myth," 155, 163.

58. Sontheimer, "The Mallari/Khandoba Myth," 15.

59. Sontheimer, "Folk Hero, King and God"; "Some Incidents," 116.

60. Sontheimer, "The Mallari/Khandoba Myth," 162.

61. Sontheimer, "Folk Hero, King and God."

62. Sontheimer, *Binoba*, 190.

63. Sontheimer, "The Mallari/Khandoba Myth," 161.

64. Stanley, "The Capitulation of Mani," 274–75.

65. Sontheimer, "The Mallari/Khandoba Myth," n. 16; citing Gangadhara's *Sri Martanda Vijaya* (composed in Marathi in 1823; ed. R. C. Dhere, 1975), 34.51ff.

66. Dhere, *Khandoba,* 31, citing *Sri Mallari Mahatmya* by Siddhapal Kesari (composed in Marathi in 1585, according to Dhere), 13.59.

67. Stanley, "The Capitulation of Mani," 28; Sontheimer, *Binoba,* 27n16, citing Gangadhara, *Sri Martanda Vijaya* (1823), 34.51ff.

68. Vinayaka, *Sri Mallari Mahatmya,* 13.24.

69. Stanley, "The Capitulation of Mani," 278.

70. Sontheimer, *Binoba,* 27, and "The Malari/Khandoba Myth," 161.

71. Stanley, "The Capitulation of Mani," 278.

72. Personal communication from John M. Stanley, from his notes on fieldwork in Maharashtra, 1986. See also Stanley, "The Capitulation of Mani."

73. Sontheimer, "The Mallari/Khandoba Myth," 162.

9. EQUESTRIAN EPICS AND MYTHIC MARES

1. Kramrisch, *Unknown India,* 51.

2. Singh, *Ancient Indian Warfare,* 63.

3. Digby, *War-Horse,* 12, 13–14.

4. Gommans, *The Rise of the Indo-Afghan Empire,* 82.

5. Digby, *War-Horse,* 21, citing Barani citing Sultan Balban.

6. Huyler, *Village India,* 245.

7. Joshi, *Painted Folklore,* 45.

8. Personal communication from Leonard Gordon, Calcutta, 1964.

9. Edwardes, *Red Year,* 121.

10. Leshnik, "The Horse in India," 57

11. Sontheimer, "The Mallari/Khandoba Myth," 162.

12. Hiltebeitel, *Rethinking,* 121.

13. Schimmel, *The Empire,* 143.

14. Hiltebeitel, *Rethinking,* 299.

15. Hiltebeitel, *Rethinking,* 2.

16. Erndl, *Victory,* 46.

17. Erndl, *Victory,* 178. Erndl notes, of her contemporary story, that there is a controversy over whether he is the same as King Harishchandra of Ayodhya (an ancestor of Rama) or a local king of Haripur in District Kangra, H.P. For Harishchandra, see Doniger, *Dreams,* 143–44.

18. Erndl, *Victory,* 96.

19. Cf. similar Tamil stories (but without the horse) in David Shulman, *The Hungry God.*

20. See the tale of Shunahshepha, *Aitareya Brahmana* 7.13–16.

21. Sontheimer, *Binoba,* chapter 4, 4–28, text 19.

22. Lockwood Kipling, *Beast and Man,* 69.

23. Brereton, *The Horse in War,* 92.

24. See https://www.youtube.com/watch?v=-AOxjLRfnlE.

25. Jairazbhoy and Kothari, "The *Par* of Pabuji."

26. Kramrisch, *Unknown India*, 87.

27. Smith, in *The Epic of Pabuji*, records several versions of the story. Parbu Bhopa told him this version, which Smith summarized on p. 493, and I have further summarized here.

28. *Rig Veda* 10.85; Doniger O'Flaherty, *The Rig Veda*, 252–56.

29. Doniger O'Flaherty, *Women*, 180–82; Doniger, *The Bedtrick*, chapter 3.

30. Tessitori, "A Progress Report," 110–14. This version "was drawn up in accordance with the account in the *Khyata* of Muhanota Nena Si."

31. Smith, *The Epic of Pabuji*, 285–87.

32. Tessitori, "A Progress Report," 111. Several Hindi/Rajasthani websites call the mare Kalavi.

33. Smith, *The Epic of Pabuji*, 484, from the version told by Mhato Nainasi (Muhanota Nena Si).

34. Smith, *The Epic of Pabuji*, 191.

35. I am indebted to Ann Grodzins Gold and Ulrike Stark for help in deciphering the name of the mare.

36. Heesterman, *The Ancient Indian Royal Consecration*.

37. Mali, *Nectar Gaze*, 82–83, 142–44, 159, 188–89, 199, 224, 229, 233–36, 249, 268–69, 377, 379–80, 399, 468–69, 471.

38. Mali, *Nectar Gaze*, 234.

39. Mali, *Nectar Gaze*, 187–88.

40. Doniger O'Flaherty, *Women*, 167–74 and 185–90.

41. Sontheimer, *Binoba*, 4–41, text 20. Basag is called Vasuki in the *Mahabharata*.

42. Mali, *Nectar Gaze*, 229.

43. Mali, *Nectar Gaze*, 234–36.

44. In Tulsi Das's Hindi *Ramayana*, Sati calls Shiva's attention to the incarnate god Rama in the same way. *Ramcaritmanas*, 1.150.1 to 1.155.5.

45. Mali, *Nectar Gaze*, 249–50.

46. Mali, *Nectar Gaze*, 468–71.

47. *Bhagavata Purana* 10.33.

48. *Bhagavata Purana* 10.8.

49. Summarized from Oman, *Cults, Customs*, 68–82.

50. Subrahmanyam, "Friday's Child," 80.

51. Subrahmanyam, "Friday's Child," 81, citing a French eyewitness account in 1714.

52. Overdorf, "Saving the Raja's Horse."

53. Subrahmanyam, "Friday's Child," 92–106, Arunachalam; *Peeps into Tamil Literature*, "Desingu Rajan Katahi," 138 ff.

54. Subrahmanyam, "Friday's Child," 108–9.

55. Arunachalam, *Peeps into Tamil Literature*, "Desingu Rajan Kathai," 138 ff., 3,800 lines.

56. Arunachalam, *Peeps into Tamil Literature*, 142, 131, and 143.

57. Recorded by Joseph C. Miller. I am indebted to Ann Grodzins Gold for sharing this data with me from an email that Joseph Miller sent to her on May 17, 2019. The passage from which I have excerpted several verses here is B.a153.1–40.

58. Ram Prakash Agravat, *Satyavadi Vir Tejapala*. I am indebted to Sandra King Mulholland for this reference.

59. Temple, *The Legends of the Punjab*, 1:121–209; Devaraja Sarma, *Guga Jahara Pira*, 83 ff.; Rose, *A Glossary*, 185.

60. Steel, "Folklore in the Panjab," 35.

61. Temple, *The Legends of the Punjab*, 1:121–209, "The Legend of Guru Gugga."

62. Vogel, *Indian Serpent Lore*, 264.

63. Crooke, *The Popular Religion*, 2:212.

64. Crooke, *The Popular Religion*, 2:211–13, citing *Indian Antiquary* 11.33ff; Cunningham, "Archaeological Reports," 17:159; and "Panjab Notes and Queries," 2:1.

65. Oman, *Cults*, 68–82; here 75.

66. Wadley, *Shakti*, Appendix 2, 198–207, esp. 202: "*Dank:* a ritual of snake possession."

67. Wadley, *Shakti*, 203, 204.

68. Sarma, *Guga Jahara Pira*, 83 ff.; also Rose, *A Glossary*, 185.

69. Oman, *Cults*, 68–82. For another version, see Crooke, *The Popular Religion*, 1: 211–13.

70. Tessitori, "A Progress Report," 113.

71. Rose, *A Glossary*, 179.

72. Personal communication from Madeleine Biardeau, August 1985.

73. Biardeau, "Brahmans and Meat-Eating Gods," 7.

74. Biardeau, "Brahmans and Meat-Eating Gods," 8–9. See also Biardeau, *Stories about Posts*, 172–78.

75. Doniger O'Flaherty, *Hindu Myths*, 238–49.

10. HORSES OF THE BRITISH RAJ

1. Lockwood Kipling, *Beast and Man*, 62.

2. Brereton, *The Horse*, 90.

3. Brereton, *The Horse*, 90.

4. Brereton, *The Horse*, 90.

5. Brereton, *The Horse*, 91.

6. Brereton, *The Horse*, 92, citing Major-General John Vaughan, in *Cavalry and Sporting Memories*.

7. Brereton, *The Horse*, 92, quoting Sergeant Burridge, of the 5th Royal Irish Lancers.

8. Brereton, *The Horse*, 90, 91.

9. Brereton, *The Horse*, 91, quoting Troop Sergeant-Major Mole.

10. Digby, *War-Horse*, 26.

11. Alder, *Beyond Bokhara*, 50–51.

12. The report was made in 1814 and "submitted to the consideration of the President and Members of the Board of Superintendence." It was reprinted in 1862.

13. Lockwood Kipling, *Beast and Man*, 72.

14. Digby, *War-Horse*, 27.

15. Moorcroft, *Observations*, 2. Further citations to Moorcroft are in the text.

16. Alder, *Beyond Bokhara*, 50–51.

17. Abu'l Fazl, *A'in-i Akbari*, 1:133; Keay, *India*, 327.

18. Dayal, "Making the 'Mughal' Soldier," 889.

19. Lockwood Kipling, *Beast and Man*, 62.

20. Personal communication from Romila Thapar, Oxford, May 25, 1986.

21. Lockwood Kipling, citing Rudyard Kipling, about a stud at Bellara, "entirely under native management," 76, 77.

22. Dayal, "Making the 'Mughal' Soldier," 878.

23. Dayal, "Making the 'Mughal' Soldier," 859.

24. Lockwood Kipling, *Beast and Man*, 70. Further citations to this work are in the text.

25. Lockwood Kipling, *Beast and Man*, 75; Rudyard Kipling to his father, 75–77.

26. Rudyard Kipling, cited by John Lockwood Kipling, *Beast and Man*, 76.

27. Rudyard Kipling, *Kim*, 161.

28. Dalrymple, *White Moghuls*.

29. "The White Man's Burden: The United States and the Philippine Islands" (1899) is a poem that urges the United States to take colonial control of the Philippines.

30. *Rig Veda* 2.20.7.

31. Finn and Smith, *The East India Company*, 8. According to Finn and Smith, Paul Benfield went out to India in 1764 as a military engineer in the service of the East India Company. He resigned his commission to become a private contractor and built a successful career as a banker and financier. Benfield was involved in a series of dubious loans to the Nawab of Arcot which ended his Indian career; he returned to England and became a prominent member of the class of nouveaux riches whose estates, political power, and respectability were bought with ill-gotten Colonial gains. He was MP for Cricklade 1780–84. He lost his money and died indigent in Paris in 1810.

32. Rudyard Kipling, *Kim*, 191.

33. Wilson, Readers' Guide.

34. McGrath, "Kipling in America," 72.

35. McGrath, "Kipling in America," 72.

36. Ure, *Shooting Leave*, 24.

37. Yang, *Bazaar India*, 116.

38. Alder, *Beyond Bokhara*, 209.

39. Yang, *Bazaar India*, 116.

40. Alder, *Beyond Bokhara*, 341.

41. Pearse, "Moorcroft and Hearsey's Visit."

42. Alder, *Beyond Bokhara*, 209.

43. Alder, *Beyond Bokhara*, 357–58.

44. Alder, *Beyond Bokhara*, 107.

45. Ure, *Shooting Leave*, passim.

46. Ure, *Shooting Leave*, 75.

47. Ure, *Shooting Leave*, 22.

48. Ure, *Shooting Leave*, 216–17.

49. Rudyard Kipling, "The Ballad of East and West" (1889). These lines are often cited in support of arguments that Kipling was racist. But the verse continues with lines that entirely contradict the first two:

Oh, East is East, and West is West, and never the twain shall meet,
Till Earth and Sky stand presently at God's great Judgment seat;
But there is neither East nor West, Border, nor Breed, nor Birth,
When two strong men stand face to face, though they come from the ends of the earth!

Note the negation of "Breed" and "Birth."

II. HORSE MYTHS AND RITUALS IN THE ABSENCE OF HORSES

1. Lockwood Kipling, *Beast and Man,* 70.

2. Chetwode, "The Horses of Kathiawar," 1.

3. Dalrymple, "Homer in India," 51.

4. Dalrymple, "Homer in India," 54.

5. Email from Gregory Alles, October 24, 2019.

6. Email from Gregory Alles, October 24, 2019.

7. Jain, "Painted Myths of Creation," 8.

8. Joshi, *Painted Folklore,* 52.

9. Stephen Inglis, personal communication, March 26, 1985.

10. Roghair, *The Epic of Palnadu,* 223–24. Further citations to this work are in the text., which often greatly condenses the full, very long, story.

11. *Panchavimsha Brahmana* 6.1.1–4.

12. Sen, *Folk Literature of Bengal,* 267–322.

13. A story by Rajaji, from a collection of short stories called *Katpanai Kadu* (*Forest of Imagination*), published in Madras in 1960; reprinted in Asher and Radhakrishnan, *A Tamil Prose Reader;* trans. Peggy Egnor (Margaret Trawick).

14. Richman, "Subramaniya Bharati's Ramayana," 15–18.

15. *Matanakamarajan katai,* 19–20; translation by David Shulman.

16. Beck et al., *Folktales of India,* 277–79.

17. Kramrisch, *Unknown India,* 58.

18. Bhattacarya, *Folklore of Bengal,* 48–49.

19. Sarkar, *The Folk Element,* 111.

20. Huyler, *Village India,* 162.

21. Huyler, *Village India,* 105, 200.

22. Hislop, *Papers Relating to the Aboriginal Tribes,* Appendix, i.iii.

23. Bhattacharya, "The Cult of the Village Gods," 19–33.

24. Kramrisch, *Unknown India,* 56.

25. Kramrisch, *Unknown India,* 57.

26. Inglis, "Night Riders," 298, 302, 304

27. Huyler, *Village India,* 113.

28. Inglis, "Night Riders," 298, 302, and 304; Kramrisch, *Unknown India,* 58.

29. Huyler, *Village India,* 105.

30. Unpublished typescript by Father Selva Raj (1952–2007), September 1992.

31. Kramrisch, *Unknown India,* 57.

32. Unpublished typescript by Father Selva Raj (1952–2007), September 1992.

33. Oman, *Cults, Customs, and Superstitions,* 68–68, 72.

34. Temple, *The Legends of the Panjab,* 1:418–528.

35. Crooke, *The Popular Religion,* 2:206, citing *Indian Antiquary* 11:325 ff. and *Panjab Notes and Queries* 2:2.

36. Personal communication from Stuart Blackburn, April 4, 1986.

37. *Gazetteer of the Bombay Presidency,* 5:242.

38. Personal communication from Suzanne Rudolph, March 1985. Similarly, the British in the eighteenth and nineteenth centuries forbade Irish Catholics to own a horse worth more than five pounds, in part to humble them, in part to keep them from owning a valuable weapon for insurrection.

39. Waida, "Central Asian Mythology of the Origin of Death," 687–88.

40. Sontheimer, "The Mallari/Khandoba Myth," 163.

41. Sontheimer, "The Mallari/Khandoba Myth," n. 18.

42. Leshnik, "The Horse in India," 57.

43. Hislop, *Papers Relating to the Aboriginal Tribes,* Appendix i.iii.

44. Huyler, *Village India,* 226.

45. Crooke, *The Popular Religion,* 2:208.

46. Kramrisch, *Unknown India,* 51.

47. Sontheimer, "The Mallari/Khandoba Myth," 163.

48. Leshnik, "The Horse in India," 57.

49. Doniger, *The Hindus,* 578, 630.

50. Kramrisch, *Unknown India,* 23 ff.

51. Kramrisch, *Unknown* India, 51.

52. Joshi, *Painted Folklore,* 52.

53. *Rig Veda* 3.31, 10.108; Doniger O'Flaherty, *The Rig Veda,* 151–58.

54. Smith, *The Epic of Pabuji,* 6, 8–9.

55. Smith, *The Epic of Pabuji,* 450–51.

56. Text in the British Library. Personal communication from Henry Ginzburg, London, January 1973.

57. *Aitareya Brahmana* 5.1; cf. *Shatapatha Brahmana* 13.4.2.2.

58. Das Gupta, "The Asvakas."

59. Kirfel, *Die Kosmographie der Inder,* 88 ff.

60. Parpola, "The Pre-Vedic Indian Background," 65.

61. Levi-Strauss, *The Jealous Potter,* 154–55, citing his *The Origin of Table Manners,* 253–59.

62. Romila Thapar, personal communication, May 25, 1986, Oxford.

63. Doniger O'Flaherty, *Other Peoples' Myths;* Doniger, *The Implied Spider.*

64. Aeschylus, *Prometheus Bound,* lines 461–68, trans. David Grene.

65. Smith, "Where the Plot Thickens," 56.

66. Raulff, *Farewell to the Horse.*

12. HORSES IN MODERN INDIA

1. Stories about human heads on (other) human bodies, sometimes transposed, are well known from the Tamil tradition: the goddess Renuka was beheaded beside a beheaded Dalit woman, and finally both were restored, but with the wrong heads. Thomas Mann developed the theme in *The Transposed Heads,* a satire on an ancient Indian myth that he

learned from Heinrich Zimmer. The detailed plot of the Indian variants is summarized by Wendy Doniger in *Splitting the Difference,* 204–16 and 235–36.

2. Satyanarayana, *Ha Ha Hu Hu,* 1–21.

3. *Mahabharata* 1.121.13–14.

4. Hiltebeitel, "*Turonaccari Yakacalai.*"

5. Herwitz, "Like Thunder and Lightning," 53.

6. Rajan, "M F Husain's 'Lightning.'"

7. Rajan, "M F Husain's 'Lightning.'"

8. Herwitz, "Like Thunder and Lightning," 47–48.

9. Herwitz, "Like Thunder and Lightning," 50.

10. Lockwood Kipling, *Beast and Man,* 77.

11. Overdorf, "Saving the Raja's Horse," 4. He writes: "[Farmers and herdsmen] bred the largest number of Marwari horses—earning their livings by providing prize horses for Hindu marriage ceremonies."

12. See https://www.quora.com/Why-do-Indian-grooms-always-come-sitting-on-a-mare-instead-of-a-horse?

13. Doniger, *Against Dharma,* 117–22.

14. The medieval romance *Prithviraj Raso* tells how the hero, unable to marry his beloved Samyukta because they came from rival Rajput clans, carried her off on his horse.

15. In the *Mahabharata,* the five Pandava brothers all married one woman, which proved highly problematic.

16. Overdorf, "Saving the Raja's Horse," 2.

17. "THE MARWARI HORSE BREED STANDARD" (http://www.horseindian.com/marwarihorsebreed.htm). *Indigenous Horse Society of India.* Archived (https://web.archive.org/web/20170312030945/http://horseindian.com/marwarihorse breed.htm) from the original on March 12, 2017, retrieved January 16, 2017.

18. Kelly, *Marwari,* 4.

19. Khan, "Horses in Pakistan."

20. Khan, "Horses in Pakistan."

21. Edwards, *The Encyclopedia of the Horse,* 162–63; also Chetwode, "The Horses of Kathiawar," 7.

22. Edwards, *The Encyclopedia of the Horse,* 162–63 and 196.

23. Bongianni, *Simon & Schuster's Guide,* entry 122.

24. Bongianni, *Simon & Schuster's Guide,* entry 122.

25. Behl et al., "Genetic Relationships," 483–88.

26. Chetwode, "The Horses of Kathiawar," 6–7.

27. Overdorf, "Saving the Raja's Horse," 4–5.

28. "Breed Information," http://www.horsemarwari.com/breedinformation.htm. Archived https://web.archive.org/web/20080509090358/http://www.horsemarwari.com/breedinformation.htm.

29. Edwards, *The Encyclopedia of the Horse,* 162–63 and 196.

30. Chetwode, "The Horses of Kathiawar." 8, citing the 1880 edition of the Bombay *Gazetteer.*

31. Edwards, *The Encyclopedia of the Horse,* 162–63 and 196.

32. Moorcroft, *Observations,* 20, 53.

33. Moorcroft, *Observations,* 16.

34. Lockwood Kipling, *Beast and Man,* 69. Further citations to this work are in the text.

35. "Marwari Horse," in *Horseman Magazine,* August 10, 2008.

36. Sirhind, "Reliving History on Horseback."

37. Mark Eveleigh, "The Marwari Horse: Divine Horses of Rajasthan," https://web .archive.org/web/2011052, June 2009. 4010359/http://www.friendsofmarwari.org.uk /_docs/Nagmag.pdf. *NagMag.* Archived from the original, http://www.friendsofmarwari .org.uk/_docs/Nagmag.pdf, on May 24, 2011, retrieved February 5, 2010.

38. Edwards, *The Encyclopedia of the Horse,* 162–63 and 196.

39. Chetwode, "The Horses of Kathiawar," 1.

40. Overdorf, "Saving the Raja's Horse," 3.

41. "Marwari Horse," in *Horseman Magazine,* August 10, 2008.

42. Overdorf, "Saving the Raja's Horse," 1; Gupta, Chauhan, and Tandon, "Genetic Diversity."

43. Overdorf, "Saving the Raja's Horse," 1.

44. Overdorf, "Saving the Raja's Horse," 1 and 3. Dundlod, generally known as "Bonnie," was a descendant of Indian nobles, though not from Marwar.

45. "Endangered," "ignorance and indiscriminate breeding," "mixed breed," "vulnerable," "crossbreeds," "bloodlines," "strict breeding," "strict selective breeding processes," "poor conformation," "the integrity of the breed," "mixed breeding," "indiscriminate breeding practices," "purebred Marwaris," "prime Marwari specimens," "top-quality horses," "suited to produce pedigreed offspring," "the breed would remain highly vulnerable," "codified breed standard," "untainted by crossbreeding," "top-quality horses," "rehabilitate the now endangered Marwari," "interbreeding," "lineage," "out-crossing," and so forth.

46. Overdorf, "Saving the Raja's Horse," 3, 3, 5.

47. Overdorf, "Saving the Raja's Horse," 1.

48. Overdorf, "Saving the Raja's Horse," 3.

49. Overdorf, "Saving the Raja's Horse," 3.

50. Email from Francesca Kelly, January 10, 2008.

51. Overdorf, "Saving the Raja's Horse," 6.

52. Doniger, "Myth and Narrative."

53. Szanton and Bakshi, *Mithila Painting.*

54. Doniger, "The Stuff that Art Is Made On."

55. Overdorf, "Saving the Raja's Horse," 5.

56. Email from Francesca Kelly, July 24, 2018.

57. I am indebted to Lorraine Daston for bringing this factor to my attention, on October 15, 2019.

58. Originally in Italian: "L'occhio del padrone ingrassa il cavallo."

59. Bongianni, *Simon & Schuster's Guide to Horses and Ponies,* entry 122.

60. Dutson, *Storey's Illustrated Guide,* 160–64.

61. Hendricks, *International Encyclopedia of Horse Breeds,* 280–81.

62. Dutson, *Storey's Illustrated Guide,* 160–64.

63. Edwards, *The Encyclopedia of the Horse,* 162–63 and 196.

64. Chetwode, "The Horses of Kathiawar," 1.
65. Chetwode, "The Horses of Kathiawar," 1.
66. Chetwode, "The Horses of Kathiawar," 2.
67. Chetwode, "The Horses of Kathiawar," 6.

13. THE GIFT HORSE

1. Davis, *Lives of Indian Images,* 113, citing Amir Khusrau.
2. Lorenzen, "Who Invented Hinduism?," 651, citing Sivaprasad Simha, *Kirtilata aur avahattha bhasa* (New Delhi: Vani Prakasan, 1988), 269–70. The *tilak* is the mark made on the forehead that indicates a Hindu's sectarian affiliation.
3. Schimmel, *The Empire,* 52–53.
4. Temple, *The Legends of the Panjab,* 1:495.
5. Email from Francesca Kelly to Wendy Doniger, October 3, 2019.
6. Beal, trans., *Si-yu-ki,* 1:20.
7. Olufsen, *Through the Unknown Pamirs,* 202.
8. I blush to say that this had not occurred to me until Lorraine Daston raised the point, on December 21, 2019.
9. Abu'l Fazl, *A'in-i Akbari,* 1:133; Keay, *India,* 327.
10. Alder, *Beyond Bokhara,* 209.
11. *Gazetteer of the Bombay Presidency,* 1880, 5:38.
12. *Gazetteer of the Bombay Presidency,* 1880, 5:38–39.
13. *Gazetteer of the Bombay Presidency,* 1880, 5:235–36.
14. Personal communication from Kirin Narayan, February 22, 1999.
15. Williams, *The Black Hills,* 83–84.
16. Jain, "Painted Myths of Creation," 24.
17. Williams, *The Black Hills,* 83; Postans, *Cutch,* 154.
18. *Gazetteer of the Bombay Presidency,* 5:235–36.
19. Kramrisch, *Unknown India,* 55.
20. Williams, *The Black Hills,* 84–86.
21. *Gazetteer of the Bombay Presidency,* 5:95.
22. *Gazetteer of the Bombay Presidency,* 5:236n. The text adds: "See Reinoud's Memoir Sur l'Inde, 125–27."
23. Williams, *The Black Hills,* 85. Further citations to this work are in the text.
24. Kramrisch, *Unknown India,* 55.
25. In discussing this argument, Joanne Waghorne invoked the equestrian metaphor, beginning with the title of her article: "Chariots of the God/s: Riding the Line between Hindu and Christian."
26. Mukherjee, *The Rise and Fall,* 300–303.
27. Bolts, *Considerations on Indian Affairs,* 194. The thumb-cutting story is found only in contemporary British accounts from the 1770s, when there was fierce rivalry between various factions of the East India Company's servants in Bengal and their supporters in London. The silk winders' incident, reported by Wilhelm Bolts, a highly disreputable and probably unreliable witness, writing against his rivals in the Company, found its way into Edmund Burke's attacks on Warren Hastings and then into Indian writings in English in the late nineteenth century. The weavers were caught between the rapacity of the Indian

agents who served as middlemen and the young Englishmen for whom they worked. But no contemporary Bengali writers, Hindu or Muslim, seem to have mentioned it, perhaps because they attached little importance to what happened to weavers, who were low-caste Muslims and Hindus. I owe my understanding of this episode to Suzanne Rudolph, March 1985.

28. Personal communication from Kirin Narayan, February 22, 1999.

29. *Mahabharata* 1.123.

30. Abu'l Fazl, *A'in i Akbari,* 1.140.

31. Bongianni, *Simon & Schuster's Guide,* entry 122.

32. Chetwode, "The Horses of Kathiawar," 7.

33. Smith, *The Epic of Pabuji,* 484, from the version told by Mhato Nainasi.

34. I heard several versions of this story from Connemara natives when I lived in Ballyvaughan in the summer of 1980.

35. Doniger, *The Implied Spider,* 79–108.

36. Williams, *The Black Hills,* 83.

37. This process of identification has been seen as a factor in the ways in which Hindus assimilated British attitudes to Hinduism in the nineteenth century. See Doniger, "From *Kama* to *Karma.*"

38. Inglis, "Night Riders," 298, 302, and 304.

Bibliography

TEXTS IN SANSKRIT AND OTHER CLASSICAL INDIAN LANGUAGES (BY TITLE)

Abhijnana-Shakuntala of Kalidasa. Bombay: Nirnaya Sagara Press, 1958.

Agni Purana. Poona: Anandasrama Sanskrit Series, 1958.

Aitareya Brahmana, with the commentary of Sayana. Calcutta: Bibliotheca Indica, 1895.

Akananuru. Trans. George Hart as *The Four Hundred Songs of Love: An Anthology of Poems from Classical Tamil: The Akananuru* (Pondicherry: Institut Français de Pondichéry, 2015).

Arthashastra of Kautilya. Ed. R. P. Kangle. 3 vols. Bombay: University of Bombay, 1960. Trans. Patrick Olivelle as *King, Governance, and Law in Ancient India: Kautilya's Arthasastra* (New York: Oxford University Press, 2013).

Ashtadhyayi of Panini. Ed. and trans. Otto Böhtlingk as *Pānini's Grammatik.* Vols. 1 & 2 in one vol. Delhi: Motilal Banarsidass, 1964.

Ashvashastra of Nakula. Ed. S. Gopalan, with V. Swaminatha Atreya, published by S. Gopalan. T. M. S. S M. Library, Saraswati Mahal Series no. 56. Tanjore, 1952.

Atharva Veda. With the commentary of Sayana. 5 vols. Hoshiarpur: Vishveshvaranand Vedic Research Institute, 1960.

Basava Purana. Trans. V. Narayana Rao with Gene H. Roghair as *Siva's Warriors: The Basava Purana of Palkuriki Somanatha* (Princeton: Princeton University Press, 1990).

Baudhayana Shrautasutra of the *Taittiriya Samhita.* Ed. W. Caland. Vol. 2. Calcutta: Asiatic Society, 1913.

Bhagavata Purana. With the commentary of Shridhara. Benares: Pandita Pustakalaya, 1972.

Bhavishya Purana. Bombay: Venkateshvara Steam Press, 1959.

Brahma Purana. Calcutta: Gurumandala Press, 1954.

Brahmanda Purana. Bombay: Venkateshvara Steam Press, 1857.

Brihadaranyaka. See *Upanishads.*

Brihaddevata of Shaunaka. Cambridge, MA: Harvard University Press, 1904.

Buddhacharita of Ashvaghosha. Trans. Patrick Olivelle as *The Life of the Buddha* (New York: New York University Press, 2009).

Devibhagavata Purana. Benares: Pandita Pustakalaya, 1960.

Gopatha Brahmana. Calcutta: Bibliotheca Indica, 1872.

Harivamsha. Poona: Bhandarkar Oriental Research Institute, 1969.

Harshacharita of Bana. Bombay Sanskrit and Prakrit Series. Bombay, 1909. Trans. E. B. Cowell and F. W. Thomas (London, 1891).

Jaiminiya Brahmana. Nagpur: Sarasvati-vihara Series, 1954.

Jatakas. Ed. E. B. Cowell as *The Jataka, or Stories of the Buddha's Former Births.* 7 vols. (Cambridge: Cambridge University Press, 1985–1907).

Kalika Purana. Ed. Sri Biswanarayan Sastri. Varanasi: Chowkhamba Sanskrit Series Office, 1972.

Kamasutra of Vatsyayana. With the commentary of Yashodhara. Ed. Devadatta Shastri. Varanasi: Kashi Sanskrit Series, 1964. Trans. Wendy Doniger and Sudhir Kakar (Oxford and New York: Oxford University Press, 2002).

Kathasaritsagara of Somadeva. Bombay: Nirnaya Sagara Press, 1930.

Kaushitaki Brahmana. 3 vols. Calcutta: Bibliotheca Indica, 1903.

Kumarasambhava of Kalidasa. Bombay: Nirnaya Sagara Press, 1955.

Linga Purana. Calcutta: Sri Arunodaraya, 1812.

Mahabharata. Poona: Bhandarkar Oriental Research Institute, 1933–69.

Mahabharata, Southern Recension. Ed. P. P. S. Subrahmanya Sastri. Madras: Vavilla Ramaswamy Sastrulu and Sons, 1931–33.

Mahavamsa. Ed. and trans. Wilhelm Geiger. London: Pali Text Society, 1912.

Manasollasa of Someshvara. Ed. G. K. Shrigondekar. Vol. 2. Baroda: G. O. S., 1939.

Manavadharmashastra of Manu. Ed. Harikrishna Jayantakrishna Dave. Bharatiya Vidya Series, vols. 20–. Bombay, 1972–78. Trans. Wendy Doniger with Brian K. Smith as *The Laws of Manu* (Harmondsworth: Penguin, 1991).

Markandeya Purana. With commentary. Bombay: Venkateshvara Steam Press, 1890.

Matanakamarajan katai. Madras: R. J. Pati Company, 1975.

Matsya Purana. Anandashsrama Sanskrit Series, no. 54. Poona, 1909.

Mrichcchakatika [Little clay cart] of Shudraka. Ed. M. R. Kale. Bombay: D. M. Tilak, Bookseller's Publishing Company, 1962.

Naishadiyacharita of Shri Harsha. Bombay: Nirnaya Sagara Press, 1986.

Padma Purana. Anandashrama Sanskrit Series, no. 131. Poona, 1894.

Panchatantra. Ed. Johannes Hertel. Harvard Oriental Series, 11. Cambridge, MA: Harvard University, 1908.

Panchavimsha [*Tandya-maha*] *Brahmana.* With the commentary of Sayana. Bibliotheca Indica. Calcutta: Asiatic Society, 1869–74.

Pandyakulodaya [Resurgence of the Pandya race] of Mandalakavi. Ed. K. V. Sarma. Hoshiapur: Vishvesvaranand Visva Bandhu Institute of Sanskrit and Indological Studies, Panjab University, 1981.

Panini. See under *Ashtadhyayi.*

Prabodhachandrodaya of Krishnamishra. Ed. and trans. Matthew Kapstein as *The Rise of Wisdom Moon.* Clay Sanskrit Library, 52. (New York: New York University Press, 2008).

Ramayana of Valmiki. Baroda: Oriental Institute, 1950–75.

Ramcharitmanas of Tulsi Das [*The Holy Lake of the Acts of Rama*]. Trans. Philip Lutgendorf as *The Epic of Ram* (Cambridge, MA: Harvard University Press, 2016).

Ravana Vaha or *Setubandha*. With commentary. Ed. Pandit Sivadatta and Kasinath Pandurang Parab. Kavyamala, no. 47. Bombay: Tukaram Javaji, 1895.

Rig Veda. With the commentary of Sayana. Ed. F. Max Müller. London: William H. Allen, 1890–92.

Sarvadarshanasamgraha of Madhava. Trans. E. B. Cowell and A. E. Gough. London: Trübner, 1914.

Saura Purana. Anandashrama Sanskrit Series. Poona, 1923.

Shankaradigvijaya of Vidyaranya. Pune: Anandashrama Press, 1891.

Shatapatha Brahmana. Benares: Chowkhamba Sanskrit Series, 1964.

Shishupalavadha of Magha. Ed. and trans. Paul Dundas as *The Killing of Shishupala* (Cambridge, MA: Harvard University Press, 2016).

Shiva Purana. Benares: Pandita Pustakaya, 1964.

Shiva Purana. Dharmasamhita. Bombay, 1884.

Skanda Purana. Bombay: Sri Venkatesvara Steam Press, 1867.

Sri Venkatesvara Laghukrtulu. Ed. Veturi Prabhakarasastri. Tirupati, 1981.

Subhashitaratnakosha of Vidyakara. Trans. Daniel H. H. Ingalls as *An Anthology of Sanskrit Court Poetry*. Harvard Oriental Series, 42. (Cambridge, MA: Harvard University Press, 1957).

Taittiriya Aranyaka of the Black Yajur Veda. With the commentary of Sayana. Bibliotheca Indica. Calcutta: Asiatic Society, 1872.

Taittiriya Brahmana. Ed. Rajendralala Mitra. Calcutta: Bibliotheca Indica, 1859; Delhi: Motilal Banarsidass, 1985.

Taittiriya Samhita. Anandashrama Sanskrit Series. Poona, 1979.

Tiruvacagam. Trans. G. U. Pope. London: Oxford University Press, 1900.

Upanishads. Ed. and trans. Patrick Olivelle as *Early Upanishads*. New York: Oxford University Press, 1998.

Vajasaneyi Samhita. Chaukhamba Sanskrit Series. Varanasi, 1972.

Vamana Purana. Benares: All-India Kashiraj, 1968.

Vayu Purana. Anandashrama Sanskrit Series. Poona, 1860.

Vishnu Purana. Calcutta: Sanatana Shastra, 1972.

Yogavasishtha [*Yogavasishtha-Maha-Ramayana*] of Valmiki. Ed. W. L. S. Pansikar. 2 vols. Bombay: Nirnaya Sagara Press, 1918.

TEXTS IN OTHER LANGUAGES (BY AUTHOR)

Abu'l Fazl 'Allami. *A'in-i Akbari*. Ed. H. Blochmann. Trans. Henry Sullivan Jarrett. Calcutta: Asiatic Society of Bengal, 1891.

———. *Akbarnama*, or *The History of Akbar*. Ed. and trans. Wheeler M. Thackston. Murty Classical Library of India. Cambridge, MA: Harvard University Press, 2015.

Agravat, Ram Prakash. *Satyavadi Vir Tejapala*. Jodhapura: Sri Uttama Ashram, Kagamarga, 1973.

Alberuni [al-Bīrūnī, Abū Rayḥān]. *Alberuni's India: An Account of the Religion, Philosophy, Literature, Chronology, Astronomy, Customs, Laws and Astrology of India*. Ed. Edward Sachau. London: Trübner & Co., 1887.

Alder, Gary. *Beyond Bokhara: The Life of William Moorcroft, Asian Explorer and Pioneer Veterinary Surgeon, 1767–1825*. London: Century, 1985.

Alexander, Mary. *Mrs. Betjeman*. London: Independently published, 2019.

Anjum, Nazer Aziz. "Horses in Mughal India." *Proceedings of the Indian History Congress* 74 (2013): 277–84.

Anthony, David. *The Horse, the Wheel, and Language: How Bronze-Age Riders from the Eurasian Steppes Shaped the Modern World*. Princeton: Princeton University Press, 2010.

Arunachalam, M. *Peeps into Tamil Literature: Ballad Poetry*. Tiruchitrambalam: Gandhi Vidyalayam, 1976.

Asher, R. E., and R. Radhakrishnan. *A Tamil Prose Reader*. Cambridge: Cambridge University Press, 1961.

Babur. *The Baburnama*. Trans. A. S. Beveridge. London: Luzac, 1921.

Barani, Ziya al-din. *Ta'rikh-i Ferozshahi*. Ed. S. A. Khan et al. Calcutta, 1862.

Beal, Samuel, trans. *Si-yu-ki: Buddhist Records of the Western World*. 2 vols. New York: Paragon, 1968.

Beck, Brenda E. F., Peter Claus, Prapulladatta Goswami, and Jawarhalal Handoo. *Folktales of India*. Chicago: University of Chicago Press, 1987.

Behl, R., J. Behl, N. Gupta, and S. C. Gupta. "Genetic Relationships of Five Indian Horse Breeds Using Microsatellite Markers." *Animal* 1, no. 4 (May 2007): 483–88.

Bhattacarya, Asutosh. "The Cult of the Village Gods of West Bengal." *Man in India* 35 (1955): 19–33.

———. *Folklore of Bengal*. New Delhi: National Book Trust, 1978.

Biardeau, Madeleine. "Brahmans and Meat-Eating Gods." Unpublished manuscript, 1985.

———. *Stories about Posts: Vedic Variations around the Hindu Goddess*. Trans. Alf Hiltebeitel et al. Chicago and London: University of Chicago Press, 2004.

Blackburn, Stuart H. "Domesticating the Cosmos: History and Structure in a Folktale from India." *Journal of Asian Studies* 45, no. 3 (May 1986): 527–43.

Bolts, Wilhelm. "Considerations on Indian Affairs; Particularly Respecting the Present State of Bengal Dependencies." London, 1772. Reprinted in *The East India Company: 1600–1858*, ed. Patrick Tuck. Vol. 3. London and New York: Routledge, 1998.

Bongianni, Maurizio, ed. *Simon & Schuster's Guide to Horses and Ponies*. New York: Simon & Schuster, 1988.

Brereton, James M. *The Horse in War*. London: Arco, 1976.

Bryant, Edwin E. *The Quest for the Origins of Vedic Literature: The Indo-Aryan Migration Debate*. New York and Oxford: Oxford University Press, 2001.

Bühler, Georg. "The Peheva Inscription from the Temple of Garibnath." In *Epigraphica Indica*, vol. 1. Calcutta: Thacker, Spink and Co., 1892, 184–90.

Butler, Robert. *The Life of the Tamil Poet-Saint Manikkavacakar*. Self-published, 2018.

Campbell, Sir James M. *Gazetteer of the Bombay Presidency in 1880*. Vol. 5: *Cutch, Palanpur, and Mahi Kantha*. [Edited by Sir James M. Campbell.] Bombay: Government Central Press, 1880.

Chetwode, Penelope. "The Horses of Kathiawar." Unpublished typescript, c. 1980.

———. *Kulu: The End of the Habitable World*. London: Transatlantic Arts, 1972.

Conze, Edward. *Buddhist Scriptures*. Harmondsworth: Penguin Books, 1959.

Crooke, William. *The Popular Religion and Folk-Lore of Northern India.* 2 vols. London: Archibald Constable, 1896.

Dales, George F. "The Mythical Massacre at Mohenjo-Daro." *Expedition Magazine* (Penn Museum) 6, no. 3 (1964): n.p. http://www.penn.museum/sites/expedition/?p =733.

Dalrymple, William. "Homer in India: Rajasthan's Oral Epics." *The New Yorker,* November 20, 2006, 48–55.

———. *White Mughals: Love and Betrayal in Eighteenth-Century India.* New York: Harper Collins, 2012.

Das Gupta, K. K. "The Asvakas: An Early Indian Tribe." *East and West,* n.s., 22, nos. 1–2 (1972): 33–40.

Davis, Richard. *Lives of Indian Images.* Princeton: Princeton University Press, 1997.

Dayal, Subah. "Making the 'Mughal' Soldier: Ethnicity, Identification, and Documentary Culture in Southern India, c. 1600–1700." *Journal of the Economic and Social History of the Orient* 62 (2019): 856–924.

Dent, Anthony, "The Earliest Wave of Domestic Horses in East Europe." *Journal of Indo-European Studies* 6, nos. 1–2 (Spring/Summer 1978): 17–64.

———. *The Horse through Fifty Centuries of Civilization.* New York: Holt, Rinehart, 1974.

Desai, Devangana. *Erotic Sculpture of India: A Socio-Cultural Study.* New Delhi: Tata McGraw Hill, 1975.

Dhere, R. C. *Khandoba.* Pune, 1961.

Digby, Simon. *War-Horse and Elephant in the Delhi Sultanate: A Study of Military Supplies.* Oxford: Orient Monographs; Karachi: Oxford University Press, 1971.

Dikshitar, V. R. Ramachandra. *War in Ancient India.* 2nd ed. New York: Macmillan, 1948.

Doniger, Wendy. *Against Dharma: Dissent in the Ancient Indian Sciences of Sex and Politics.* New Haven: Yale University Press, 2018.

———. "Another Great Story." Review of *The Roots of Hinduism,* by Asko Parpola. *Inference: International Review of Science* 3, no. 2 (August 2017).

———. *The Bedtrick: Tales of Sex and Masquerade.* Chicago: University of Chicago Press, 2000.

———. "Diary: Crazy about Horses." *London Review of Books,* September 23, 1993. Reprinted in *Broom, Broom,* LRB collection 7, "Writing about Witches from the London Review of Books." London, 2019.

———. "The Deconstruction of Vedic Horselore in Indian Folklore." In *Ritual, State and History in South Asia: Essays in Honor of J. C. Heesterman,* ed. A. W. van den Hoek, D. H. A. Kolff, and M. S. Oort. Leiden: E. J. Bill, 1992, 76–101.

———. *Dreams, Illusion, and Other Realities.* Chicago: University of Chicago Press, 1984.

———. "Ekwos, Equus, Asva, Eoh or The Land East of the Asterisk." Review of *Indo-European Poetry and Myth,* by Martin L. West. *London Review of Books,* April 10, 2008, 27–29.

———. "From *Kama* to *Karma:* The Resurgence of Puritanism in Contemporary

India." *Social Research* 78, no. 1 (Spring 2011): 49–74. Reprinted in *India's World: The Politics of Creativity in a Globalized Society,* ed. Arjun Appadurai and Arien Mack (New Delhi: Raintree, 2012), 47–70; and in Doniger, *On Hinduism,* 396–408.

———. *The Hindus: An Alternative History.* New York: Penguin Press, 2009.

———. "'I Have Scinde': Flogging a Dead (White Male Orientalist) Horse." The 1998 Presidential Address for the Association of Asian Studies. Published in *Journal of Asian Studies* 58, no. 4 (November 1999): 940–60. Available online at www.jstor.org /view/00219118/di015153/01p0195c/0.

———. "Impermanence and Eternity in Hindu Epic, Art and Performance." In *On Hinduism,* 509–23.

———. *The Implied Spider: Politics and Theology in Myth.* New York: Columbia University Press, 1998.

———. "Indra as the Stallion's Wife." In *On Hinduism,* 473–47.

———. *The Mare's Trap: Nature and Culture in the* Kamasutra. Delhi: Speaking Tiger, 2015.

———. "Myth and Narrative in Indigenous Indian Art." In *Many Visions, Many Versions: Art from Indigenous Communities in India.* Washington, D.C.: International Arts and Artists, 2017, 32–43.

———. *On Hinduism.* Delhi: Aleph Book Company, 2013. 2nd ed., New York: Oxford University Press, 2014.

———. "Sacred Cows and Beefeaters." In *On Hinduism,* 501–8.

———. "Saranyu/Samja: The Sun and the Shadow." In *Devi: Goddesses of India,* ed. John Stratton Hawley and Donna M. Wulff. Berkeley and Los Angeles: University of California Press, 1996, 154–72.

———. *Splitting the Difference: Gender and Myth in Ancient Greece and India.* Chicago: University of Chicago Press, 1999.

———. "The Stuff That Art Is Made On: Impermanence and Meaning in Art." *Aspen Institute Quarterly* 2, no. 4 (Autumn 1990): 62–139.

———. "A Symbol in Search of an Object: The Mythology of Horses in India." In *A Communion of Subjects: Animals in Religion, Science, and Ethics,* ed. Paul Waldau and Kimberley Patton. New York: Columbia University Press, 2006, 335–50.

Doniger O'Flaherty, Wendy. *Asceticism and Eroticism in the Mythology of Siva.* Oxford: Oxford University Press, 1973.

———. "Contributions to an Equine Lexicology, with Special Reference to Frogs." *Journal of the American Oriental Society* 98, no. 4 (October–December 1978), 475–78.

———. *Dreams, Illusion, and Other Realities.* Chicago: University of Chicago Press, 1984.

———. *Hindu Myths: A Sourcebook, Translated from the Sanskrit.* Harmondsworth: Penguin Classics, 1975.

———. "Horses and Snakes in the *Adi Parvan* of the *Mahabharata.*" In *Aspects of India: Essays in Honor of Edward Cameron Dimock,* ed. Margaret Case and N. Gerald Barrier. New Delhi: American Institute of Indian Studies and Manohar, 1986, 16–44 and 172–73.

———. *Karma and Rebirth in Classical Indian Traditions.* Berkeley: University of California Press; Delhi: Motilal Banarsidass, 1980.

———. *The Origins of Evil in Hindu Mythology.* Berkeley: University of California Press, 1976.

———. *Other Peoples' Myths: The Cave of Echoes.* New York: Macmillan, 1988.

———. *The Rig Veda: An Anthology.* Harmondsworth: Penguin, 1980.

———. "The Tail of the Indo-European Horse Sacrifice." *Incognita* 1, no. 1 (1990): 18–37.

———. *Tales of Sex and Violence: Folklore, Sacrifice, and Danger in the Jaiminiya Brahmana.* Chicago: University of Chicago Press, 1985.

———. *Textual Sources for the Study of Hinduism.* Chicago: University of Chicago Press, 1990.

———. *Women, Androgynes, and Other Mythical Beasts.* Chicago: University of Chicago Press, 1980.

Dubey-Pathak, Meenakshi. "The Rock Art of the Bimbetka Area in India." *Adoranten* (Sweden) (2014): 1–18.

Dumézil, Georges. "L'*asvamedha* du colonel de Polier." In *Pratidanam: Indian, Iranian, and Indo-European Studies Presented to Franciscus Bernardus Jacobus Kuiper on His 60th Birthday.* The Hague, Paris: Mouton, 1968, 430–35.

———. "Bellator Equus." *Rituels Indo-European à Rome.* Paris: C. Klincksieck, 1954, 73–91.

———. "Derniers soubresauts de Cheval d'Octobre." In *Fêtes romaines d'été et d'automne.* Paris: Gallimard, 1975, 177–219.

Dutson, Judith. *Storey's Illustrated Guide to 96 Horse Breeds of North America.* New York: Storey, 2005.

Earles, J., trans. *A Treatise on Horses, entitled Saloter, or, A Complete System of Indian Farriery, Compiled Originally by a Society of Learned Pundits, in the Shanscrit Language: Translated Thence into Persian, by Abdallah Khan Firoze Jung . . . which is Now Translated into English, by Joseph Earles.* Calcutta: George Gordon, 1788.

Eaton, Richard. *India in the Persianate Age: 1000–1765.* London: Allen Lane, 2020.

Edwardes, Michael. *Red Year.* London: Sphere Books, 1975.

Edwards, Elwyn Hartley. *The Encyclopedia of the Horse.* 1st American ed. New York: Dorling Kindersley, 1990.

Epstein, Hellmut. *Domestic Animals of China.* Buckinghamshire: Commonwealth Agricultural Bureau, 1969.

Erndl, Kathleen M. *Victory to the Mother: The Hindu Goddess of Northwest India in Myth, Ritual, and Symbol.* New York: Oxford University Press, 1993.

Fairservis, Walter. *The Ancient Kingdoms of the Nile.* New York: Mentor Books, 1962.

Festus. *Breviarium rerum gestarum populi Romani.* Paris: Belles lettres, 2002.

Finn, Margo, and Kate Smith, eds. *The East India Company at Home, 1757–1857.* London: UCL Press, 2018.

Gangadhara. *Sri Martanda Vijaya.* Ed. R. C. Dhere. Pune, 1975.

Gazetteer of the Bombay Presidency in 1880. Vol. 5: *Cutch, Palanpur, and Mahi Kantha.* [Edited by Sir James M. Campbell.] Government Central Press, 1880.

Giraldus Cambrensis. *Topographia Hibernica.* Ed. J. S. Brewer. Vol. 5 of *Opera.* London, 1861–91.

Gode, P. K. "Studies in the History of Indian Plants; History of Canaka (Gram) as Food for Horses Between c. A. D. 800 and 1870; Together with Some Notes on the Import of Foreign Horses into India in Ancient and Medieval Times." *Annals of the Bhandarkar Oriental Research Institute* 26, nos. 1–2 (1945): 89–105.

Gommans, Jos. L. "The Horse Trade in Eighteenth Century South Asia." *Journal of the Economic and Social History of the Orient* 37, no. 3 (1994): 228–50.

———. *The Rise of the Indo-Afghan Empire, c. 1710–1780.* Leiden and New York: E. J. Brill, 1995.

Gopinatha Rao, T. A. *Elements of Hindu Iconography.* 4 vols. Madras: The Law Printing House, 1914.

Gottschalk, Peter. *Beyond Hindu and Muslim: Multiple Identity in Narratives from Village India.* New York: Oxford University Press, 2000.

Griffith, Ralph T. H. *The Texts of the White Yajur Veda.* Chowkhamba Sanskrit Series, vol. 95. Benares, 1899.

Grottanelli, Cristiano. "Yoked Horses, Twins, and the Powerful Lady." *Journal of Indo-European Studies* 14, nos. 1–2 (Spring 1986): 125–53.

Gupta, A. K., M. Chauhan, and S. N. Tandon. "Genetic Diversity and Bottleneck Studies in the Marwari Horse Breed." *Journal of Genetics* 84, no. 3 (December 2005): 295–301.

Gupta, C. "Horse Trade in North India: Some Reflections of Socio-Economic Life." *Journal of Ancient Indian History* 14 (1983–84): 186–206.

Hayes, Matthew Horace, *A Guide to Training and Horse Management in India, with a Hindustanee Stable and Veterinary Vocabulary and the Calcutta Turf Club Tables for Weight for Age and Class.* Calcutta: Thacker, Spink, and Co., 1875.

Heesterman, J. C. *The Ancient Indian Royal Consecration.* The Hague: Mouton, 1957.

———. *The Broken World of Sacrifice.* Chicago: University of Chicago Press, 1992.

Hendricks, Bonnie. *International Encyclopedia of Horse Breeds.* Norman: University of Oklahoma Press, 2007.

Herodotus. *History.* Trans. David Grene. Chicago: University of Chicago Press, 1987.

Herwitz, Daniel. "Like Thunder and Lightning." In *Lightning by M. F. Husain,* ed. Marguerite Charugundla. New York: Asia Society Museum; Ahmedabad: Mapin Publishing, 2019, 47–53.

Hiltebeitel, Alf. *Criminal Gods and Demon Devotees: Essays on the Guardians of Popular Hinduism.* New York: SUNY Press, 1989.

———. *The Cult of Draupadi.* Vol. 1: *Mythologies: From Gingee to Kurukshetra.* Chicago: University of Chicago Press, 1988.

———. "Muttal Ravuttan: Draupadi's Muslim Devotee." Unpublished paper, August 1985.

———. *Rethinking India's Oral and Classical Epics: Draupadi among Rajputs, Muslims, and Dalits.* Chicago: University of Chicago Press, 1999.

———. *Rethinking the Mahabharata: A Reader's Guide to the Education of the Dharma King.* Chicago: University of Chicago Press, 2001.

———. *"Turonaccari Yakacalai,* 'Dronacarya's Sacrificial Hall.' A play." Ms. Retold in Hiltebeitel, *The Cult of Draupadi,* 1:191–92.

Hislop, Stephen. *Papers Relating to the Aboriginal Tribes of the Central Provinces.* Ed. R. Temple. Nagpur, 1866.

Holt, John Clifford. *The Buddha in the Crown: Avalokitesvara in the Buddhist Traditions of Sri Lanka.* New York: Oxford University Press, 1991.

Hooykaas, C. *Agama-Tirtha: Five Studies in Hindu-Balinese Religion.* Verhandelingen der Koninklijke Akademie der Wetenschappen, 70, no. 4. Amsterdam: Noord-Hollandsche Uiigevers Maatschappij, 1964.

Hopkins, Edward Washburn. *Epic Mythology.* Strassburg: K. J. Trübner, 1915.

Huda, M. Z. "Faras-namah-i-Hashimi and Shalihotra." *Journal of the Asiatic Society of Pakistan,* 14, no. 2 (1969): 144–65.

Huntington, Susan L., and John C. Huntington. *The Art of Ancient India: Buddhist, Hindu, Jain.* New York: Weatherhill, 1985.

Huyler, Stephen P. "Folk Art in India Today." In *The Arts of India,* ed. Basil Gray. Oxford: Oxford University Press, 1981, 191–201.

———. *Village India.* New York: Harry Abrams, 1985.

Inglis, Stephen Robert. "Night Riders: Massive Temple Figures of Rural Tamilnadu." In *A Festschrift for Professor Shanmugan Pillai,* ed. M. Israel et al. Madras: Madras Kamaraj University, Muttu Patippakam, 1980, 297–307.

Iskandar, Kai Ka'us Ibn. *A Mirror for Princes (the Qabus Nama).* Trans. Reuben Levy. London: Cresset Press, 1951.

Ivanow, W. "The Sect of Imam Shah in Gujurat." *Journal of the Bombay Branch of the Royal Asiatic Society,* 1937.

Jahangir. *The Tuzuk-i-Janhangīrī or Memoirs of Jahāngīr.* Trans. Wheeler Thackston. Oxford: Oxford University Press, 1999.

Jain, Jyotindra. "Painted Myths of Creation: The Art and Ritual of an Indian Tribe." *India Magazine* 5, no. 2 (January 1985).

Jairazbhoy, Nazir, and Komal Kothari. "The *Par* of Pabuji." In *Puppetry at the Smithsonian,* comp. and ed. Jeffrey LaRiche, 4–5. Smithsonian Folklife Program, June 1980.

Jamison, Stephanie. *Sacrificed Wife, Sacrificer's Wife.* New York: Oxford University Press, 1996.

Jettmar, Karl. *Die Religionen des Hindukusch.* Stuttgart: W. Kohlhammer, 1975.

Johannson, K. F. "Über die altindische Göttin Dhisana und Verwandtes." *Skrifter Utgifne af Kuninjlik Humanistike Vetenskaps-Samfundet i Uppsala,* 1917–19, 97–120.

Joshi, Om Prakash. *Painted Folklore and Folklore Painters of India: A Study with Reference to Rajasthan.* Delhi: Concept Pub. Co., 1976.

Kapp, Dieter B. "Ein Menschenschopfungsmythos der Mundas und seine Parallelen." *Abhandlungen fur die Kunde des Morgenlandes* (Wiesbaden) 43, no. 2 (1977).

Karnad, Girish. *Three Plays: Nagamandala, Hayavadana, Tughlaq.* Delhi: Oxford University Press, 1996.

Keay, John. *India: A History.* New York: Grove Press, 2000.

Kelly, Francesca. *Marwari: Legend of the Indian Horse.* Prakash Book Depot, in Association with Dundlod International, 2000.

Khan, Bakhat B. "Horses in Pakistan." *Agrihunt,* November 13, 2011.

Kipling, John Lockwood. *Beast and Man in India: A Popular Sketch of Indian Animals in Their Relations with the People.* London: Macmillan and Co., 1891/1921. Kindle edition, December 18, 2012.

Kipling, Rudyard. *Kim.* Ed. with an introduction and notes by Edward W. Said. Harmondsworth: Penguin Books, 1987.

——. "The Maltese Cat." In *The Day's Work.* London: Macmillan, 1895.

Kirfel, Willibald. *Die Kosmographie der Inder nach der Quellen dargestellt.* Bonn and Leipzig, 1920.

——. "Siva und Dionysos." *Zeitschrift für Ethnologie* 78 (1953): 83–90.

Klostermaier, Klaus K. *A Survey of Hinduism.* 2nd ed. Albany: SUNY Press, 1994.

Kossack, Steven M. *Indian Court Painting, 16th–19th Century.* New York: Metropolitan Museum of Art, 1997.

Kramrisch, Stella. *Unknown India: Ritual Art in Tribe and Village.* Philadelphia: Philadelphia Museum of Art, 1968.

Lapoint, Elwyn. "The Epic of Guga: A North Indian Oral Tradition." In *American Studies in the Anthropology of India,* ed. Sylvia Vatuk. New Delhi: Manohar, 1978.

Lariviere, Richard. "More Equine Lexicography: The Hamstring Is Not Connected to the Nose." *Journal of the American Oriental Society* 103, no. 2 (April–June 1983): 421–22.

Law, B. C. "Animals in Early Jain and Buddhist Literature." *Indian Culture* 12 (July–September 1945): 6–117.

——. *Tribes in Ancient India.* Baroda: Baroda Oriental Research Institute, 1944.

Leshnik, Lawrence S. "The Horse in India." In *Symbols, Subsistence and Social Structure: The Ecology of Man and Animal in South Asia,* ed. Franklin C. Southworth. Philadelphia: University of Pennsylvania, South Asia Regional Studies, 1977–78, 56–57.

——. "Some Early Indian Horse-Bits and Other Bridle Equipment." *American Journal of Archaeology* 75, no. 2 (April 1971): 141–50.

Lévi-Strauss, Claude. *The Jealous Potter.* Chicago: University of Chicago Press, 1996.

——. *The Origin of Table Manners.* Chicago: University of Chicago Press, 1990.

Lommel, Herman. *Kleine Schriften.* Wiesbaden: Otto Harrassowitz, 1978.

Lorenzen, David N. "Who Invented Hinduism?" *Comparative Studies in Society and History* 41, no. 4 (1999): 630–59.

Macdonell, Arthur Anthony. *Vedic Mythology.* Strassburg: K. J. Trübner, 1897.

Mahadevan, T. M. P. *Ten Saints of India.* Bombay: Bharatiya Vidya Bhavan, 1961.

Mahalingam, T. V. "Hayagriva—the Concept and the Cult." *Adyar Library Bulletin* 29 (1965): 188–99.

Maitra, Nabanjan. "The Rebirth of Homo Vedicus." Ph.D. dissertation, University of Chicago, 2021.

Majumdar, R. C., and A. D. Pusalker. *The Struggle for Empire.* Bombay: Bharatiya Vidya Bhavan, 1966.

Mali, Aditya. *Nectar Gaze and Poison Breath: An Analysis and Translation of the Rajasthani Oral Narrative of Devnarayan.* New York: Oxford University Press, 2005.

Mann, Thomas. *The Transposed Heads: A Legend of India.* New York: Alfred Knopf, 1941.

McClish, Mark. *The History of the Arthashastra: Sovereignty and Sacred Law in Ancient India.* Cambridge: Cambridge University Press, 2019.

McGrath, Charles. "Kipling in America." *The New Yorker,* July 8 and 15, 2019, 69–72. A review of *If: The Untold Story of Kipling's American Years,* by Christopher Bentley (New York: Penguin Press, 2019).

Meech-Pekarik, Julia. "The Flying White Horse: Transmission of the Valahassa Jataka from India to Japan." *Artibus Asiae* 43, no. 1/2 (1981): 111–28.

Monier-Williams, Sir Monier. *Sanskrit-English Dictionary.* Oxford, 1899.

Mookerji, Radhakumud. *The History of Indian Shipping.* Bombay: Longmans, 1912.

Moorcroft, William. *Observations on the Breeding of Horses within the Provinces under the Bengal Establishment.* Published by the Royal College of Veterinary Surgeons, Central Library for Animal Diseases. Calcutta: Military Orphan Press, 1862.

Mukherjee, Ramkrishna. *The Rise and Fall of the East India Company.* Delhi: Popular Prakashan, 1975.

Nagaswamy, R. "Gateway to the Gods. 1. Sermons in Stone." *Unesco Courier,* March 1984.

Narayan, Kirin. "Who is Vishwakarma's Daughter? Divine Kinship and Goddess Randal Worship in a Gujarati Artisan Community." In *In Search of Vishwakarma: Mapping Indian Craft Histories,* ed. Vijaya Ramaswamy. Delhi: Primus Books, 2019, 95–116.

Narayana Rao, V., trans., with Gene H. Roghair. *Siva's Warriors: The Basava Purana of Palkuriki Somanatha.* Princeton: Princeton University Press, 1990.

Ohnuma, Reiko. *Unfortunate Destiny: Animals in a Buddhist Cosmos.* New York: Oxford University Press, 2017.

Olufsen, Ole. *Through the Unknown Pamirs: The Second Danish Pamir Expedition, 1898–99.* London: William Heineman, 1904.

Oman, John Campbell. *Cults, Customs, and Superstitions of India.* London: T. F. Unwin, 1908.

Overdorf, Jason. "Saving the Raja's Horse: British Horsewoman Francesca Kelly Brings India's Fiery Marwari to the United States in Hopes of Reviving the Breed." *Smithsonian Magazine,* June 2004, 1–6.

Ovid. *Fasti. Ovid,* vol. 4. Trans. Sir James George Frazier. Loeb Classical Library. Cambridge, MA: Harvard University Press, 1931.

Parpola, Asko. "The Pre-Vedic Indian Background of the Srauta Ritual." In *Agni: The Vedic Ritual of the Fire Altar,* by Frits Staal. 2 vols. Berkeley: Asian Humanities Press, 1983, 2:41–75.

———. *The Roots of Hinduism: The Early Aryans and the Indus Civilisation.* Oxford: Oxford University Press, 2015.

Pattanaik, Devdutt. "What Puranic Historians Won't Accept." *The Hindu,* September 18, 2019.

Pausanias. *Description of Greece.* Trans. W. H. S. Jones. Vol. 2, Books 3–5. Loeb Classical Library. Cambridge, MA: Harvard University Press, 1931.

Pearse, Hugh, Colonel. "Moorcroft and Hearsey's Visit to Lake Mansarowar in 1812." *The Geographical Journal* 26, no. 2 (August 1905): 180–87.

Pinault, David. *Horse of Karbala: Muslim Devotional Life in India.* New York: Palgrave, 2001.

Platte, Ryan, *Equine Poetics.* Washington, D.C.: Center for Hellenic Studies, 2017.

Plutarch. *Questiones Romanae. Moralia,* vol. 3. Trans. Frank Cole Babbitt. Loeb Classical Library. Cambridge, MA: Harvard University Press, 1931.

Polo, Marco. *The Book of Ser Marco Polo, the Venetian, Concerning the Kingdoms and Marvels of the East.* Trans. George B. Parks. New York: Macmillan, 1927.

——. *Marco Polo: The Description of the World.* Trans. A. C. Moule and Paul Pelliot. London: George Routledge, 1938.

——. *The Travels of Marco Polo.* New York: Dutton, 1908.

Polybius. *Histories.* Vol. 4. Trans. W. R. Paton. Loeb Classical Library. Cambridge, MA: Harvard University Press, 2011.

Pope, G. U., trans. *Tiruvacagam.* London: Oxford University Press, 1900.

Postans, Marianne [later Young]. *Cutch. Or, Random Sketches, Taken During a Residence in One of the Northern Provinces of Western India.* London: Smith, Elder and Co., 1839.

——. *Western India in 1839.* 2 vols. London: Saunders and Otley, 1839.

Propertius. *First Roman Elegy. Elegies.* Trans. C. P. Goold. Loeb Classical Library. Cambridge, MA: Harvard University Press, 1990.

Puhvel, Jaan. *Comparative Mythology.* Baltimore: Johns Hopkins University Press, 1987.

——. "Vedic Asvamedha and Gaulish IIPOMIIDVOS." *Language* 31 (1955): 353–54.

Rajan, Sujeet. "M F Husain's 'Lightning' Strikes New York, Again." *News India,* March 21, 2019.

Raulff, Ulrich. *Farewell to the Horse: A Cultural History.* London: Liveright, 2018.

Rawson, Philip. *Erotic Art of the East.* New York: G. P. Putnam's Sons, 1968.

Richman, Paula. "Subramaniya Bharati's Ramayana." *Manushi: A Journal about Women and Society* 116 (January–February 2000): 15–18.

Robertshaw, David. Notes from discussions at the College of Veterinary Medicine, Cornell University, in 1989.

Roghair, Gene Henry. *The Epic of Palnadu: A Study and Translation of Palnati Vitrula Katha.* Oxford: Clarendon Press, 1982.

Rose, H. A. *A Glossary of the Tribes and Castes of the Punjab and North-West Frontier Province.* Vol. 1. Lahore: Government Printing Office, 1919.

Rousselet, Louis. *India and Its Native Princes. Travels in Central India and in the Presidencies of Bombay and Bengal.* London: Biskers and Son, 1878.

Sarkar, B. K. *The Folk-Element in Hindu Culture.* London: Longmans, Green, 1917.

Sarma, Devaraja. *Guga Jahara Pira.* Rataihala: Jila Bilasapura, 1974.

Satyanarayana, Viswanadha. *Ha Ha Hu Hu: A Horse-Headed God in Trafalgar Square.* Trans. Velcheru Naryana Rao. Delhi: Penguin Random House, India, 2018.

Scharfe, Hartmut. *The State in Indian Tradition.* Leiden: Brill, 1989.

Schimmel, Anne-Marie. *The Empire of the Great Mughals: History, Art and Culture.* London: Reaktion Books, 2004.

Sen, Dinescandra. *Folk Literature of Bengal.* Calcutta: University of Calcutta, 1920.

Sherratt, Andrew. "Plough and Pastoralism: Aspects of the Secondary Products Revolution." In *Patterns of the Past: Studies in Honour of David Clarke,* ed. I. Hodder, G. Isaac, and N. Hammond. Cambridge: Cambridge University Press, 1981, 261–305.

Shulman, David Dean. "The Green Goddess of Tirumullaivayil." *East and West* (IsMeo), n.s., 30 nos. 1–4 (December 1980): 117–31.

———. *The Hungry God: Hindu Tales of Filicide and Devotion.* Chicago: University of Chicago Press, 1993.

Singh, S. D. *Ancient Indian Warfare with Special Reference to the Vedic Period.* Leiden: E. J. Brill, 1965.

Sirhind, Manish. "Reliving History on Horseback." *The Tribune,* Haryanna ed. June 8, 2008.

Smith, John D. *The Epic of Pabuji: A Study, Transcription and Translation.* Cambridge: Cambridge University Press, 1991.

———. "Where the Plot Thickens: Epic Moments in Pabuji." *South Asian Studies* 2 (1986): 53–64.

Sontheimer, Gunther Dietz. *Binoba, Mhaskoba und Khandoba: Ursprung, Geschichte und Umwelt von Pastoralen Gottheiten in Maharastra.* Wiesbaden: Otto Harassowitz, 1976. Trans. Anne Feldhaus, typescript.

———. "Folk Hero, King and God: Some Themes According to the Folk and Textual Traditions in the Khandoba Cult." Typescript, November 1984.

———. "The Mallari/Khandoba Myth as Reflected in Folk Art and Ritual." *Anthropos* 79 (1984): 155–70.

———. "Some Incidents in the History of the God Khandoba." In *Asie du sud: Traditions et changements,* ed. M. Gaborieau and A. Thorner Paris: Editions du Centre National de la Recherche Scientifique, 1978, 111–17.

Stacul, Giorgio. *Prehistoric and Protohistoric Swat, Pakistan (c. 3000–1400 BCE).* Rome: ISMEO, 1987.

Stanley, John M. "The Capitulation of Mani: A Conversion Myth in the Cult of Khandoba." In *Criminal Gods and Demon Devotees: Essays on the Guardians of Popular Hinduism,* ed. Alf Hiltebeitel. New York: SUNY Press, 1989, 271–98.

Steel, F. A. "Folklore in the Panjab." *Indian Antiquary* 2 (February 1882).

Storey, C. A. *Persian Literature: A Bibliographical Survey.* Vol. 2, part 3. Leiden: E. J. Brill, 1977.

Subrahmanyam, Sanjay. "Friday's Child: Or How Tej Singh Became Tecinkurajan." *Indian Economic Social History Review* 36 (1999): 69–113.

———. *The Political Economy of Commerce: Southern India 1500–1560.* Cambridge: Cambridge University Press, 1990.

Szanton, David, and Malini Bakshi. *Mithila Painting: The Evolution of an Art Form.* N.p.: Ethnic Arts Foundation; Pink Mango, 2007.

Tavernier, Jean-Baptiste. *Travels in India.* Translated from the original French ed. of 1676, &c., by V. Ball, &c. 2 vols. London: Macmillan and Co., 1889.

Temple, Sir Richard Carnac. *The Legends of the Panjab.* 2 vols. Bombay, 1884–1900.

Tessitori, L. P. "A Progress Report on the Preliminary Work of Translation of a 17th century Chronicle of Pabuji, Done during the Year 1915 in Connection with the Proposed Bardic and Historical Survey of India." *Journal of the Asiatic Society of Bengal,* 1916, 57–116, esp. 110–14.

Thapar, Romila. *Early India: From the Origins to 1300.* London: Penguin, 2002.

Trautmann, Thomas R. *Aryans and British India.* Berkeley: University of California Press, 1997.

———. *Elephants and Kings: An Environmental History.* Chicago: University of Chicago Press, 2015.

Ure, John. *Shooting Leave: Spying Out Central Asia in the Great Game.* London: Constable, 2009.

Vaudeville, Charlotte. "Evaluation of Love-Symbolism in Bhagavatism." *Journal of the American Oriental Society* 82 (1962): 35–36.

Vinayaka. *Sri Mallari Mahatmya.* Bombay, 1972.

Vogel, J. Ph. *Indian Serpent Lore, or The Nagas in Hindu Legend and Art.* London: Arthur Probstain, 1926.

Wadley, Susan Snow. *Shakti: Power in the Conceptual Structure of Karimpur Religion.* Chicago: University of Chicago Press, 1975.

Waghorne, Joanne. "Chariots of the God/s: Riding the Line between Hindu and Christian." *History of Religions* 39, no. 3 (November 1999).

Waida, Manabo. "The Central Asian Mythology of the Origin of Death." *Anthropos* 77 (1982): 681–91.

Waugh, Evelyn. *Helena.* London: Chapman and Hall, 1950.

West, Martin L. *Indo-European Poetry and Myth.* New York: Oxford University Press, 2007.

Williams, L. F. Rushbrook. *The Black Hills: Kutch in History and Legend. A Study in Indian Local Loyalties.* London: Weidenfeld and Nicolson, 1958.

Wilson, Alistair. Readers' Guide, Notes, Kiplingsociety.co.uk, January 30, 2006.

Witzel, Michael. "Harappan Horse Myths and the Sciences." *The Hindu,* March 5, 2002.

Witzel, Michael, with Steve Farmer and Romila Thapar. "Horseplay in Harappa." *Frontline,* October 13, 2000, 4–16.

Xenophon. *Anabasis.* Trans. Carleton L. Brownson. Loeb Classical Library. Cambridge: Harvard University Press, 1998.

———. *Cyropaedia.* Trans. Walter Miller. Vol. 2. Loeb Classical Library. Cambridge: Harvard University Press, 1914.

Yang, Anand A. *Bazaar India: Markets, Society and the Colonial State in Bihar.* Berkeley: University of California Press, 1999.

Yocum, Glenn E. "Brahmin, King, Sannyasi, and the Goddess in a Cage: Reflections on the 'Conceptual Order of Hinduism' at a Tamil Saiva Temple." Paper presented at a meeting of the Association for Asian Studies, March 25, 1984. Typescript.

———. *Hymns to the Dancing Shiva: A Study of Manikkavcakar's Tiruvacakam.* New Delhi: Heritage Publishers, 1982.

Young, Serinity. *Women Who Fly: Goddesses, Witches, Mystics, and Other Airborne Females.* New York: Oxford University Press, 2017.

Zeuner, F. E. *A History of Domesticated Animals.* London: Hutchinson, 1963.

Index

art (*continued*)
ings, 13, 223n32; Chinese, 189; of celestial horses, 19; composite figures in horse shape, 66, *67;* contemporary, 19, 115, 188–90, 216; of gods vs. anti-gods, 117; Gupta, 4, 73; horse heads in, 43; horses fading from, 186; horses trampling people in, 205, *206, 207;* by Indo-European speakers, 22; of Krishna as charioteer, 49; by Mithila women, 201–3; Mughal, 19, 105, 121, 192; murals, 12, 117, 164, 165, *166,* 189; Rajasthani or Rajput, 120, 129; sculptures, 4, 22, *61,* 73, 99, 120, 184; starving horses in, 4, 183; of St. George on horseback, 28; stirrups in, 120; temple sculptures, 175–76; tribal, 180–81; Veda with horse head in, 98; vehicles (*vahanas*) in, 73
Arthashastra, 75–78; *Ashvashastra* compared to, 85; on feeding, 8, 76–77; on gaits, 77–78; on importing horses, 11; on Janamejaya, 41; on stables, 76, 78; on types of horses, 77, 108
Arunacalam, M., 137
Aryans, 22, 25, 211, 223n21
ashva, 22, 35, 36, 44, 173
Ashvaghosha, 93, 97
ashvamedha. See horse sacrifices
Ashvamukhas/Ashvamukhis, 98, 184, 230n15. *See also* horse-headed beings
ashvashastras: audience for, 89–90; authors of, 79, 152; beauty standards of, 202–3; on best horses, 96, 153; dates of, 79; elephants vs. horses in, 219n2; on "family line" (*kula*), 81, 157; geographic not genealogical typology of, 153; on horse types, 77, 81, 82, 108, 152–53; manuscripts of, 79, *80;* Mughal knowledge of, 85, 105; Nakula's, 79, 85; omens in, 79, 80, 82, 87, 96; Persian, 85–88, 105; practical

vs. magical/mythical in, 78, 79, 83, 85, 88, 90; satire of, 154; Shalihotra's, 82, 85; topics covered in, 79–83; on winged horses, 17, 79; women riders not mentioned in, 120
Ashvavaikyaka of Jayanta Suri, 88
Ashvins: Dadhyanch and, 43, 62, 68, 226n67; in horses' ears, 84; Nakula and Sahadeva as sons of, 49, 79; Pedu given horse by, 28; Saranyu and, 31–34, 68, 224n6
asuras. *See* anti-gods
Auckland, Lord, 145
Aurangzeb, Emperor, 116, 136, 139
Aurva, 60–64, 66
Avalokiteshvara, 103

Babur, Emperor, xv, 105
Babur (horse), xv
Bahlika, 77, 108, 153
Baladasti horses, 107
Balochi horses, 194
Bana, 107
Barani, Ziya-al-Din, 107–9
Barasari, 137
barbarians, 73–74, 154
bards, 48, 107, 120, 129, 150, 211
Barha Kotra, 99, *101*
Basak, 139–41
Basava, 110, 112
Baz Bahadur of Malwa, Sultan, 121, *122*
beauty, 149, 165, 195, 202, 217
Benfield, Paul, 159, 236n31
Bengal, 127, 212; Abu'l Fazl mentions, 108; breeds or breeding in, 107, 146; clay or wooden horses in, 116, 174–75; folk art in, 164; horses in, 155–56; Malancha and Pakshiraj story from, 170–71; three-legged-horse satire from, 173–74; tribal story from, 180; weavers in, 212, 241–42n27
Berners, Lord (Gerald Hugh Tyrwhitt-Wilson), xiii–xiv

Recent books from the
PAGE-BARBOUR AND RICHARD LECTURES

Three Rings: A Tale of Exile, Narrative, and Fate
Daniel Mendelsohn

*Reading the Hindu and Christian Classics: Why and How Deep Learning
Still Matters*
Francis X. Clooney, SJ

Philosophy as Poetry
Richard Rorty

Treasure in Heaven: The Holy Poor in Early Christianity
Peter Brown

Hope without Optimism
Terry Eagleton

Structural Intuitions: Seeing Shapes in Art and Science
Martin Kemp

From Theology to Theological Thinking
Jean-Yves Lacoste, translated by W. Chris Hackett, with an introduction by
Jeffrey Bloechl

Dialect Diversity in America: The Politics of Language Change
William Labov

The Witch in the Western Imagination
Lyndal Roper

Fatalism in American Film Noir: Some Cinematic Philosophy
Robert B. Pippin

The Reason of the Gift
Jean-Luc Marion, translated by Stephen E. Lewis

The Virtues of Mendacity: On Lying in Politics
Martin Jay

*Fathoming the Cosmos and Ordering the World: The "Yijing" ("I Ching," or
"Classic of Changes") and Its Evolution in China*
Richard J. Smith